MORE THAN
MONEY

MORE THAN MONEY

TRUE STORIES OF PEOPLE WHO
LEARNED LIFE'S ULTIMATE LESSON

NEIL CAVUTO

10 ReganBooks
Celebrating Ten Bestselling Years
An Imprint of HarperCollins*Publishers*

HarperCollins books may be purchased for educational, business, or sales promotional use. For information please write: Special Markets Department, HarperCollins Publishers Inc., 10 East 53rd Street, New York, NY 10022.

FIRST EDITION

Designer: Publications Development Company of Texas

Printed on acid-free paper

Library of Congress Cataloging-in-Publication Data

ISBN 0-06-009643-8

04 05 06 PDC/QWF 10 9 8 7 6 5 4

To Mary, for always being there
And Tara for just being

CONTENTS

INTRODUCTION

"MY HEROES"

This book won't make you money. It has no stock tips. No hot investment opportunities. No meaningful investment insights. This book is not about moguls or their schemes. Nor is it about takeovers and their players. There are no management tips here; no ten-step guide to the corner office—none of that.

I've been a business journalist for twenty years, and I have nothing against wealth and success. But now I measure them in other ways.

I admire business titans who've made the journey to fame and fortune. But I'm more impressed with leaders and others who've overcome enormous odds to achieve what they have. That's the real story—*how* they got there.

To me, greatness is defined not by how we handle all that goes well for us, but how we deal with all that does not.

This book is about personal and professional tragedies and triumphs, and those who've made the most of their difficult and painful lives. People who achieved and regained success and wealth, and people who didn't. It's about how they chose to fight, rather than whether they won or lost. Their stories are all a testament to dignity and courage under fire.

What's vital isn't the riches they have, but the inner riches they gained along the way. It's about the clock inside all of us that says life is short . . . let's go long.

All of these struggling people—some very well known, others less so—and their inspiring outlook on life, passion, commitment, and compassion, have helped me put my own life in perspective.

I've had multiple sclerosis for more than six years. There's no cure for MS, and there's not much likelihood of one any time soon. It's a strange, almost mercurial illness that compromises the nervous system, leaving affected nerves unsheathed and unprotected (much like a live wire). The only thing you can predict about MS is its unpredictability—the numbness, the tingling, and the blinding attacks that are its better-known symptoms. These symptoms hit me in waves, more on some days than on others, but always frightening, and always there.

I also "had" cancer, which has been in remission for more than sixteen years, but could return at any time—the perpetual fear of every cancer survivor.

MS and cancer have changed my life, and what I consider important in life. Illness and hardship can do that to you. Living, wondering, and worrying day-to-day can force you to stop and think about what *really* matters.

There were many years when my life, even as a cancer survivor, was defined more by what I accomplished professionally than what I did personally. This didn't mean I was a bad father or husband (at least I hope not!). I was just increasingly wrapped up in doing good work. Money and status mattered a lot more than contentment and meaning. I was more comfortable committing free time to my work than to my family. To be candid, in those years I was a jerk: obsessed more with what I was professionally building than what I personally already had.

In a profession consumed by one-upmanship, I was all business, all the time. I'd put in more hours, read more research, cull through more magazines and newspapers, books and reports, call more contacts, and doggedly pursue more stories than anyone, just to get the edge.

My increasing success in the tough, competitive world of television reinforced my workaholism.

When I first discovered I had MS, I was angry and bitter—especially after having fought off cancer a decade earlier. Why is God punishing me? I wondered. What the hell did I do? Why another illness, and this time with no cure in sight? I'm a good husband, a good father. So why? Why?

Doctors have since told me that my reaction was as predictable as my anger; that it's natural, after being diagnosed with a disease, to lash out—loudly. But what made my diagnosis all the more troubling, and worrisome, was the fact I make my living on TV. People *see* me every day.

I remember being convinced that my professional life would suffer every bit as much as my physical life. What are my viewers going to be watching? My slow demise? My twisted retreat? What happens to me? To my show? To my previously promising career? I had recently launched my own business show on the Fox News cable channel, and was doing well enough against the entrenched competition to continue into what was now my second year.

Everything seemed overwhelming. It was as if my mind was working on two distinct tracks: surviving MS, and somehow functioning on the job with it.

I had a lot of self-pity—sometimes way too much.

For a while, I was self-centered enough to think I was the only one suffering, the only one getting knocked in life.

And then, I don't know quite when or how, I snapped out of it.

I began thinking less about myself, and spending more time longing for meaning, for an understanding of how *others* go through pain and difficulty, how they deal with their crosses, challenges, and suffering.

When I looked around, I discovered many, many others who are dealing with far heavier crosses than I am. In the very world I covered every day, there was plenty of suffering going on—even in the lives of some of the most powerful people in the world.

I began studying many of those people, watching them, even marveling at them:

- The company founders and leaders Jon Huntsman and Patrick Byrne, and the top-ranking executive Harry Pearce, who beat back cancer and turned it into a lifelong mission to prevent others from ever having to go through the same hell. Huntsman himself, a two-time cancer survivor, held his mother in his arms as *she* died of cancer.

- Aaron Feuerstein, Milton Cole, and the father-son team of Jack and Suren Avedisian were chief executives who saw their businesses go up in flames, who could have cashed out on some fat insurance policies and lived happily ever after, but who chose not to; who were more concerned with paying their out-of-work employees than enriching themselves with a fat bank account.

- The shy chairman Paul Orfalea, who endured a life of ridicule and abuse, labeled an idiot who'd never amount to anything, only to go on and build one of the world's most widely recognized and innovative companies.

- Jim Langevin, the quadriplegic who became a United States congressman.

- Geraldine Ferraro, the first female vice presidential candidate, who became the foremost crusader against an insidious, almost entirely unknown form of cancer.

- The novel humor and textbook-insane responses to career challenges of Richard Branson, Roger Ailes, and Herb Kelleher, irreverent CEOs who founded some of the most creative and enjoyable consumer brands in the world.

- Fred Alger, semi-retired, who had to resume leadership of his premier Wall Street money management firm after his younger brother died in the 9/11 attack on the World Trade Center.

- The fatherly guilt of Michael Wilson, the distinguished Canadian banking and government veteran whose son's suicide led him to launch an international education campaign.

- Michael Walsh, the legendary CEO of a giant corporation, who carefully chose Dana Mead, a fast-rising young executive, to train as his heir apparent. When Walsh eventually retired, Mead would be a well-prepared new CEO. But their close mentor/heir relationship and executive positions were suddenly and shockingly changed when Walsh was diagnosed with terminal brain cancer—at 50.

- The ever-smiling entrepreneur Wally Amos, who lost control and ownership of his own company, and finally the legal right to use even his name.

I decided to write this book and tell the stories of these folks and the special other people I selected, because they all mean something to me. They taught me, by example, that difficulty can be made a positive element of living.

Some of them talked to me about their experiences. Others preferred to let their lives speak for themselves.

After all my years of covering Wall Street and business in general, I've discovered that the tools we use to measure financial success fail miserably when used to define deeper success.

There is no multiple for personal happiness or grateful workers. You can't buy a stock based on whether a given workforce feels fulfilled, or a company's customers know they're being treated ethically and fairly. But there *should* be such standards and measures.

In a business world dominated by money and power, and in the larger world we live in, we need to be able to evaluate and share our determinations of honesty, compassion, and honor.

This book is my personal effort to contribute to that noble cause.

The people I've written about are not heroes in the conventional sense. They are everyday people in an unconventional sense, and in a very unconventional world. But they are *my heroes*. They met their obstacles head-on—some successfully, others not, but all fully engaged in life, as described by the poet John Dryden, "never ending, always beginning, fighting still." And all dedicating their lives to doing good and helping others.

The inspiration I've gained and lessons I've learned from their efforts have clarified and changed my priorities, ambitions, and values.

My illnesses helped humble a jerk, a guy who was more focused on becoming something big than on doing something big, and more inclined to measure the greatness of a business titan by what he had in the bank than by what he had in his heart.

They've also helped me become more of a human being. It's one of the reasons I tell people I'm *lucky* to have come down with cancer and now MS.

I know I'm different now from the way I was when I was healthy and well. I've gained more than I've lost. I think I'm a better person, more appreciative, compassionate, and properly focused.

I bring a deeper sense of purpose to my life and my job. I believe that my daily show on Fox News, *Your World,* has succeeded precisely because, as its title suggests, it's the one business show that isn't about numbers. It's about the stories behind those numbers, about the simple drama of everyday life.

Your World's emphasis on people and their stories has made it, and kept it, the most-watched business news show on cable TV.

Each day I spend with MS reminds me that life is fragile, too short and too beautiful to get wrapped up in insignificant details.

And my heroes' continuing lives and actions offer a shining example not only of what could be, but of what is. Each of them made a mark by thinking less about their odds and more about their possibilities, less of themselves and more of others. They are a reminder that there is greatness in our ranks.

They are collectively greater than the sum of their fears, and our fears. They are the embodiment of our hopes and dreams, for ourselves and others, despite and because of all of the obstacles and difficulties we're certain to encounter on our journeys through life.

I hope, as you read on, that you will be as motivated and inspired as I am by the lives of those who decided to do more—and never quit.

There are many "unlucky bastards" in life. The lucky ones are the people who make their suffering and losses the sources of new, powerful, enduring motivation.

"LUCKY BASTARD"

Looking back on it, I don't know what worried me more: sitting half naked on a cold examination table, desperately hoping someone wouldn't barge in, or knowing I was running late for work—very late.

Meanwhile, my wife, Mary, was waiting in another room.

I couldn't understand what was taking the doctor so long. By the time he'd finished making me parade around his office, walk a straight line with my eyes closed, walk backward the same way, and then repeatedly touch my nose and cross my arms, I didn't know whether this was a doctor's visit or the making of a gag videotape for the next neurologists' convention.

It was September 1997, and I was sick. I just didn't know what was making me sick. But both the timing and the year had me worried, because ten years earlier—almost to the day—I had been feeling pretty sick too. After being admitted to the hospital for what turned out to be a case of viral meningitis, the doctors had discovered more trouble: a massive tumor in my chest, reportedly the size of a football. After a biopsy, doctors told me I had advanced Hodgkin's disease, a form of cancer.

Just hearing the "C" word had scared me. My mother had died only seven months earlier of a brain tumor, so I feared the worst. And hearing about the treatment regimen—six to eight months of intensive chemotherapy and another three months of radiation—hadn't improved my spirits.

"Figure a year of bad stuff," my oncologist, Dr. James Salwitz, told me at the time. "I won't lie to you. This won't be fun, but a year from now, it will all be over."

He was right on both counts. It was bad stuff. But after a year it was over, and I was in remission. They never say "cured," but full remission was just as good and just as comforting.

As the years went on, I remained cancer-free. The memories of that wretched year of nausea, steroid-induced weight-gain, mood swings, hair loss, and general misery gradually faded, until it was almost as if it they'd never happened. But I knew otherwise.

Every cancer survivor's nightmare is getting the damn thing all over again. That's why ten years later I was worrying again. Weird things were happening, and I didn't know why. I was getting headaches, feeling pain in my back, tripping and stumbling, just feeling "out of it" . . . again.

It all began innocently enough. I started seeing spots, then having extended periods of blurred vision. Sometimes I had no vision at all. What's more, it was beginning to affect every aspect of my life. I was forgetting things, and I was constantly tired.

Even my infamously bad tennis game, never a source of worry for most opponents, had become a worry for me. During a game with Mary on vacation in New York's Adirondack Mountains, I simply couldn't follow the ball. My legs were like stilts; my sense of balance was off. She was wiping me out—and she was just about the only person on the planet I could beat at tennis!

When we returned home, I told Mary, "I don't know. Something's not right. But I don't know what it is. I just think I should go see a doctor."

Mary knew that if I was volunteering to see a doctor, that itself was cause for concern. No offense intended to the medical community, but I hate doctors. I mean, I *really* hate doctors. And my one-year-long cancer torment a decade earlier hadn't helped matters any.

For some time, Mary had been advising me, sometimes urgently, to check out my unsettling symptoms. She would take it upon herself to call my former oncologist, but I never followed up. I didn't want to go back there, not again. I hoped the symptoms would just go away, but they never did. In fact they increased—and so, inexplicably, did the pain, a shooting, lightning-like attack on my spine, so crippling at times it would make me drop. Only the excruciating, escalating pain made me finally agree to see my old friend and oncologist, Dr. Salwitz. He brought me in, tested me from head to toe, drew enough blood to keep Lon Chaney going for ten movies, and then followed up with more tests on top of those tests.

But after all that, nothing. "I don't know what to tell you," he said. "It's not cancer, but something is going on." He recommended a good neurologist. I was actually relieved it wasn't cancer; anything else, I thought, would be a piece of cake. I could get back to work knowing I wasn't about to die. My life, and my job as a television anchorman and business news executive, were secure. I figured that any future doctor visits would produce nothing more serious than a pinched nerve, or Lyme disease, which was particularly prevalent in the densely wooded areas near my western New Jersey home.

The neurologist put me through the mill: walk a straight line; open your eyes, close them; look at this odd drawing and tell me what you see. After the first visit, I underwent a battery of tests that seemed odd—a full CAT scan of my head and spine, a spinal tap, in which fluid is taken from inside the spine for examination, and still more blood tests.

What the heck were they looking for, I wondered that chilly fall morning as I sat on that equally chilly examination table, looking like John Candy in *Stripes* (or at least that's how out-of-shape I felt). I feared someone would barge in and see me like this as much as I feared the doctor telling me about my condition.

After what seemed like an eternity, he walked back in. His manner had always struck me as cold, abrupt, indifferent, and way too "medical." Mary liked him even less. And true to form, without preamble, he told me his diagnosis. "Mr. Cavuto," he said in a monotone, "You appear to be the unluckiest bastard on the planet. You have MS."

That was it. That's all he said for the next few minutes—minutes that seemed like hours—as I just sat there, taking it all in. MS—Multiple Sclerosis. I knew very little about the disease, only that it affected the nervous system, something about the myelin sheath-protected nerve endings that somehow went wacko.

Now I had this weird thing called MS. I already knew of others who had it, including former Mouseketeer Annette Funicello and comedian Richard Pryor. Both were in pretty bad shape. Actually, *really* bad shape. I wasn't encouraged.

The doctor explained my options. I would have to cut back at work, if I could continue to work at all. My fatigue would steadily increase, and so would the blackouts and stumbling episodes. My form of MS had tentatively been labeled a "remitting progressive form" of the disease. I understood what that meant: My MS would keep getting worse, but at a varying, not constant, rate. There were treatments to slow down its acceleration, but no cures.

"Surely there must be something coming down the pike."

"Nothing," he responded. "But at least, for the most part, it's not a death sentence."

His cool, almost icy dismissal of my concerns really angered me. He wanted to schedule another appointment. I told him I would seek a second opinion, that this diagnosis couldn't be right. Statistically, it seemed darn near impossible that he could be right—or even close! And I preferred never to see him again anyway.

The doctor nodded and left. Mary and I went home. All I can remember doing is collapsing on our bed and crying. The MS diagnosis was so sudden, unequivocal, and irreversible.

I almost wished I had cancer again; at least with that I would have a fighting chance to get well. Not so with MS. I also was angry. How could this possibly happen? The odds of getting cancer *and* MS in the same life were something like two million to one. Leave it to me to defy the odds. A *doubly unlucky bastard.* I remember writing in my calendar at the time, "Everything sucks. Let's plan for the end. Gather all the papers and see what I've got to muddle through financially."

If Mary was tortured or panicked, she didn't (or wouldn't) show it—at least in front of me. For the benefit of our twelve-year-old daughter, Tara, Mary had the composure to keep a stiff upper lip. She had done this before, all of it, just ten years earlier. Back when I had cancer, she was carting along two-year-old Tara to chemotherapy and radiation treatments. Now she once again proved a rock of pure strength.

I would joke with her; the prospect of giving a dinner party would cause her to fall apart. Throw her a life-threatening illness and a routine turned upside down, and she handled it with ease. Amazing.

To this day, I don't know what thoughts went through Mary's head when I was first diagnosed with cancer, or what she thought when we first learned about my MS. All I kept thinking was that Mary was once again getting the ever-shorter end of the marriage stick. When the priest said "in sickness or in health," I don't think she knew what she was signing up for! All I knew then—all I know now—is that I'm grateful she did.

Mary gave me time to vent and stew, while she spent two days compiling a list of top-notch neurologists, including one of the world's best at Johns Hopkins in Maryland.

The neurologist there was kind enough to schedule an appointment only one week later. By the time I got down there, he had received and reviewed all my tests and blood work. He conducted his own examinations, as much to rule out things, such as Lyme disease, as anything else. By the time he rejoined me and Mary, he was direct, but compassionate. "It is definitely MS, Mr. Cavuto. No two ways about it."

But he was optimistic. "You can live a very productive life with this disease," he told me. "But your attitude accounts for a lot."

He went on to explain treatments and regimens, and volunteered his services. As kind and well-credentialed as he was, though, having a neurologist five hours away wasn't an option.

Moreover, I still couldn't accept the diagnosis. I felt there was an outside chance this doctor could be wrong too. It happened all the time, I figured. My symptoms could just be a pinched nerve or a virus, I told myself—maybe both. But not MS, please, God.

Back home, I began asking for recommendations of a top New York City neurologist, a true MS expert. The name Dr. Saud Sadiq kept popping up. Year in and year out, he topped *New York* magazine's "Best Doctors" lists. He was frequently described as one of the country's premier *and* progressive MS experts. He seemed like exactly the neurologist I should talk to.

We called, and he offered to see us immediately. If there's such a thing as falling in love with a doctor, we did with Dr. Sadiq. He listened for more than an hour as I recounted our ordeal and the diagnoses of the first two neurologists. He quietly reviewed my charts and scans, peering through files that had become as thick as the Pentagon Papers.

He talked to me alone. Then Mary alone. Then the two of us together. Then he went off and studied all my materials alone. Some two hours later, he returned. He recommended another spinal tap, some motor-sensory tests and still more blood work. He too was convinced it was MS. He just wanted to ascertain exactly what kind of MS we were talking about.

Somehow, this time, with this doctor on this day, I felt okay. I was almost resigned to the illness, even curiously upbeat about my prospects for tackling it. Dr. Sadiq had a lot to do with that. His positive, encouraging manner, progressive approach to MS, and willingness to combat and forestall any new attack, all made a big difference.

What's more, his office and my Fox News offices were both in Manhattan, adding some needed security. If anything went wrong for me at work, he was right there. He would be my doctor. He would lead my physical journey. That much I knew. Everything else was doubt and uncertainty. Mary and I left his office not happy, but not hopeless. Later tests would confirm Dr. Sadiq's conclusion.

By then, I was ready to tell my boss at Fox News, Roger Ailes. I have never been more anxious in my life.

It helped that Roger had been my boss and friend for nearly four years; I'd been a close friend of his wife, former CNBC producer and executive Beth Ailes, even longer.

I'd been at CNBC for its launch in 1989, and Roger became my boss in 1993 when he took over the channel as the new CEO. We'd worked so well together that when he left in the fall of 1996, to launch a new, all-news channel for Rupert Murdoch at the Fox Network, I soon left CNBC and joined him there.

During the past year, I'd come to admire Roger even more, watching him build Fox with his inspirational leadership and remarkable speed, from nothing but a concept into a small but solidly successful cable channel. Unfortunately, my own news show wasn't getting high ratings, or pulling in a sizable audience.

I knew Roger never cared about such things. He was extremely patient, as willing to wait for my show to get its footing as he was to spend years developing Fox into the major news force he thought it should be. But I was still very worried. MS was another matter entirely, and business was business. As CEO, Roger had responsibilities that far outweighed our friendship, and understandably so.

It was easy to understand why it would be in the best interests of Fox for Roger to let me go. His cable channel was successful, but only a year old, building but not yet established, with a startup's inherent risk of failure.

Why would he want to stick with me? I couldn't think of any good business reasons. Treatments alone would take me out of work from time to time. And after I'd finished them, the progressive, degenerative nature of my disease would make my absences more frequent, and my symptoms more visible and debilitating—*on daily television.*

I'd be much less useful, probably a lot less productive. I worked out the scenario in my head: so-so host of a so-so program with a not so so-so illness that was unlikely to get better over time. Surely, I thought, I was toast!

But I couldn't, and wouldn't, hide this illness. Believe me, the thought had crossed my mind. *Just don't tell them at work, don't tell anybody. They'll be none the wiser.*

I had done that ten years ago when I was diagnosed with cancer, and endured and concealed a grueling year of treatment. It was the wrong decision, a major error in judgment, and one I'll always regret.

When you keep something so big so secret for so long, it hurts you in almost innumerable ways. You're living a lie, constantly hiding, pretending, deflecting. I sure as hell wasn't going to make that mistake again.

Besides, it wasn't even an option now. My body wouldn't let me lie. Everyone had noticed my extreme fatigue, my occasional stumbling bouts. More of the same, and worse, would be coming in the future. What were they thinking now? What would they be thinking later, if I didn't tell the painful truth? Living a lie creates spiraling problems. Nasty rumors start. Soon my colleagues would be assuming I was on my deathbed—and I'm not even dying!

No, I wouldn't do with MS what I'd done with cancer, when I worked for PBS as the New York bureau chief for the *Nightly Business Report.* I was young and nervous, and told only a precious few. If news of my cancer spread, I worried, I would be a professional dead man walking. So through the chemotherapy and radiation, weight gain, nausea, and so much more, I didn't breathe a word. My superiors knew only that I had Hodgkin's disease; I tried to leave out as many of the ugly details as possible.

I was more lucky than perhaps I deserved to be that my immediate boss and executive producer, Barry Nemcoff, and his boss, Linda O'Bryon, were very kind, and more than flexible about the days I took off—days that became increasingly frequent as the cancer treatment wore on.

What's more, I later found out that unbeknownst to me, some of my colleagues, led by Washington bureau chief Helen Whelan, had "volunteered" their vacation and sick time to accommodate my days and weeks away from work. The lies I'd tortured myself with for so long had fooled no one.

I'll always be grateful for the striking compassion of my coworkers, the extent of their sacrifices and efforts to help me deal with my cancer and treatment, and their success in keeping all that kindness hidden from *me*.

Still, there was too much going on at the time for any of us to focus substantially on me and my problems. Only two months after my Hodgkin's diagnosis, for example, came the great 1987 stock market crash, and I was the guy in New York assigned to cover this moment in history. Somehow I managed to work straight through this hell, although to this day I don't know how.

I recall doing one report outside the New York Stock Exchange, and after finishing it, promptly puking all over the sidewalk. My cameraman told me I hit a couple of passersby! Sick, weakened, and ashamed, somehow I found the energy to pray that no one would report my actions back to the *Nightly Business Report* offices. That's how scared I was.

With those panic-stricken memories and useless, selfish lies vivid in my mind, I went to Roger's office. It wasn't easy, but when I got there I didn't stop moving. I went right in.

Roger looked at me, ever-perceptive, no-nonsense. All he said was, "What's wrong?"

I tried to compose myself, but I couldn't. Roger's number two and trusted confidante, Chet Collier, was also in the room. I saw them both as my bosses, but also as my priests (a comparison that will no doubt raise Roger's eyebrows!).

They had an enormous empathy for people around them, and an acute sense of people's suffering. Contrary to the often harsh press coverage Roger receives, he is a deeply caring and sensitive individual. It was the real Roger who'd asked the question, and Chet, an equally emotional soul, reinforced my sense of compassionate concern. They knew this was a difficult moment, and that I wasn't there on a routine visit.

I valued my friendship with Roger and had vowed never to abuse it. I liked him for who he was, not for what he could do for me. I lived and acted that way at work, often erring on the side of being remote for fear of being thought a suck-up. But now I had no choice; I trusted Roger to know that I was here on a professional basis only.

Somehow I stammered through, telling Roger and Chet everything my neurologists had told me: I had MS, it was a progressive disease, and I had no way of knowing how far the deterioration would go, or how much it might incapacitate me.

I told them . . . the truth. Telling them was difficult, but it was wonderfully refreshing and relaxing to be so open—right away.

Roger looked at me, his famous blue eyes deeply concerned. His gaze seemed to burrow straight through me.

Then I heard three words: "Is that it?"

"Yes," I answered. "You know what I know."

Roger nodded. "Well, it doesn't sound so bad to me. Just take care of yourself. Do what you have to do. Neil, we're with you. I want you to know that." His gaze intensifying, he repeated for emphasis, "*Do what you have to do.*" Chet seconded his sentiments.

I felt as if the weight of the world had been lifted off my shoulders. My bosses were behind me and I wasn't hiding anything.

The next day I told my staff. I refused to make a federal case out of it. I was very straightforward. "You've already seen some of my odd, maybe troubling, physical symptoms, without knowing the cause or what was wrong with me." I saw heads nodding. "I'm sorry for any distress or concern I may have caused you, and I wish I could have told you sooner. But now you know.

"I'm afraid you're going to see more of my struggles, and they'll gradually get worse. But I'm the same guy, and I want to do the same job. I just may have to ask for a little help now and then."

Their smiling faces told me that wouldn't be a problem.

"Unless I tell you differently, please do your jobs as usual, and treat me as a boss trying to do the same."

My staff was great, They formed a SWAT team to take care of the details I couldn't. Research on guests for my show was presented earlier. The writing that I routinely handled was quietly done for me.

Even my talent back-ups—including Karen Gibbs, and later Brenda Buttner and Terry Keenan—jumped in willingly to be there whenever and wherever.

It must have been an enormous strain on them all, especially given the disease's unpredictable nature. But they were always there, willing, and smiling.

And Roger and Chet often tag-teamed, making frequent calls, checking in, and following up on whatever they thought was necessary.

Since those two days, that double catharsis, my MS has often been difficult, but it has been manageable, with some hospital visits and continued medication and steroid treatments. All in all, not bad.

Dealing with cancer and then MS hasn't been easy, but the way I see my life, I'm one of the *"lucky bastards."*

CHAPTER 1

WHEN LIFE THROWS
YOU A CURVE BALL

'm not a huge baseball fan, but I like the game, and I *am* impressed by the New York Yankees. Because they've won so many championships and World Series, and because they embody the character of New York: unyielding, cocky, very much in-your-face.

That makes all the more odd the unassuming skipper who runs this bunch. In the hurricane that is the big media in the Big Apple, Yankee Manager Joe Torre is the calm eye in the storm: solid, sure, dependable.

I marvel at the way this thrice-fired manager, in a job that tends to age men quicker than the U.S. presidency, only grows calmer over the years, and more self-assured.

He never screams or throws fits. He never berates his players on national TV. If they get hot, he lets them cool down. He prefers talking to each of them privately, rather than en masse or in public.

As he told a gathering of hospital executives in June 2001, "I like communication and talking to people one on one. I don't like screaming. I like to make sense."

Torre makes plenty of sense to his team, and to New Yorkers, and he surrounds himself with people who are much like him: diplomatic doers, not brash talkers.

A good example is Mel Stottlemyre, the quiet, modest pitcher-turned-coach who, like his boss, insists on working out his Yankee pitchers' troubles harmoniously, without fanfare or bravado. He has a rapport with his players that press reports about him understate.

Like Torre, players don't just like him, they trust him. They know he'll be there to shield them from the New York media glare. Pitchers like Dwight Gooden, Mike Hampton, and Andy Pettite, have all said that they wouldn't have become the successes they did become had it not been for Stottlemyre.

Torre and Stottlemyre proved to be powerful dynamos behind the Yankees' success and all those post-1996 division, league, and World Series championships.

As significant as their baseball achievements are, though, it's the way each man handled personal crises that made me decide to include them in this book.

Torre, in 1999, and Stottlemyre, in 2000, had bigger worries than winning baseball games and titles on their minds.

They each had cancer, and their initial prospects looked dicey. Stottlemyre was afflicted with multiple myeloma, a form of cancer that's usually fatal. Torre had a particularly virulent form of prostate cancer—what doctors call a fast-moving malignancy.

Any time you hear the word cancer, you're rightly shell-shocked. Just the word scares people. Cancer: the Big "C."

Years before my mother was diagnosed with a brain tumor, I remember being aware that her biggest fear was getting cancer.

It wasn't so much the hopeless prospects for the disease at the time, but its debilitating final days.

For strong and vibrant people like my mother it was particularly cruel, sapping them of the energy and determination that made them unique, in the end reducing them to little more than human vegetables, painfully closing out their final days.

Heart attacks and car accidents actually take more lives, but cancer and its consequences have a singular dominance of our psyche and fears.

People who *do* survive cancer feel special. I know I do.

Not a day goes by, even with my MS, that I don't think of cancer returning: maybe another bout of Hodgkin's, maybe some lymphoma.

You name it, I worry about it.

And no cancer survivor ever loses that queasy feeling that it could happen all over again.

As traumatizing as it is to learn the diagnosis, and understand how your life has been changed forever, it's worse when you're in a very public job. There's nowhere to hide. Nowhere to cry. Nowhere to gather your senses.

There's an intense pressure on public figures who have to work through very private issues. Almost as important as how they privately deal with their issues or diseases, is how they do so when many people, sometimes across the country, are watching them closely.

Some handle the pressure and personal issues well. Sadly, a lot of them do not.

Magnifying the stress on Torre and Stottlemyre, as they dealt with scary, preferably private, life-threatening cancers, was that they were in a profession that transcends business and inspires kids of all ages, working in the sports world's biggest fishbowl—New York—and with America's most scrutinized baseball team—the New York Yankees.

Unlike business leaders being watched by shareholders curious about how they were doing, the Yankees manager and coach knew that millions of fans were wondering and worrying.

My father once said that you can tell a lot about a person by how he or she handles sickness. The way these two baseball veterans handled theirs is revealing and admirable.

As I discovered, they focused far more on others than on themselves. I'm sure that in private they had their difficult periods, dealing with the stark fact of cancer and their individual fears and doubts. Publicly, though, they put it all aside and led by example.

No matter what their pain and suffering, they were going to hold it together—not only for the team, but for the world. That's an enormously selfless act, at a time when it would have been understandable to be selfish. These men were not.

NOT JUST YOUR ORDINARY JOE

Here I am, not much of a baseball fan, and even I call him "Joe." *Everyone* calls him Joe. He's the guy next door, a pal down the block, an uncle and friend rolled into one. The guy so familiar to millions he's never met, whose hands he's never shook, and whose good words he's never heard, that when they see him they shout, "You da man, Joe!"

Joe Torre is every guy's ideal guy. He comforts the pitcher who just got blown out in a horrible inning, and cries for his team after winning the big one. He wears his emotions on his sleeve and his low-key humor on the field. He is the comfortable shoe, who doesn't act like a heel.

I know this sounds corny, but as an Italian American (with a little Irish thrown in for good measure), Joe makes me proud. He's the kid who's done good. But he's also the kid who's overcome so much, and done so with dignity and determination.

In him, we can see a model for ourselves. Why vent, when you can just do? Why rant, when you can just roll?

Joe was the guy who took it all on, and took it all in.

Maybe his strength and graciousness began to develop during his childhood battles with self-esteem. Overweight and self-conscious as a kid growing up in Brooklyn, Joe apparently lacked the athletic gifts that had propelled his older brother Frank into the major leagues. To critics watching his earliest baseball playing, young Joe Torre was just a fat kid with no speed.

So much to overcome. So many doubters. So many problems. So little time to prove himself. Yet the fact that he did gives us all hope.

Joe *did* follow his older brother into the big leagues, and an April 2001 *Fortune* magazine profile on Joe attributed his rare ability to motivate players to his having been a player himself, and a damn good one.

He spent sixteen years in a player's uniform, mostly as a catcher for the Atlanta Braves, St. Louis Cardinals, and his first New York team, the Mets. That experience taught him about slumps (and how they come and go), and batting averages (and how they rise and fall). It certainly taught him about dealing with difficult players and demanding bosses. Ted Turner in Atlanta and August Busch III in St. Louis are considered two of the toughest owners in baseball, and they scrutinized everything Joe did, as a player, and later as a manager.

Joe also had to suffer through the tragic death of his oldest brother, Rocco, and later the ordeal of his now-retired brother, Frank, as he waited desperately for a heart transplant.

What always helped Joe endure and ultimately triumph was the special closeness of his family, including his two sisters, one of them a nun in Queens. The Torres were every family, yet like no other family. Through it all they held together, and helped each other get back up.

After making the uncommon and estimable transition from player to manager, which requires a very different set of skills, Joe had more obstacles to overcome. Before coming to the Yankees, he was fired as a manager from all three of the teams he'd played for: In his years with the Mets, Braves, and Cards, he amassed more than 1,000 losses.

The rap was always the same. He was too close to the men he managed, more inclined to baby them than challenge them.

Then Yankee owner George Steinbrenner offered Joe the big Bronx job.

Joe has said that a lot of luck has come his way. I prefer to think that luck follows those who work the hardest. And Joe had *worked* for this singular opportunity. After decades in baseball and repeated "failures" and firings, he was now in the most important and challenging position of his career.

He was the manager of the New York Yankees, the most storied and successful team in the history of baseball—and reporting to the most stress-producing owner, even by the standards of Turner and Busch.

Torre's critics were certain that his time in the Bronx would be short-lived. How, they asked, could this calm and deliberate fellow, never prone to temper tantrums, ever survive working for Steinbrenner, who seemed to make it his life's mission to destroy his managers?

What most impressed me in watching Joe take over the Yankees in 1996 was how self-assured he was coming into the job.

Legend has it that, upon arriving in New York, Joe asked Yankee owner George Steinbrenner whether he should buy or rent an apartment. Steinbrenner reportedly shot back, "Rent!"

Joe opted to buy. He hung pictures in his office as if he planned to stay a while. Keep in mind that, before Joe came along, Steinbrenner had made twenty-one managerial changes in his first twenty-two years of ownership. Who but Joe could have anticipated that in the years to come he would manage more games than Billy Martin did in all five of his tenures *combined*?

Joe calmly sensed that unexpected longevity before anyone else inside or outside the Yankee organization. He knew the Yankee squad had the talent. They just didn't have the motivation. They didn't have someone solid or consistent in their corner. Joe decided he would be that man.

In short order, he instilled a loyalty in the players, between him and each other, the likes of which hadn't been seen in American sports since the days of Vince Lombardi.

I recall an April 2001 *Fortune* magazine profile on Joe, that described how the Yankee boss could teach executives of all stripes a thing or two:

No this isn't Jack Welch in pinstripes. Let's be clear: Joe Torre knows no more about running a Fortune 500 company than Shakespeare or Elizabeth I or Jesus or any of the other figures who have lately been transfigured into management savants. Understanding ERA does not make one a master of EVA. But chances are, Joe Torre knows something about managing people that you don't.

Leave it to Yankee owner George Steinbrenner to tell *Fortune* this about his under-the-magnifying-glass manager: "For a guy who was fired three times, he's done pretty well. He has respect for me and the organization. Maybe that comes from getting fired three times."

Even with tongue-in-cheek praise, the message was then and is now clear: Joe Torre connects with everyone he meets, whether a down-and-out player, or an in-your-face owner. New Yorkers hadn't seen it before. They're not likely to see it again.

The "Torre method" consists of sitting tight the day of the bonehead move, and taking it up the next day. His goal is to wait out the emotion of the moment, and hopefully engage in productive discussions later, when emotions have cooled.

Also, Joe's not a showoff, and he didn't want his players to be showoffs either. If you're good, his thinking went, it should be obvious. You don't have to persuade people, and you shouldn't brag about it.

The world is legion with Yankee-haters. But Joe's 1996 Yankee squad, and the teams that followed in coming years, gave them no reason to continue such bad feelings. These guys knew they were good. They just stopped acting like it.

Joe's message was unmistakable: Let them hate us, if they want to, but only because we're so good, not because we act so bad.

When I discussed his people-management skills with Joe during a fall 2001 visit he made to my show, he described how his approach extended beyond his own Yankees. Teamwork means understanding your team, he said, but more important, it means understanding the personalities of *all* the players, especially the more difficult ones. It also means having the right amount of patience, varying it from player to player.

"What I think we have to do, Neil," he added, "is treat everybody with respect. But not only your teammates. I think what helps us and what has helped us be successful as a team, is we treat the other team with respect also. We don't spike the ball. We don't go and say, 'Hey, look how good we are.' We play. We win. We know we're good. We have what I like to call, '*inner conceit.*' Nobody has to know it but us."

With no disrespect to Mr. Torre, I prefer to think of his exemplary approach as "*humbled power.*" No "conceit."

Because of his compassion and respect for others, Joe sticks by people whom others love to abandon when trouble comes up. It's why he was supportive of Darryl Strawberry after he was arrested in Florida for picking up a prostitute. "I just saw a guy who had been on an emotional roller coaster," Joe said.

Later, in 1998, he cried when he told the team that Darryl Strawberry was battling colon cancer. Later, he told his star player Bernie Williams to go home, be with his gravely ill father, and not worry about hurrying back.

Joe knows what the true priorities are. He also knows that when you get your team to focus on the big things, they tend to do better at the little things. They're more cohesive, and in the end they're more content.

Joe's famous calmness, respect for the feelings of others, and patience are so completely a part of the man that when it was time to handle a different, decidedly more personal pressure and issue, he stayed the same "Joe." On the field or off, he is true to himself and others.

He tries to understand, not just players, but life. He knows both can be fleeting. Players can be stars one moment, then duds the next. And life? Well, no guarantees there either.

When he announced early in the 1999 spring training season that he had prostate cancer, what struck me first was how routinely he treated it, how consistent his perspective on life and the game were.

"I feel fine," he announced at the time, "and I am looking forward to taking care of this problem and getting back to work."

There were reports that team doctors thought Joe's disease was in its early stages, that owner George Steinbrenner thought the tests were encouraging and Joe would be back in three weeks, in time for the season opener on April 5.

What wasn't talked about was how much of a jolt the news was to the Yankee organization.

Word of Joe's condition came only days after Yankee great Joe DiMaggio died from lung cancer, and on the same day Darryl Strawberry returned to the lineup for the first time in five months, after battling his own cancer.

Suddenly, cancer was popping up a lot in the baseball world. Atlanta first baseman Andres Galarraga had just been diagnosed with a cancerous tumor in his lower back and was undergoing chemotherapy. And Florida Marlins third baseman Mike Lowell had been diagnosed with testicular cancer a month earlier.

Still, people were hopeful. Marv Levy, the former Buffalo Bills football coach, had undergone prostate cancer surgery a few years earlier, and was back coaching only weeks after the operation.

Joe was more concerned with how his team was doing, than how he was. He met with every one of his coaches, then individually with veteran players, including Joe Girardi, Paul O'Neill, and David Cone.

But privately, he would later say, he was stunned. Speaking to *In Touch* in July 2001, Joe talked about how the whole episode was "so different from the way I think in baseball."

"You know, when you're out there playing against another team, one of the two teams has to win—so you preach positive and tell the players to 'stay aggressive.' But when you're waiting to hear if you have cancer, it's pretty much out of your hands. It's a different mental preparation."

With very different priorities. "When a doctor is talking to you about possible side effects—you know, incontinence, impotency, and so on, at that point you're so driven by wanting to live that those things seem insignificant."

As he would later say about those earliest days with the disease: "My first thoughts centered on my family. I have four kids, including a three-year-old daughter named Andrea Rae. This was one of those moments that clarifies personal priorities; the needs and concerns of my family were front and center. Certainly, baseball is my life, but being diagnosed with a serious disease like prostate cancer makes you realize what's really important!"

With the support of his wife and children, and the members of the extended Torre family, Joe concentrated on getting well—which, after surgery, he did.

His next priority was helping other men avoid the same fate. No sooner had Joe beat cancer, than he was out on the road preaching cancer prevention and treatment.

Within months of his recovery, there was Joe in Washington, D.C., speaking before Senator Arlen Specter's Subcommittee on Labor, Health and Human Services about prostate cancer. "I am the manager of the New York Yankees," he stated. "I am also a prostate cancer survivor."

The committee was riveted on every word, not just because Joe Torre was the guy talking, but because of what he was talking about: the randomness of a disease that was far more pervasive than many on that committee might have thought. "A man has a one in six chance of getting prostate cancer in his lifetime," he said. "If he has a close relative with prostate cancer, his risk doubles. With two close relatives, his risk increases five-fold. With three close relatives, his risk is nearly 97 percent. Make no mistake, this can be a family disease."

Joe went on to explain the risk to African Americans in particular: They have the highest prostate cancer rate in the world, up to 50 percent greater than the rate for white males. African American men are also twice as likely to die.

"I'm here to tell you that prostate cancer doesn't discriminate based on age," he said. "This is not an old man's disease. About one in four prostate cancer cases strikes a man during his prime working years, under the age of sixty-five. I am fifty-eight years old and the number of men in their forties and fifties who are battling prostate cancer is increasing. Doctors around the country report seeing more aggressive forms of the disease in younger men."

I always marveled at the impact Joe was having on that committee, and the accompanying media attention he was getting. This sounds horrible, but prostate cancer couldn't have found a better target, or a more vocal one.

Joe did everything in his power to warn anyone who would listen that this disease was growing, and social demographics supported his conclusion.

"Don't forget," he warned, "as the baby boom generation ages, its risk of prostate cancer, if unchecked, will continue to increase. That's why this hearing is so crucial and why Congress's role in protecting men and their families from prostate cancer will make such a tremendous difference in the lives of millions of Americans."

With Father's Day just days away, Joe opted for one hell of an emotional close. "I'm happy to be able to spend this holiday with my loved ones. I am also happy to be able to be a spokesman for Cap Cure's 'Home Run Challenge,' its annual week-long effort with Major League Baseball, centered on Father's Day, to raise awareness and private-sector funding for prostate cancer research."

"For too many families, this holiday is a time to remember the fathers, husbands, and brothers who have been lost to this disease. By providing increased research funding, you can stem rising rates of prostate cancer and protect future generations of men and their families from its devastation."

Committee members were shell-shocked. Joe had hit an emotional home run. Prostate cancer, a disease many men felt uncomfortable talking about, was suddenly the disease *everyone* was talking about. So impressed were cancer-fighting advocates of all sorts, that Joe became their pitchman of choice. It didn't matter the particular cancer, just make sure you have Joe talking about its dangers.

No one seemed to connect with audiences like the Yankee boss. Oddly, with women and men, young and old, Joe was a sizzler on the stump. Some audience members would ask him if he'd ever run for office. Joe would just smile.

Suddenly Joe was popping up at one cancer event after another. He would join celebrities like Paul Newman, Rosie O'Donnell, Harry Belafonte, and Hillary Clinton to pitch cancer prevention.

The size of the audience didn't matter as much as the message. You'd see Joe in hospitals and bookstores, fancy banquet halls and gymnasiums. It didn't matter. Anywhere he could get the word out, the Yankee skipper was preaching.

They say you can tell a lot about a person by how he handles success. Does he still remember his roots? Does he deny his past? Is he more interested in being with the in crowd than the old crowd? When I hear about his family gatherings and his cross-country pitch for cancer-fighting causes no matter how small the venue, I see a guy who gets it. I also see a guy who tries to share it.

His whole approach to cancer, and turning a bad thing for himself into a potentially instructive thing for others, always told me a lot about Joe Torre. He was and continues to be every bit the powerful, spiritual, and philanthropic chief executive wielding power and influence from one hell of a powerful public relations perch.

Making living more important than winning, and prioritizing others above himself, are part of what keeps Joe at peace. Those values held him together when his Yankees were ending the 2000 season losing sixteen of nineteen games. He refused to panic or throw tantrums in front of the media. He kept himself calm and his team focused.

The Yankees went on to win games when they *really* counted, ultimately winning the World Series that year.

With that continuing success, I worried about Joe professionally. How does a guy who's given New Yorkers so much, so many titles over so many years, keep raising the bar? I brought this question up with Joe in that 2001 interview.

"People are getting kind of used to winning these titles, Joe. They want to see them all the time," I suggested.

"I understand," Joe answered. "And I think it's pretty good working for George Steinbrenner, because he feels he owes it to the people of New York to keep the ball club on top."

Joe said that he welcomed the pressure. "It makes my job easier."

I told him I had my doubts. "Well, people asked me, Neil, when I was first named manager, 'What happens? What are you gonna do when George does this or when George does that?"

"I always say I don't *What I am gonna do?* It depends on the mood I am in, and the circumstances that are involved, and then I'll decide what I do. But I wasn't going to waste my time trying to project my answer to a certain criticism when I didn't know what the criticism was, and if it was ever going to come."

Joe knows he can't control events or people. He strongly believes in what I suggested were "schmuck-free" zones. "Bad guys are gonna be bad guys," he said. "It's gonna come out. But I think you should let them know the way you feel about things."

And when it comes to his own players, just let them know where you stand, then "turn them loose. I never try to dictate to my players, other than some rules. We all follow some basic rules."

I now saw more deeply that Joe just knows how to handle pressure, from physical pain to professional pain. Just like he knew what he was coming into working for Steinbrenner back in 1996. "You have to understand," he told me. "When you play thirty years, a combination of playing and managing, and you have never been to a World Series. And knowing that George is a tyrant, sure. But he is going to put the players on the field, and try to win. And I'm going to try to win. We both agree."

Many say he works for the most difficult boss in the world. "He does second-guess you a lot, doesn't he?" I ask.

"That's fine," he answered. "I mean, ask my wife. My sister too, and she's a nun."

"But does it bug you," I ask, "when he just comes in and says, 'that was a bonehead play. Why did you do that?' I mean, how do you deal with that?"

"You listen to it."

"But do you get mad or angry?"

"I get angry. Sure."

He talks about one episode in the 1996 series, when Derek Jeter was thrown out trying to steal third base. Joe was furious.

"He was trying to go to third base with two out, and it was the third out of the inning. And I slammed something down, and threw things. And I said to [assistant coach Don] Zimmer, 'I can't talk to this kid, because he is just a kid. And I'll get him tomorrow.'

"After the inning was over, Jeter came in and sat between Don and myself. And I said, 'This kid is special.' I hit him in the back of the head, and just said, 'Get the hell out of here.'"

Obviously, Joe's "angry" isn't like anyone else's. He might get upset, but he never gets mad. That's a significant distinction in the Torre school of interpersonal skills.

"I can tell you from being treated for cancer that you go through a lot of emotions. Not that there's any excuse for that, but I try to understand."

He once spoke of the fickleness of the lives of baseball managers, heroes one moment, heels the next. He knows nothing is guaranteed in life, so he refuses to take advantage of it. He talks about things that matter, not titles and riches that ultimately do not.

As he pushes on in sports, it's what Joe teaches us about life and living well, by doing good for others, that's more enduring than his baseball achievements.

History will record him as one of the most successful managers ever. I will remember his courage under fire, and his generosity after fire—with his time, his money, and his heart.

I'll also remember the way Joe lives his life with dignity, reminding those who have suffered illnesses of their own, or endured personal and professional failures, that these challenges can devastate you or define you.

Joe Torre chose to be defined, and in doing so achieved an unexpected, unselfish greatness.

Millions of us are grateful he did.

ALMOST OUT-PITCHED

Sometimes I wonder if the Yankees are as much cursed as they are gifted. Sure, they won all those World Series titles, along with dozens of other championships, but it seems they get more than their fair share of pain to go along with the triumphs.

After Joe Torre battled prostate cancer in 1999, with pitching coach Mel Stottlemyre always at his side, the following year Stottlemyre had his own immensely challenging struggle with cancer.

What made his battle so daunting and terrifying is how hopeless it seemed. Multiple myeloma is an incurable blood cancer, carried in the bone marrow, often lethal, and very difficult to treat. This particular type of blood cancer erodes the bones, and for more than half the victims leads to death within five years or less.

Its rarity is part of the problem, because not enough is known about this form of cancer. Multiple myeloma is the second most prevalent blood cancer, but it accounts for only 1 percent of all cancers, and 2 percent of cancer deaths.

Only three new cases per 100,000 people are diagnosed every year. Often undetected until it's too late, multiple myeloma usually becomes a death sentence, as devastating as it is quick.

The odds and statistics were *not* in Stottlemyre's favor.

If he was shaken by the diagnosis, though, he didn't show it, and he didn't share the news. Through the summer of 2000, no one detected that the Yankees pitching boss was sick at all. He'd stroll through the clubhouse, smiling at players and visitors alike—his vise-like handshake as strong as ever.

His cheerful demeanor is classic Mel Stottlemyre. Never a complainer, he was always the unheralded guy doing big things, often against big odds.

He was the promising pitching prospect called up from the minors in August 1964 to join the Yankees' starting rotation. From that point on, through the end of the regular season, Stottlemyre won nine games and pitched a 2.06 earned run average. The league batted a meager .219 against him.

He won a crucial rubber game of a three-game September series against the Baltimore Orioles, leading his Yankees to the divisional championship, and ultimately the World Series. In that series, the rookie Stottlemyre picked up a crucial win against Bob Gibson, the St. Louis Cardinals pitcher who'd later be chosen for the Hall of Fame.

As a Yankee pitcher, he'd go on to win twenty games in a season no less than three times, and pitch in five All-Star games. His lifetime ERA is an enviable 2.97.

No wonder teams clamored for Stottlemyre's coaching services when he retired—and got plenty of success if they had him on their staff.

When he was the Mets' pitching coach during manager Davey Johnson's tenure, the team finished first or second in its division for seven straight years, including a World Series win in 1986. He'd enjoy even more success, and titles, with the Yankees.

He'd also experience a pain that was worse than losing games or titles. During that summer of Stottlemyre smiles, he was already months into chemotherapy that was being absorbed through tubes in his chest. He was taking up to twenty-four pills a day, all charted and organized by his wife, Jean, who transformed a big Yankee pitching chart into a medicine schedule prominently displayed on the Stottlemyre refrigerator.

"It was scary when I read the med sheet and saw what Mel had to take," she told *New York Post* reporter George Willis months later, in April 2001. "I thought to myself, Dear God, how will I ever get this straight? That was one of my biggest problems in the beginning. I knew it was important to get all those meds right. It was quite a process."

Through much of the first half of the season, Jean was traveling with her husband to make sure he was taking his medication properly.

I really think Stottlemyre, who has the true Yankees grit, would never have told a soul about his cancer if he hadn't needed a stem-cell transplant in September 2000. Such treatment often is considered a medical Hail Mary pass, in which stem cells are transplanted after a high dose of chemotherapy. The goal is to trigger the normal production of blood cells again, after chemotherapy has destroyed bad cells.

His medical emergency forced him not only to tell his beloved Yankees the shocking news, but to leave his position as their pitching coach.

With a severely weakened immune system, he couldn't risk being around people. Exposure to something as slight as a cold could prove fatal. Stottlemyre would later say he had hoped the transplant could be put off, maybe until after the end of the season, but the danger was too great, so on September 11 he ceased his active duties.

Characteristically, though, instead of focusing exclusively on his life-and-death struggle, he remained very involved in his team's rough and rocky ride to and into the American League championship series.

He stayed in touch with Joe Torre and members of his pitching staff, so he could contributing indirectly, as much as possible, to the Yankees' progress in the playoffs. He even found a way to visit the

Yankees clubhouse, albeit carefully. On doctor's orders, he had to wear rubber gloves and a mask, and stay away from as many people as possible.

Stottlemyre would later watch Games 1 and 2 on a television in Torre's office. And he found a way to be directly involved when he needed to be.

The *New York Post*'s George Willis described how Stottlemyre communicated with Roger Clemens after the volatile pitcher threw that infamous bat in the direction of Mike Piazza in Game 2. Stottlemyre said, "I just told him he had to turn the page and go on with the game, and not let that be a distraction to what he was trying to accomplish."

Sometimes I wonder what I would be thinking if it were me. I'd probably be ignoring a temperamental pitcher, and paying more attention to my temperamental body! But not Stottlemyre. And though his intention was to help his players, I think he benefited medically from his prioritizing. That he was as much, if not more, focused on others as he was on himself, seemed to strengthen and speed up the healing process.

Innately modest, he supervised one of the most closely scrutinized and praised pitching staffs in baseball history. But he refrained from shining the spotlight on himself, and even more from looking for sympathy.

Sure, he'd have his moments, commenting at the time that the chemotherapy would make him nauseous or weak, but he never made a big deal of it.

What did matter was that the Yankees had a third straight World Series championship in reach. That motivated Stottlemyre to focus on keeping his staff on course, and assisting his boss and his team in winning the famous New York Subway series, as the Yankees and Mets clashed for baseball's highest honor.

He succeeded on both counts, and happily resumed his active duties when the stem-cell transplant proved effective in pushing the cancer into remission.

He also became an inspirational victor in another, even more important way.

Just as prostate cancer sufferers couldn't have hoped for a better spokesman than Joe Torre, those dealing with the vagaries of multiple myeloma couldn't have had a bigger champion than Mel Stottlemyre.

He knew that the key to helping others was getting the word out. He energetically used his fame, success, and clout to educate as many people as he could, and lent his name to the efforts of others who were fighting the illness, and increasing awareness of it.

His wife, Jean, was equally committed. They were already heavily involved in finding cures and treatments for leukemia, a blood cancer; their third son, Jason, had died of leukemia in 1981 at the age of eleven.

Rather than keep their pain inside, Mel and Jean were eager to see some good come out of their tragedy, raising money for and awareness of the disease that took Jason's life.

In 1992, Mel and Jean received the National Recognition Award from the Leukemia Society for all their efforts. Another son, Todd, a promising pitcher for the Arizona Diamondbacks at the time, donated $1 million to leukemia research. It was and is a family affair.

Building on almost twenty years of experience in cancer education, and only months after Mel's own grueling battle, Mel and Jean established the Mel Stottlemyre Multiple Myeloma Foundation. Together they reminded sufferers that their prospects weren't hopeless; that new research and technologies had vastly improved over the years; that more than fifty thousand people with multiple myeloma were living with hope rather than fear.

Now multiple myeloma patients are getting the same treatment, the same undivided attention and support, as most cancer sufferers.

I'll never forget an interview I read in the *Chicago Tribune* in March 2001, in which Phil Rogers asked if Stottlemyre ever felt sorry for himself. He'd lost a son to cancer and almost died from it himself.

"I never said, 'Why me?' " the embattled pitching coach replied. "I could also say, 'Why not me?' "

〰〰

L iving in the glare of the media can make even healthy guys go bonkers. Suffering a disease in tough enough on the person suffering it. Doing so under public scrutiny only makes it tougher. Understandably, some sick people go even more bonkers.

But Joe and Mel aren't your typical sick guys. They turned the media spotlight around, and used their success and fame to benefit others—far less well known, and professionally and financially fortunate.

They battled cancer the way they played, coached, and managed baseball, with unrelenting drive and complete commitment, and they learned from their illnesses, painful as they were, as they've learned from their thousands of defeats and victories.

They relish helping others beat the odds, even more than they delight in defeating other teams in championship series.

They have lent their name, time, effort and money to getting the word out—about early detection, constant check-ups, and staying alert about the little things so they don't become big things.

In life, as in baseball, they are scrupulous "coaches" who constantly remind cancer sufferers and potential victims that it's the details, the small, overlooked symptoms that make a big difference in a big game—whether it's a World Series or a person's health and life.

Thousands of men have gotten off their duffs and tested for prostate cancer because Joe Torre said it can happen to anyone, even big league managers.

Thousands of women and men alike have talked to their doctors because they know that rare blood abnormalities can hit anyone at any time. Mel Stottlemyre has reminded them that such abnormalities are indeed rare, but if caught early, they need not be fatal.

All of these people and more continue regular testing and visits with their doctors because two baseball guys have changed their lives forever.

It's hard to say how many potential victims have been spared by prevention, or how many people are alive today because of early treatment. Whatever the totals are, they're the most vital statistics in the careers of Joe Torre and Mel Stottlemyre.

CHAPTER 2

WHO CARES IF THE COOKIE CRUMBLES?

Can you imagine being the name behind Famous Amos Cookies, and not being allowed to capitalize on it? Or even use the name? Imagine being Wally Amos, the cookie entrepreneur, whose own cookie empire crumbled—on him!

If something like that happened to me, I can't help thinking I'd be bitter, and probably poor. But not Wally Amos. To this day, he maintains his good humor and sharp wit. Far from being devastated by the events that ripped his own company from his hands, he remains strong and remarkably upbeat.

I don't think I've ever heard or read of his getting depressed, or beaten down. Each new challenge only brings out the kidding, jovial bearded visionary who made Famous Amos a household name.

For most people, a professional defeat can cause very real and profound emotional damage. But Wally Amos is not most people. And it's precisely his dogged optimism and good humor that have helped him triumph where most others would have been resigned to failure.

Many have joked that Wally's cookie empire "crumbled," but Amos enjoys correcting the metaphor. In countless interviews and speeches, he points out that "the cookie never does crumble. That phrase demeans the cookie, actually. I mean, once it breaks up, you just have little, smaller cookies. It multiplies." Talk about optimism!

A high school dropout who earned his GED in the Air Force, Wally didn't seem to have any of the makings or trappings for greatness. But he did have a knack for seizing opportunities.

In 1961, he moved to New York and got a job as a mail clerk at the powerful William Morris Agency in New York. He helped out wherever he could, including serving as a receptionist or secretary when needed. He even replaced toilet paper in the company's men's rooms when it needed to be done.

As he later observed in *The Famous Amos Story:* "Working in the mailroom was a job that required you to listen, be observant, have initiative, plenty of patience, and do what you were told to do as quickly and efficiently as possible. It was also the perfect place to be to see how the agency functioned; you could literally see the business from the ground up."

He saw it well. After only two months of shuffling mail, he was promoted to substitute secretary, and a few months later he was made secretary to Howard Hausman, a senior vice president.

Hausman immediately took a liking to Wally, allowing him to attend strategy meetings and even listen in on phone calls. It was Hausman who later recommended the young Wally Amos for a new music department the firm was starting. Wally would report to that department's supervising agent, Jerry Brandt, who taught the young man all the industry ropes.

Wally Amos was coming on strong. Within a few months, he was an assistant agent, and by 1962, only a year after starting at the agency, he was a full-fledged William Morris talent agent.

But he had moral ambitions, too. "Agents, I realized, had shady, underhanded images, and I wanted to clearly establish that that was not the manner in which I operated."

He successfully combined being a *different* kind of agent with a knack for spotting talent in as yet, unknown entertainers. It was Wally who booked a singer/songwriter by the name of Paul Simon and his partner, Art Garfunkel. He later represented the Supremes, Dionne Warwick, Sam Cooke, and Marvin Gaye.

Wally was clicking, and he was convinced the firm would recognize his contributions when the top position in the music department opened up. But despite his seniority and accomplishments, he didn't get that job. That was probably the only time in his professional life he may have felt some bitterness. But it didn't last long.

He continued developing his agenting skills, and expanding the impressive list of talented entertainers he represented.

In 1967, when he was ready to become independent, he left William Morris and started his own firm in Los Angeles. He'd thought the move would make his work easier and smoother, but soon he was sorely disappointed.

One of his earliest acts, on whom he had bet a great deal, was a well-known trumpeter. Wally was arranging a concert in New York City's Philharmonic Hall, now Avery Fisher Hall, when the trumpeter terminated their business relationship, still owing Wally thousands of dollars. Other disappointments would follow over the next six years.

"I would put all my hopes in my clients, and then nothing would happen," he wrote in *The Famous Amos Story*. "I grew tired of never having any money and never knowing how I was going to get money to pay my expenses."

To console himself, Wally started baking cookies, then bringing them in to work. He'd pass them out to anyone in the office, from his own staff to visiting producers and entertainers. Suddenly the cookies were bigger talking points than any potential business deals. Among those impressed was B. J. Gilmore, a secretary to musician Quincy Jones. She told Wally his cookies were good enough to sell; maybe this talent agent should become a cookie agent.

To Wally, it sounded like a dream—that he could turn into a real business.

Continuing his client work, Wally began seeking out investors who'd help him get his cookie company started. His ambitious and daunting goal was to raise $25,000 to buy baking equipment and cover rent for a store. To his relief and delight, Wally soon attracted some powerful backers, Marvin Gaye and Helen Reddy among them.

Indeed, support for Wally's cookie venture came so fast and furious that within months of that now-famous chat with Gilmore, he was hosting a Hollywood pre-opening-day party outside his Sunset Boulevard store. More than 2,500 attended the gala event; when the store opened for business the next day, customers were lining up outside the door.

Suddenly his cookies were a cult, successfully pitched for their sinfully plentiful ingredients, with the image of the smiling Wally "Famous" Amos on the packaging, reflecting the pleasure they brought in the eating.

They were the Lays potato chips of the chocolate chip world: Nobody could eat just one. And for a good while, it seemed that nobody did. In an increasingly crowded market for premium cookies, Famous Amos was the brand of choice. And there never seemed to be enough to go around.

By the summer of 1975, the Famous Amos Chocolate Chip Cookie Corporation was going wholesale, selling directly to Pasadena, California, grocer Jurgensen's, and later the Macy's branch in San Francisco. Little more than a year after that, Wally was selling in upscale department stores Bloomingdale's and Nieman Marcus. His list of flavors grew, and so did the business line that went with them. There were Famous Amos T-shirts and umbrellas, duffel bags, and jewelry.

Wally himself was as close to a rock star as the clients he used to represent. He was riding on floats in Macy's Thanksgiving Day parade and popping up on television and radio shows, and newspaper and magazine covers. *Time* featured him among "The Hot New Rich" in a June 13, 1977, cover story. By that time, Famous Amos cookies were being produced at a rate of six tons every week. Earnings had already crossed a million dollars.

But the cookie market remained hotly competitive, and price wars ensued. Wally was a great visionary for the company, but by his own admission, not so great a day-to-day business guy. And as *Forbes* magazine later reported, the people he trusted to run the business weren't a whole lot better. The company seemed to be forever short of cash for expansion. By the mid-1980s, the Famous Amos company was losing money.

Wally made a fateful move. Desperate for investments from outsiders, he entertained even those who would drain his own equity in the company. By some accounts, the company changed hands no less than four times, with Wally ultimately reduced to little more than a pitchman. By the time the company was sold to a Taiwanese corporation in 1992, Wally received nothing—not one red cent.

"I take responsibility for what happened to me," Wally told *Parade* writer Michael Ryan in 1994. "When my company rejected me and gave me lemons, I decided to turn those lemons into lemonade. I remembered that doors had slammed in my face before, yet others had always opened to more brilliant prospects . . . . I knew that the proper use of this period in my life was to benefit people in need."

He devoted more time to charitable causes, including Literacy Volunteers of America and Cities in Schools, a national dropout-prevention program.

Wally's business connections were, for all intents and purposes, completely severed. Not only had he lost majority control, and then ownership, of his own company; because of a legal document he'd signed, he lost the right to start or enter into any business that had anything to do with his old one. This was more than a noncompete clause, it was basically a *no-business* contract. He had to refrain for two years from "conducting business on behalf of any other organization engaged in the production or marketing of cookies."

As bad as things were, they got even worse. The owners of the Famous Amos company obtained a court order forbidding Wally from using either his name or likeness, or even his voice, in conjunction with *any* food-related business. The man who made "Amos" famous couldn't use the name himself. Not only could he not use his own good name; he had to watch others cash in on it!

It was a professional disaster.

In the annals of entrepreneurial businesses, it isn't unusual for the guy who starts the company to get fired. Steve Jobs, the co-founder of Apple Computer, got forced out in a power struggle, only to return in triumph years later. But it is very unusual for a company founder to be legally prevented from ever using his own name in a business enterprise again.

I can't imagine the pain of seeing the baby you created effectively turn on you, even dump you. How do you recover from such a humiliating professional catastrophe?

Wally's answer is, you don't dwell on it. You don't seek revenge, or obsess about the loss and pain. You carry on, with your head held high, and your ego in check. You remind yourself that the sum of your talents vastly exceeds the sum of your shortcomings. And you chuckle at the fickleness of life, the silliness of it all.

I'm convinced that Wally would have gladly skipped out on anything he was doing, if he wasn't having a good time. That's why he decided not to stay on at a revamped and re-owned Famous Amos as some sort of goodwill ambassador. He owed himself, and those who knew him best, more than that. And, in the end, he gave the world much more.

I've covered thousands of chief executives in my life. They range from those who've enjoyed steady success, those who've thrived, failed, and rebounded, and those who've fallen, and not even tried to come back.

I've known many executives who grew angry at the world after failed ventures. I knew one, in fact, who left his wife and kids and retreated into a hermit-like existence because he was so bitter.

Usually, the ones who quit trying don't gain any valuable insights from their experiences—probably because they're too proud or ashamed to face their failures. For the same reason, they don't talk about their mistakes.

Not Wally Amos. Far from avoiding discussing his problems, he showcases them. He doesn't waste time making excuses for his failures. He points the finger right back on himself. He writes and talks often about how his own arrogance and business shortcomings doomed his initial venture.

What Wally's example teaches us is that there's not much use in agonizing over the might-have-beens. In order to move on professionally, you have to move on mentally. "Attitude is the magic word," he writes.

Wally *is* what he writes. He's so positive and upbeat, you get the feeling he could be left with nothing at all, and still laugh about it. It's the adventure that matters to him, not whether he's made money, or even done well.

Enjoy the ride, up and down. Seize it, appreciate it, understand it, and learn from it. The problems and failures can make you bitter and angry, but they shouldn't. They can make you want to quit, but don't.

"The only thing you can do by yourself is fail," he told a Purdue University audience in November 2002. "If you're determined to really succeed, you absolutely can. I learned not to focus on problems, focus on the solution."

What was the solution to the absolute loss of Famous Amos cookies?

"Since I lost the company," he told *Newsday* in November 2002, it had "always been in the back of my mind" that he wanted to go back to cookies. As he waited through the two-year, no-cookie-business period, Wally prepared to launch a new company "Most people said I couldn't even get the one cookie store off the ground," he recalled. "They had no faith in my ability. I think I got so intent on proving people wrong that I got a little big-headed. Ultimately, through my own missteps and arrogance, I wound up losing the company."

But he learned something from that initial failure. He couldn't retail a product with no retail expertise. He correctly surmised that his product was much better suited to a wholesale environment, entrusted to experienced managers who really knew the retail trade.

Using his original cookie recipe, but legally prevented from using the Famous Amos name, the crafty Wally launched Uncle Noname Cookies in 1992, poking fun at his legal predicament.

The competition was, if anything, more daunting than it was when he first started out. There were all those entrenched competitors to worry about—big names like Nabisco, Pepperidge Farm, Mrs. Fields, and Keebler.

But Wally wasn't much impressed by competition. Something inside him aims to correct past mistakes, to "vindicate myself for screwing up Famous Amos," as he would later put it.

Although that brand didn't take off, the fact that Amos was back in the business generated a lot of good buzz, and he started a new brand called Aunt Della's Cookies, in tribute to the aunt he'd moved in with at age twelve when his parents divorced.

Aunt Della's had little difficulty securing deals with Pathmark and Wal-Mart stores within months of its launch.

Building on that success, Wally branched out into Uncle Wally's Rich & Moist Muffin, selling sinfully delicious muffins in two, three, and four-pack sizes. Like his cookies, they featured the best ingredients, and a lot of them.

Wally quickly discovered that a good product can overcome not-so-good marketing, or a not-so-hot name. Word of mouth does the job. And with Wally as the guy leading the charge, the word spread fast. From virtually nothing, Uncle Wally's Muffins now does more than $20 million a year.

Venture capitalists didn't turn things around for Wally Amos. He did, because he believed. Through some competitors' laughter, even jeers, he carried on, with that beguiling smile and contagious laugh. Now it's Wally Amos who's having the last laugh.

Never in the business world, at least to my knowledge, has someone who has failed so big, later come back bigger still.

Today, the Famous Amos name and formula endure with the Keebler family of cookies, and the Keebler folks love him, even hiring him to spread the good word and the good name that is Famous Amos.

For Wally, the money, fame, and success are nice to have, but have never really mattered. It's the sheer thrill of the experience and having a good time that move him—and now he's turned that enthusiasm into a new career as a hot motivational speaker. Companies clamor to book him; colleges pay top dollar to hear him. His message remains the same: Go ahead and fail. You'll get more chances. And you can always turn adversity into opportunity.

As of this date, he's written four inspirational books: *The Cookie Never Crumbles: Inspirational Recipes for Everyday Living, Man With No Name: Turn Lemons into Lemonade, Watermelon Magic,* and *The Power in You.* In each book, he trumpets the power of a good attitude.

Each book starts with some of his business ventures that have not succeeded, each providing another learning lesson, and becoming another bestseller.

I'm a sucker for these kind of books. I put much greater stock in people who talk about valuable life lessons than business lessons. The extra kicker with Wally Amos is that he gives you both. And he does so with remarkably good humor.

Here was a guy considered finished, who later thrived. Now the very people who tried to put him down and out, are gone and forgotten.

Life has come full circle for the man once given up as financially dead. He wasn't then, and he isn't now.

As he told the *Dayton Daily News* in April 2002, he won't retire until "I quit breathing.

"The whole retirement thing is a human concept. What else would I do?

"I take care of my body and watch what I eat," he says. "but more important than all that is watching what I think. You can't let negative people determine what your future is going to be."

And he doesn't.

No one knows the company honchos and lawyers who shut him down all those years ago. But everyone knows Wally Amos—his cookies, his muffins, his speeches, and his books, his inspirational message and infectious smile.

All in all, not bad for a guy with a high school diploma who made his living off cookies. Not bad for a guy who's been inducted into the Babson College Academy of Distinguished Entrepreneurs, received the Horatio Alger Award, the President's Award for Entrepreneurial Excellence, and the National Literacy Honors Award.

And not bad for a guy whose shirt and battered Panama hat now sit proudly in the Smithsonian Institution's Business Americana Collection.

Wally's life is not perfect. Even now he talks of mountains of debt. But so what, he says. "There are people who are dealing with issues far, far, far graver than mine."

Rare is it to find an executive or up-and-coming star who thinks of anyone but himself, but then again, Wally Amos is a rare bird. Life's challenges come in many forms: illness, loss, even death. Losing money, failing in business, and suffering a damaged professional reputation might not top everyone's list of life-destroying events, but in our money and status-obsessed culture, they come close.

Wally Amos just refused to see things that way. He saw in himself not a business guy revolutionizing an industry, but a fun-loving chap who liked to make cookies.

His original cookie empire "crumbled." But Wally is right. In the end it just made for a lot more cookies—and they were even better.

CHAPTER 3

THE SADDEST DAY

I've always said that the saddest day in my life was not when I was first told I had cancer, or later informed I had MS. No, the saddest day I can remember was when my mother died on February 23, 1987, after a long and difficult battle with brain cancer.

Our family had tried everything to save her, to little avail. New treatments and technologies that seemed promising only ended up extending her agony. When she passed away, it was as if an era had passed. I guess everyone says his or her mother is great. I was fortunate to know many, many people who happily shared my view. Losing someone so dynamic changed my world, and from that day forward made it a decidedly more empty one.

The next most difficult day for me came a little more than five years later when my father joined her, succumbing to a heart attack after a nearly year-long battle with prostate cancer. He had tried to be the family rock after her passing, and he succeeded measurably.

But with both gone by the time I was thirty-four, I felt I had been robbed of some of the pleasures my colleagues enjoyed—of parents who were still vibrant, still so much a part of their lives; of loving grandparents, enjoying their kids' kids.

I know from painful experience that there's no more crushing loss than to see a loved one go. But it's even worse to see that loved one go quickly or suddenly or unexpectedly. It's much worse still to see it happen violently or cruelly.

As a nation we recoil in horror at the senseless tragedies we see, the eleven children of the Columbia shuttle astronauts suddenly left without fathers and mothers. Car accidents. Plane crashes. Shootings.

The very surprise of these tragedies, their unpredictability, rattles and unnerves us. We are left devastated and desperately searching for meaning. We invariably find ourselves asking, why do bad things keep happening to good people?

In recent memory, perhaps the most striking example of such an unanticipated disaster was September 11, 2001. So many of the people I interviewed regularly died that day. But I had no idea how much the living suffered as well—the survivors.

There's John Duffy, the chairman and CEO of the brokerage firm Keefe, Bruyette & Woods, who lost not only a third of his staff that day, but his son as well. All perished in the eighty-eighth and eighty-ninth floors of Two World Trade Center.

Just a twin skyscraper away were the offices of Fred Alger Management. Fred's brother, David Alger, and thirty-six of their employees died in the attacks. They were on the ninety-third floor of One World Trade Center when hijacked American Airlines Flight 11 slammed into the building just two floors above them.

Imagine being Fred, coming back to his namesake firm, to help rebuild what his brother and colleagues had left behind.

Or John Duffy, coming back to a shell of a company, and now without his son.

Neither was required to return, and God knows their hearts were aching so much, that coming back probably intensified their suffering.

Nothing impresses me more than people who deal with tremendous loss and turn it around into something constructive, meaningful.

These gentlemen were more than rich enough to leave the workaday world behind and wallow in their misery, and most people would have sympathized and understood.

But they *had* to come back. They had a profound sense of duty, purpose, mission, and obligation, not only to their families, but their colleagues.

Their quiet dignity, honor, compassion, and coolness under enormous personal pressure stand out in a world we often find lacking in such qualities.

"MANY TEARS"

It was September 11, 2002, one year after the terrorist attacks on the World Trade Center and the Pentagon. Like all news organizations at the time, Fox News was providing around-the-clock commemorative specials.

I had my own approach, revisiting the people I had talked to just after the attacks to see how they were getting on with their lives.

There were many people I talked to over those days leading up to and including that first anniversary, but the toughest of all the interviews—and the one in which I had to work hardest at controlling my emotions—was my chat with John Duffy. My interview with him remains, to this day, one of the most engaging and intensely personal I've ever conducted.

The investment bank he ran, Keefe, Bruyette & Woods, lost sixty-seven employees. Among them were the company's co-CEO, four other board members, and Duffy's son, twenty-three-year-old Christopher, who had joined the firm on the trading desk just a year before.

Duffy had come on my show to reflect on September 11, and what was running through his mind at the time. He is a big bear of a man, and true to everything I had heard about him: quiet, driven, compassionate, deeply sensitive, the antithesis of what you'd expect to see in the cool, money-centric world of Wall Street.

His recounting of what happened that day, and what he did as he moved through it, stands out for his bravery, and his simple passion to find meaning in something so dreadful.

He was also a master of understatement. "I'm coming along," he told me. "The firm's coming along."

I already knew how much had happened in so little time. Duffy had written a book about those experiences, *Triumph Over Tragedy: September 11 and the Rebirth of a Business.* It remains, for my money, the single best reflection from someone directly affected.

As Duffy recalls, that Tuesday morning started as usual. Soon that changed. Duffy was driving along New York City's West Side Highway when he heard something on the radio about a plane crash at the World Trade Center.

"At first I thought, like probably everyone else, that this had to have been some mistake by an inexperienced pilot, probably flying a private plane.

"A little farther along, I found out it was a commercial jet. Well, I knew it would be mayhem downtown, so I got off the highway at 30th Street in midtown Manhattan and figured I would take the subway."

He parked his car and walked over to the Broadway line, but by the time he got there it was out of service. Next stop, Herald Square, to get the Sixth Avenue line. That train too had been taken out of service. Authorities were already stopping train service to and from downtown New York.

Since that happened from time to time in Manhattan, Duffy had no reason yet to think that the day's events would have such magnitude.

He walked over to a hotel across the street from Penn Station and began making calls. When efforts to reach his firm prove fruitless, he called home to his wife to tell her he was okay. "I got my daughter on the phone and she told me one of the World Trade Center towers had collapsed. Which one, I asked. She wasn't sure."

Duffy was panicked now. Keefe Bruyette was located at Two World Trade Center, the south tower. Not knowing was causing his pulse to race.

"I got back into my car and headed home."

His son Christopher had moved out of the house just ten days earlier, taking an apartment in Manhattan with some college friends.

He'd been happy at the firm, and shared his Dad's garrulous good humor. He'd enjoying being part of what some in the industry called the "Cult of Keefe."

Over the decades, the familial Keefe work environment had drawn so many talented people that it had long been a legend on Wall Street.

Keefe, Bruyette & Woods (KBW) had started about forty years earlier, when three young—some said crazy—investment professionals from Hartford, Connecticut, decided to strike out on their own with a firm focused solely on bank stocks.

Harry Keefe, Gene Bruyette, and Nobert "Nobby" Woods had sensed that the demand for finance-related information was beginning to soar. Their specialty couldn't be more timely.

As the firm grew, so did the number of workers—and in turn the firm's commitment to those workers. KBW was well known for granting employees lucrative stakes in the company.

As it ballooned to hundreds of stockbrokers, stock analysts, and investment bankers, so too did its cities of operation: from Hartford to New York, San Francisco, Boston, Chicago, Columbus, and Richmond.

By the mid-1980s, KBW was bursting at the proverbial seams. The company needed space, particularly in New York, and found it at the World Trade Center's south tower, Two WTC, starting out on the eighty-fifth floor, then moving to still larger quarters on the eighty-eighth, and eighty-ninth floors.

Years later, on that dark Tuesday morning, workers in KBW's Hartford offices weren't sure whether it was Keefe's tower that had been hit by the first plane. They frantically called to make sure their colleagues were okay.

They were, but from their KBW offices on the eighty-eighth and eighty-ninth floors, those colleagues had witnessed the first plane striking the World Trade Center's north tower, less than a hundred feet away.

When the Hartford workers heard it was the other tower into which the plane had crashed, of course they were horrified at the event, but they were relieved that their own people weren't harmed. They never expected that the safety of those employees would be all too brief.

When the second plane hit a few minutes later, workers in Hartford were watching on TV. They could see it had struck the south tower, the Keefe tower, crashing into the building only ten floors below Keefe's offices.

The phones in Hartford suddenly went dead. Computers shut down. All communication to and from the World Trade Center offices stopped.

"I soon knew that the second tower had collapsed and, as I drove home, I was thinking, my God, who got out? It seemed like I was stuck on the highway for a very long time. I got home and started calling our office in Hartford, Connecticut, which became something of a central information depository. That is when I found out my son was missing."

Duffy immediately called back Chris's two brothers and sisters, who'd been waiting to find out what had happened to their brother.

They were a close family, and Chris was a spark. Friends and family recounted his "Duff Jam" parties in high school, always when his parents were away. "They covered their tracks," his Dad told the *New York Times*. "But over the years we learned the extent of the parties."

Those who knew Chris talked of his sense of humor and an equally uncanny sense of style. A sister later remarked that he had a knack for finding great clothes.

According to his sister Kara, although Chris was fond of wearing Hugo Boss clothes at work, he was partial to flip-flops and Hawaiian shirts outside the office.

"Two of the children were away at college," Duffy told me. "My son Kevin was up at school in Vermont and my daughter Kara was in school in Rhode Island. One of the other daughters who was going to school in California was supposed to leave the next day, so she had not yet left. So I brought Kevin and Kara home."

Duffy, his family, and the surviving KBW workers would learn later that a shocking sixty-seven KBW employees, including young Christopher—a full third of the workforce—were dead.

Duffy knows that only a few ran for the exits when the first plane hit. Most stayed at their desks working. After all, the trading day was about to begin, and true to KBW form, the employees wanted to be ready for it.

Whether KBW workers lived, survived, or died that day was determined by happenstance and heroism.

Tom Michaud, KBW's director of equity sales, had been at a Michael Jackson concert just the night before. He decided to sleep late. He normally got to his desk by 7:30 A.M., but not that day. He lived.

Bob Planer, another KBW worker, had spent six hours stuck in an elevator in the 1993 attack. During this second attack, after the first plane struck, Planer called his wife, who immediately urged him to "just get the hell out of the building and out of New York." He did.

Then there's J. J. Aguiar, who could have saved himself, but spent all his time on the eighty-eighth floor, after the first tower was hit, urging colleagues to flee, sometimes literally pushing them out the door. J. J. didn't make it.

One KBW worker had taken the day off to plan her wedding; another overslept.

While most of the research team died, some managed to escape—a couple escaped only temporarily. An express elevator arrived amazingly fast, and Dean Eberling, Russell Keene, Lauren Smith, and Linda Rothemund were able to get on it, and start descending just moments before the second jetliner hit the floors directly above them.

But when the plane did smash into their tower, it severed the cable of their express elevator, which had only reached the seventy-eighth floor, and sent the car free-falling dozens of floors before emergency brakes kicked in just above the concourse level.

But there was only about an eight-inch gap at the floor where the elevator had buckled—too small for the men, but just big enough for Rothemund and Smith to squeeze out and run for help.

They got out. Eberling and Keene never did.

John Duffy found himself consoling other families as much as his own.

There were many tears, and constant memorial services, including the one for twenty-three-year-old Chris. His twelve closest friends, honorary pallbearers at the memorial mass, wore suits—and flip-flops—in his honor.

The Sunday after the attacks, employees, relatives, clients, and friends gathered for a memorial service at the Fifth Avenue Presbyterian Church, followed by a reception at the Helmsley Palace. Duffy said he planned on a few hundred people showing up. It ended up more like two thousand.

The hotel was instructed to keep the food and drink flowing all night, until the last guest left. The food bill alone amounted to $200,000.

But that still left the very real practical issue of getting the firm operating effectively again—a lot easier said than done.

"My first priority was to get us back," Duffy said, in memory of Chris and all the other loyal KBW workers who'd perished—but also to help the employees who'd survived.

But how do you do that when you've lost your co-CEO, all the company's records, and your New York offices? As Duffy said, you start slowly.

The company rented some space at the nearby Palace Hotel as a grief center, with counselors for employees and family members.

"We wanted to let people respond to the situation instead of imposing any notion of how things should unfold," KBW president Andrew Senchak, told *U.S. News.* "Whoever showed up, we put to work."

The twenty-eight-member research team was down to just six people, the sales and trading staff of thirty down to five.

But this is where Duffy's good name and the firm's good standing helped. Offers came in from everywhere to help get the company back up and running. The company's law firm offered space; competitors actually offered them business.

Across the street, the French investment bank BNP Paribas volunteered extra space on its trading floor. Rivals Merrill Lynch and Salomon Smith Barney included KBW on some deals.

KBW officially restarted operations on Tuesday, September 18, one week to the day after the terrorist attacks. The market had technically opened for the first time on Monday, but KBW had decided to wait until the following day, as much for the families to continue visiting the grief center, as for the survivors to get their financial act together.

Somehow they managed the first day of business just fine. Although trading volume was three times its normal level, the KBW workers handled things just fine, with Duffy watching over each and every one of them—part father, part conciliator, all professional.

Within weeks of the attacks, Duffy put out a statement saying simply: "Right now, we are totally committed to rebuilding Keefe, Bruyette & Woods and helping the families of our lost colleagues."

Although business was coming the company's way, manpower was a big issue. KBW needed more workers. "I must say that space is a secondary priority," Duffy said at the time.

"The most important thing is to rebuild our research team, which has been hit so hard, and to restore our trading operation." That meant hiring people who knew they were replacing dead people. Duffy recalled how difficult that process was. Candidates would be awkward in interviews, but Duffy himself would calm their fears and hear them out. He wanted to reassure them that new people were welcome. This was going to be a new KBW, but with the same legendary KBW spirit.

Duffy's timing was as good as the market was bad. Because of tough conditions, brokerage firms were laying off people. "The DLJ [Donaldson Lufkin & Jenrette] layoffs were serendipitous," Duffy recalled. He managed to pick up three or four veterans from the well-respected brokerage firm, since merged with Credit Suisse First Boston. He also added top people from Salomon Smith Barney and other companies.

Within months of the attacks, KBW had more employees than it did on September 10, 2001; even more remarkably, the firm was generating revenues and returns on equity at the same levels as they were before the attack—an amazing accomplishment given the huge market falloff since that time.

There's talk that the new KBW doesn't look a lot like the old KBW, that veteran employees are still adjusting to all the new faces at the firm. But Duffy is proud of his troops and how they rallied. "I definitely think Keefe is back."

And he's paying at least as much attention to the little things that make a difference with workers as to the big things. He still has his Junk Food Fridays, where employees can indulge in chicken wings or Big Macs. Workers still kid each other, and Duffy often leads the kidding.

Then there's the commitment to the families. All proceeds from Duffy's best-selling book went to a special Family Fund. The fund continues to grow to this day, with more than $10 million collected—a lot of that coming from KBW employees donating commissions and their own money.

The firm also made a substantial donation to the Central Park Zoo, where there's now a bench with the names of the sixty-seven who died, including Duffy's son Chris.

Duffy often thinks back to September 11. "Not a day goes by that I don't," he says. And he thinks of Chris.

"Horrible way to die," he adds. "Just horrible. I think it reemphasizes or reinforces the attitude that we kind of can't let the bad guys win."

I ask him what he thinks of so many countries criticizing American efforts to go after terrorists.

"I think if it happened to them, they would have a different reaction. I do not think you truly appreciate the horror and how it changes you life until it hits close to home."

And Christopher is always close to home. "What about your kids?" I ask.

"It has been an awakening for them," he says. "I think they handled it very well. We don't forget Christopher. We have pictures of him all over the place. And they talk about him, you know, with great regularity."

"Yes, we kind of feel we've had more than our share of bad luck. So maybe we've gotten some good luck in the past few months. I think we've been able to attract some very good people.

"Sometimes it is hard to see the good luck or good fortune we have had, but I think net-net with whatever luck we've had, our attitude is, let's get it done."

Duffy speaks as much for the son and coworkers he lost, as for the hundreds more who survived them.

MY BROTHER, MY WORK

Fred Alger and David Alger were brothers. To many, though, that's where the similarities ended. Fred was the teacher. David, nine years younger, was the student. Fred was quiet, David often loud and boisterous.

Fred was no slave to fashion, David the epitome of style. Fred was born for the boardroom, David for CNBC.

Fred ran Fred Alger Management, one of Wall Street's premier money management firms. What Alger lacked in size, it more than made up for in stature. And a lot of that was because of Fred's professional achievements.

He was a dynamo, and the Fred Alger method was legendary. When Fred was only thirty, he'd already established a reputation for huge financial bets, supported by dogged research, and during those early years in the 1960s he was becoming the financial hotshot of the decade. In 1965, his Security Equity fund returned an astonishing 77.8 percent, a performance virtually unheard of at the time.

Part of Alger's method was to avoid the herd, and he trained his growth-oriented managers to do the same.

Institutional investors swarmed to Alger, and his uncanny read of the markets and the economy. Considered a one-stop financial shop, Alger Management did it all, its own research, its own transfer agency, handling the sales and redemptions of fund shares. And there to help his brother do it all was David, who joined Fred and his firm in 1971, three years after graduating from the University of Michigan's business school.

Like Fred, David was big on research—and on making sure Alger Management's exhaustive technical and fundamental examination of stocks and sectors was second to none.

The idea of not relying on traditional Wall Street research gave Alger an important leg up on its competitors. Fred first preached and practiced it. But it was David who extended it and built on it.

David shared his brother's discipline for covering all contingencies—and perhaps more important, Fred's uncanny marketing sense. David had a way of grasping the big picture and seeing how certain stocks and sectors fell into that picture.

It was the same knack that saw Fred recommending Polaroid in the 1960s, long before most appreciated what Polaroid was and how it fit into the go-go strategy of that decade.

David was equally fervent about technology, and how it would shape a similar boon in the 1980s and into the 1990s. It was David who took a relatively obscure closed-end fund, Spectra, and made it into a regular no-load superstar fund that became the single most successful diversified fund of the 1980s.

His success continued into the next decade. His impressive money management skills and market timing, combined with his continually brilliant insights about technology's moneymaking potential, made him among the top-performing fund managers of the 1990s.

David was among the first, for example, to use computer modeling to forecast everything from revenue growth and profit margins to cash flow and long-term corporate survival.

David also was passionate about having all his fund managers explain their position in, and fondness for, a stock. His rapid-fire questions to analysts were part of his own method. People who worked at the firm knew they had to be on top of their game there. It made many nervous. But it kept Alger on top.

David was onto Yahoo!, America Online, and Amazon.com early, sensing that each company was a category leader long before most analysts even recognized its category. And when these companies eventually fell on hard times, David trimmed positions just in time. He had an eye for stocks that could sizzle and experience enormous run-ups, but his eye was just as good for stocks that could fizzle, and he'd have the firm cash out before they did.

With decades of his own professional success, and having helped his brother make Fred Alger Management even more legendary, the charming, talkative David was a favorite television pundit.

David was a frequent guest on my show and countless other financial programs. I liked him for his clarity. Our viewers liked him for his trend picks.

What was less public about the brothers' activities—but vital to the firm's reputation for serving its clients at standout levels—was its constant effort to cover all contingencies. Fred was convinced that firms with all their eggs in one financial center basket, risked big problems if trouble came along.

In following through on their fail-safe security plan, Alger made sure to have off-site locations, where records would be backed up and duplicated. If any office went down, the others could pick up the slack.

Every shareholder's records, every fund's net asset value, every dividend paid and capital gain distributed, would be tallied and stored, for easy reference . . . just in case.

Their sense of world affairs was as acute as their market timing, and years before the 1993 World Trade Center bombing, Fred was publicly predicting the possibility of terrorist attacks on New York. His words struck some at the time as alarmist. Few said that later.

Alger Management's main base of operations was housed in One World Trade Center, but most of the firm's back office functions were handled out of Jersey City, just across the Hudson River, with an eagle's eye view of the Trade Center. Another office in Morristown, New Jersey, about forty miles west of New York, originally relegated to little more than telemarketing, gained even greater stature after the 1993 attacks.

After twenty-four years of working together, Fred was very proud of how his younger brother was aggressively taking the firm to the next level, and in 1995 he easily passed the baton of running the firm to David.

Fred settled into semi-retirement, living in Geneva, Switzerland. He remained chairman and the largest shareholder of Alger Funds, helping where and when he was needed, but day-to-day it was David's firm.

And David ran the firm well, building it over the next six years to managing about $16 billion in assets, while maintaining the firm's legendary quality of service and return on investment.

For the Alger brothers, quality and results were more important than trying to match the managed assets of such goliaths as Deutsche Bank Asset Management, with about $700 billion, or even downtown New York neighbor Fiduciary Trust's $44 billion.

David and Fred, at their different levels of involvement, enjoyed the firm's steady growth and success through the summer of 2001, and into the bright, crisp morning of September 11.

That day, Fred and his wife were locking up their vacation rental home in East Hampton, New York, when they heard that a plane had rammed into One World Trade Center, at the ninety-fifth floor.

The alarmed Algers thought about the firm's offices on the ninety-third floor. The north tower was reported to be spewing heavy smoke, and visibly on fire.

As the authorities later realized, the heat from the explosion alone had to have been intense. Thousands of gallons of jet fuel were spilling and igniting simultaneously.

Alger Management had a fifty-five-person staff, including David. Fred was almost certain his brother would be in his offices at that time of day, but he and his wife had no way of knowing how many staff members would be at work at that particular time on that Tuesday morning. Their feelings of horror made even breathing painful.

Fred immediately called the Alger satellite offices and told them their mission was to learn all they could about their coworkers' fate. But it was next to impossible to find out anything.

Fred couldn't stop thinking about David and the Alger workers who'd been with him at the time of the attack.

Now and then, he received some comforting news. One mailroom clerk, who was late getting to work that morning, phoned in to say he was okay. Another employee, Monica Smith, whose job it was to recruit analysts, was traveling elsewhere that day.

Sometimes, though, the news was bad.

Fund manager Ron Tartaro had phoned to say he and eight others were trapped in the southwest corner of the building. Another woman named Bonnie said she'd heard something about a plane crashing just above her and that everyone was all right and heading out. But then nothing.

Bonnie, Ron, and Ron's eight coworkers were never heard from again.

Fred spent much of the next day just trying to get into Manhattan on the train. Accounting for the missing was proving a Herculean task. The death toll at the time was thought to be into the tens of thousands. The whereabouts of so many, including David and the others who worked at Alger, were a complete mystery. It was as if they had disappeared from the face of the earth.

What the evidence finally clarified was that thirty-six people, a majority of Alger's staff—were at work at the time, and died as a result.

Containing his grief and sense of loss, Fred took on David's responsibilities, and concentrated on getting the firm running again. He owed his brother and deceased employees that much. He owed it to the survivors all the more.

By September 13, he was in the Morristown office, taking charge and desperately trying to right a battered financial ship.

Fred's first order of business was centralizing operations in Morristown. Chief Financial Officer Greg Duch ordered 160 workers to evacuate the Jersey City office and move to the western New Jersey outpost.

Grief counselors were brought into Morristown and were made available around the clock.

Fred's early preparedness, begun more than a decade ago, was paying off. All account information and details were backed up. As Fred told clients on a conference call that morning, "From a technological and systems standpoint, every account is intact and nothing is lost."

Fred chose not to show his personal pain to coworkers. He knew that his tone and emotion would set the mood for everybody.

Workers remarked with admiration on how focused and disciplined he was. They marveled that a man handling such intense personal grief could find a way to channel that emotion into bringing a firm back from the brink, and his surviving employees along with it.

As was happening with John Duffy and his firm, Keefe, Bruyette & Woods, Alger's biggest competitors became its biggest backers and friends.

From small financial planners to Fidelity Investments, all offered condolences and even office space and phones to get Alger up and running. The fact that Fred himself was coming back to steer day-to-day operations added to the Alger allure.

Fred wasted little time putting key people in key posts. Within days of the disaster, he promoted two key staffers to prominent positions. Dan Chung, Fred's son-in-law, who had been out of the office at a conference on the day of the attacks, became chief investment officer. David Hyun, a former comanager of Spectra before joining Oppenheimer in 2000, returned to manage Spectra and other mutual funds, including Capital Appreciation. Both men were appointed to co-manage another Alger Fund, LargeCap Growth.

Hyun was part of a growing team of returning, loyal Algerites, who made it their goal to shepherd back to financial health and success the firm that had made their careers.

Teresa McRoberts came back as a health care analyst and portfolio manager, after three years at the helm of Morgan Stanley Health Science Fund. Retailing analyst Amy Ryan returned to Alger, after a decade at Prudential Securities.

Fred knew that the key to keeping clients was reminding them regularly that the firm was very much still in business. He stressed that nearly 90 percent of the $16 billion managed at the time was invested in companies followed by analysts who had survived. As Alger vice-chairman Jim Connelly told *Kiplinger's* only weeks after the disaster: "We feel able to manage the money we have with the minds we have."

That confidence would prove well-founded. *Kiplinger's* noted that Chung, in particular, had every bit of David's keen sense of stock timing. James Morton's bestseller, *Investing with Young Guns: Next Generation of Investment Superstars,* tells the story of how Chung steered Alger toward AOL in 1995, then had the firm unload it in 1996—after doubling its money, and before the stock's infamous plunge.

Over the next few years, Alger's funds overall have performed no worse than others in their category, and a surprising number have done measurably better. Those are some of the reasons so many original investors stuck with the company, and more to the point, stuck with Fred. They valued the firm's long-term track records, enviable to say the least, more than its short-term problems.

Although American Skandia Investment Services took $835 million out of their mutual fund and variable-annuity assets with Alger, it was about the only big name that did.

Alger's current stature, and excellent management of the billions entrusted to its care, are a remarkable testament to a firm that lost a majority of its fund managers on September 11, and whose prospects at the time were considered by many outsiders to be shaky at best.

Most credit Fred himself for the turnaround, but this pensive Wall Street legend is not given to cockiness or boasting. Instead of thinking about how much credit he may deserve for Alger's survival and strong recovery, in quiet moments, he thinks of the life he had and the brother he loved.

"I mean, I really anticipated that [David] would retire," he told *Money* magazine, "and we might build a compound together in Florida. I even had a place in mind. And we would, you know, play family tennis and watch the grandchildren grow up."

That will not happen now. As for where Fred goes from here, confidantes say even he doesn't seem to know. His three-year visa to stay in this country is renewable, but Fred refuses to discuss his plans, besides commenting that "this is a young man's game."

In a sense, Fred built two firms, and each essentially from scratch. On the first go-round, the odds were considered next to impossible. The second time? Even more so.

The first Fred Alger Management was launched by Fred alone because his younger brother was too young to help him then, but David would join him a few years later. The second firm was built from the ruins of what remained of Alger after September 11. This time, when Fred got the new Alger Management up and running, he again did it without David, but for a very different and heartbreaking reason: His brother was gone.

And that loss made Fred's starting up that second Alger firm a moral mission as much as a financial one. The Alger Management of today is a tribute to David and the thirty-five Algerites whose lives were lost—because they were in their offices, doing the work they loved to do.

Fred respected and honored his brother in life. In death, he honors what was so important to David and those who perished with him on that fateful day, all the more.

CHAPTER 4

SQUIGGY'S GREAT
ADVENTURE

From 1976 to 1983, David L. Lander wasn't just any actor. He was a star. His character, Squiggy, on the sitcom *Laverne & Shirley* had made him a much-loved, much-imitated sensation. I can remember several Halloweens in those years when kids would dress up as Squiggy, the lovable, spitcurled character who helped to make Penny Marshall's show the hit it was.

Lander also has appeared in a number of highly acclaimed feature films, including *A League of Their Own, Scary Movie,* and *Who Framed Roger Rabbit?* He's guest-starred in more than thirty television shows, including *Mad About You, Twin Peaks,* and *Pacific Blue.*

A longtime fan of his, I'd seen him often on the big and small screen. I'd always appreciated his stardom, the longevity of his career, and his acting achievements. But I and his thousands of other fans now know that behind the fame and success there were many years of secret darkness, pain, and suffering.

What Lander had kept secret for long so, he shared openly and honestly when he published his autobiography, *Fall Down Laughing,* in 2000. In telling his story, he also made us laugh very hard, bringing back memories of how Squiggy kept us cracking up.

Laughter and pain. How often they go together.

In 1983, during the sixth and last year of *Laverne & Shirley,* Squiggy may have been funnier than ever. But the people who worked with him knew *something* was wrong.

No one knew what was ailing Squiggy, and even Lander only knew what his early symptoms were: a strange numbness in fingers and limbs, a certain clumsiness, a feeling of vertigo when he wasn't much higher than a flight of stairs.

In the months after the end of the series' long run, the symptoms were happening more frequently and severely. Lander didn't know what he had. He just knew it was something *bad,* powerful enough to make his once athletic body go haywire.

Lander *had* to find out the cause, but he was totally unprepared for the actual diagnose: multiple sclerosis.

Lander's disease, as I'd find out myself fourteen years later, gradually broke down the body's nervous system, steadily increased the duration and depth of fatigue, and caused more and more frequent stumbling episodes and blackouts. Work might be possible for a while, but at a diminishing level—and then, at some unknowable time, not possible at all.

As almost anyone who has endured a serious illness will tell you, the toughest part is hearing about it, and then deciding whom to tell. There's great pressure in our society not to look vulnerable. Lander found that particularly acute in Hollywood, where looking good and feeling good aren't just a way of life. They're practically gospel.

For a still-young and successful actor, the terror was overwhelming. As disastrous and horrifying as having MS was, almost as terrifying was the prospect of the professional consequences, if the news of his disease should leak out, or he began telling people about it.

He was sure that coming out with news of his MS would mean the immediate end of his career, so he made the difficult but almost inevitable decision to keep his condition a secret, and manage his debilitating symptoms as best he could.

There are many people in the entertainment industry who have dealt with and continue to deal with MS. And there are many who have made the disease a cause, and contributed mightily. Montel Williams is perhaps the best example.

What differentiates Lander from these celebrities is that his professional fears kept his struggle with MS a secret for such a long time.

As an actor who was desperate to continue working, he hid his neurological disease for *sixteen years.* It's hard to imagine.

But I can empathize and understand, because Lander's fears and secrecy closely paralleled my own emotions and actions—not when I was diagnosed with MS, but when I learned I had cancer ten years before.

We both suffered from the fear of being found out—the fear of being ostracized, of being professionally finished, and the additional stress and pain of concealing our illnesses from almost everyone.

Over the years, we would rely heavily on our wives and daughters for their support. And like Lander, I grew to worry about the toll that our diseases—and our families' constant preoccupation with them—were taking on them, especially our young daughters. There are themes in our lives that are remarkably similar as I learned when I talked with Lander in September 2000, soon after the publication of *Fall Down Laughing,* which is one of the best personal accounts of dealing with MS I have ever read.

He talked of being constantly on guard. "I got by," he told me, "but when someone would say we think you have a problem, I would go, 'Oh my God, they know I have MS. I will never work again." So Lander continued to keep the secret, having told only his wife, and hoping for the sake of his new baby girl, Natalie, that she would be shielded from the trauma.

At first I had done the same, initially telling only my wife, and hoping too that Tara, my two-year-old daughter, would be free to grow up as untroubled as possible.

Lander and I were wrong on both counts, though we both meant well.

As I knew from my experience, deciding to keep a secret is hard enough. Living the lie is worse.

When Lander started showing signs of MS, he revealed, "I began walking in strange ways and people thought I was drinking."

That's what happens when you battle serious illnesses in private. I discovered the same thing: The more you don't say, the more people wonder what *is* wrong. I'll never forget taking the PATH train in one morning to my PBS offices in New York, and tripping and stumbling with each jerk of the train. One man stormed off to the other end of the car after I had fallen on him. "Sober up, pal!," he blurted. "It's not even seven in the morning."

I recall the icy stare of every passenger in that train car. That feeling of shame was a hell of a lot worse than the nausea I still had from the chemotherapy the night before.

I had a friend who *did* tell me what his own suspicions were. Because I was getting nauseous so often, and coming in late to work more and more, my friend had pulled me aside and asked me if I had AIDS. I probably should have leveled with him and just told him about the Hodgkin's, but I didn't. Soon others were gossiping about the possibility that I was HIV positive.

Serious illness plays off one's worst paranoid fears. As Lander and I learned, not telling people what ails you can make them suspect much worse. But as painful and humiliating as those experiences are, you still don't tell the truth. Reason doesn't prevail. Paranoia does.

Lander kept his disease a secret, as I had, but for much longer.

He recalls in his autobiography shooting a scene for *The Love Boat* in 1983. "There was one scene in which I had to walk down the boat deck behind my boss, played by Ben Vereen, an old friend from Performing Arts. I found myself having difficulty keeping up with Ben and hitting the mark in time to say my line. We kept cutting and retaking the shot. The director was growing very irritated, but for some reason my legs would not move fast enough. In a fit of frustration, I finally said, 'What difference does it make if I hit the mark? The laugh machine will get the joke.'

"But the director was not amused. 'I don't know how you did it over at L and S, but here we take our comedy very seriously.'

"It may have been the funniest line he heard that day."

But the string of embarrassing incidents continued. One got him knocked off a movie shoot with Arnold Schwarzenegger; another had him almost falling off a stage with comedian Buck Henry. And there was the taping for the *Hollywood Squares,* when Lander was very concerned about getting up and down to his middle box. "I didn't know if I could make it," he recalled. "I refused to come down throughout the taping of all five shows because I was pretty sure I wouldn't be able to climb back up. When we broke for lunch, I had it sent up to my square. You might say I ordered square service."

Only days later there was another problem, this time at a Hollywood audition. Lander had parked in a nearby garage, but when he got out on the street, he couldn't get down off the curb. "My foot just wouldn't work," he remembered. "By this time, I had completely lost faith in my legs. I didn't trust them to be able to step off a curb without buckling."

When Lander was dealing with MS back then, AIDS was just coming on to the national scene. With actor Rock Hudson's revelations in 1985 and subsequent death, all anyone could talk about was AIDS: who had it, how they got it, and who else might be next.

In that environment, Lander was dealing with another very real and debilitating condition, about which there was little public interest, or understanding. People would have been deeply shocked if he'd told the truth, but they wouldn't care much about the disease itself, and might care even less about Lander and his MS-caused suffering.

Lander was determined not to tempt fate. He told me, "The main reason I kept my MS a secret was I just felt people didn't understand it. And I was at a point in my career where I didn't think that by coming out I would really be able to help anyone, especially when I was first diagnosed."

There is also something about MS that mystifies people. Lander's comment that during that time many people confused multiple sclerosis with muscular dystrophy is as true today as it was then.

When I was diagnosed with MS in 1997, more than a few mistook me for one of Jerry's "older" kids. That's how little was known about the disease—even those few years ago.

Lander calls Hollywood especially unforgiving—at any time. For him, that period was a time *not* to be sick, look sick, act sick, or appear vulnerable.

And it was certainly not a time to tell the truth, not even to friends, not even close friends. As Lander jokes in his bestseller, "Squiggy caught multiple sclerosis and didn't tell nobody." Not even his close friend Michael McKean, who played Lenny to his Squiggy. Whenever McKean was curious about his former costar's tripping, stumbling, and other visible problems, Lander would dismiss them as related to some old back injuries—which he didn't have. And that would be that.

His guardedness continued throughout the 1980s and 1990s. It was bad enough to be associated with an old TV show; it was another thing altogether to face the prospect of being "that Squiggy guy, who has MS."

Lander felt he couldn't afford medical honesty. But his very real physical problems only worsened.

As recounted in *Fall Down Laughing,* he arrived at film shoots barely able to control the pain in his legs, hobbled by the familiar MS fatigue and clumsiness. All the old, early, professional problems and misunderstandings continued. Directors yelled at him, colleagues snickered, others suspected the worst. Lander was so overtaken by fatigue on one shoot that he collapsed in his trailer and slept for more than a day. When he woke up, he was fired.

As his symptoms became more obvious, Lander found it harder to get new roles, and even tougher to keep them.

Working in Hollywood with a serious illness is a double-edged sword. You lose roles because of the effects of your secret disease, but if you tell your fellow professionals you're sick and that's why you're flubbing lines or parts, you don't get the lines or parts—period. Lose, lose.

I think the same can be said, in varying degrees, about any profession. Darwinism rules: Only the strongest survive. Once you're known to have an illness or a problem of any sort, you are marked forever. Even if it's not a kiss of death, it's a distinction just the same. And generally not a good one.

In work, as in life, most people prefer to be surrounded by others who are strong and "normal." "Different" is potentially threatening, and that's another aspect of Darwinism.

There's also what's arbitrary, like personal or professional preferences. Hollywood, like the business world, allows certain things, and doesn't allow others. Some human foibles, like drinking, are okay. Others, like serious illnesses are not. Go figure.

As Lander told me in September 2000, in Hollywood it's almost chic to be alcoholic. "They have a Betty Ford clinic," he said. "There are a lot of drinkers in Hollywood. 'Oh, I know the problem you're going through.'

"But MS is unclean. Even now people say, does this make you one of Jerry's kids? There is so much stuff that people don't understand about it. People think you can catch it from someone. You can't. People think that you inherit it, but that's not really true. I mean anyone can get this thing, [usually] between the ages of 20 and 40. But people don't understand. They just don't understand."

Years later, although he was aware of the risk and the isolated emotional stress of dealing with MS in secret, Lander would every so often publicly identify the cause of his symptoms. In his book, he described complaining to his pal Harry Shearer about how poorly *Saturday Night Live*'s Lorne Michaels was treating him. Shearer wanted to know why Lander would even care, and why he would want to work on a show like that anyway.

"Because I have to, Harry," he replied forcefully. "I can hardly work anymore. I have MS, okay? I don't know when I'm ever going to get a job."

He later told the blunt truth again, after he and his buddy Michael McKean cowrote a script about Lenny and Squiggy. McKean was complimenting his friend, urging him to pursue producing TV shows and be more involved in the entertainment industry. Then he noticed the stationary bicycle in the corner of Lander's office, and asked about his back problems, thinking they might hinder Lander's plans for the future.

"Oh, it never was [the] back, Michael," Lander shot back. "It's multiple sclerosis."

McKean was stunned by the news of the devastating disease—*and* the fact that his close friend had kept him in the dark about such a serious matter.

I asked Lander if McKean had been ticked off about his secrecy. "Yeah," he remembered. "I think he was a little bit miffed that I didn't tell him. But it was basically one of those things; we weren't working together every single day by then. Maybe if we were, I would have, but I would see him maybe three, four times a year. It would seem weird for me to just say, 'Oh, by the way, I have MS.'"

Lander meant no slight, to McKean or anyone else, when he decided to keep his illness secret. As he explained in his book: "I didn't want pity, or even sympathy, from anyone. If I was going to fail or succeed in my career and in life, I always wanted to do it on my own terms. I never wanted to suspect that I was being given special treatment or opportunities because I was sick. I also never wanted to put Michael in a position where he'd have to make excuses for me. If he didn't have information about my illness, he wouldn't have to defend me."

I understood Lander's thinking perfectly. You don't want to be pitied, or worse, patronized. I was certainly that way with cancer; I don't know if it was my Italian-Irish heritage, mixed with some good, old fashioned Catholic guilt, but I never felt myself worthy of extra attention and sympathy, so I neither sought it, nor, when it came to me, strongly embraced it.

You just want to be accepted for who you are, not what you have. The trouble is that friends feel slighted when you don't confide in them. Some wonder if you were ever really close to them at all. It is doubly painful for the person suffering the condition, because they have to explain themselves to the friends they've hurt, and keep struggling with a disease that hurts even more.

Even so, Lander has regrets about keeping something so important a secret for so long. "Honesty truly is the best policy after a while," he told me. "But that's a decision someone has to come to on his own."

Lander knows full well there are bosses who aren't understanding, companies that aren't tolerant, and working environments that aren't giving. That means an employee with a degenerative condition, who can't do his job properly may lose it.

Compared to Lander's incredible difficulties in keeping his MS secret for sixteen years, I've been relatively more fortunate, because my bosses have been sympathetic and supportive as I battled both cancer and MS. While I kept my cancer a secret from almost everyone through a year of brutal chemotherapy and radiation, I'd told my supervisors at PBS that I had Hodgkin's disease shortly after I was diagnosed.

When my cancer went into remission and I started to discuss it more freely, I discovered that many of my compassionate coworkers had long known of my condition and had been discreetly helping me out. I was also lucky to be a business journalist: Even in TV news, where image does matter and suppressing the visible symptoms of a disease is crucial, for an actor, looking *good* is almost everything. The professional costs to Lander were almost certainly much greater than they were for me, even if I was just as terrified.

Also, MS was Lander's first battle with a serious disease. When I was diagnosed with MS, in 1997, I'd been dealing with cancer for ten years, the first year in treatment, the next nine in remission. That full decade of living as a cancer survivor made me a bit better prepared to handle MS than Lander was. By then, I was also more secure in my career and more confident about being able to disclose that I had a debilitating disease without damaging or destroying my career.

I was also comparatively lucky in having just two sets of supervisors to tell. For Lander, working in Hollywood meant dealing with dozens of bosses over the years, changing with each new, often short-term role. Usually he worked with people who were complete strangers to him before he was cast.

When Lander finally revealed his disease, he had little choice in the matter. His MS had become public before he'd decided to widely disclose that fact to those in his profession, finding out that news of his condition had leaked in the most curious of ways.

It was an early evening in February 1999 when Lander got a call from Penny Marshall. Out of the blue, she asked, "David, are you fighting MS?"

Lander recalled his stomach feeling like it had dropped to the floor.

Marshall told him she was calling at the personal request of Tom Sherak, the head of Twentieth Century Fox. Sherak's daughter, Melissa, had MS, and he was a big fund-raiser for and active participant in the National MS Society.

He'd asked Penny Marshall, whom he knew to be a close friend of Lander's after their six years together on *Laverne & Shirley,* to call Lander on his behalf. Because of the sensitivity of the issue, Sherak had thought it best that Lander hear first from a friend that the fact of his multiple sclerosis was known in Hollywood, rather than being told in an unexpected call from the head of a major studio.

Marshall explained that Sherak wanted to honor Lander at the Society's Dinner of Champions, a huge fund-raiser for MS research that the studio head managed every year. Penny said that she and Sherak both hoped that Lander would be willing to at least consider appearing at the event, even with all the attendant publicity and unwanted attention.

But Lander was reluctant and worried. After sixteen years of secrecy, concealing his illness had become an enormous part of his life. As he recounted in his book, "I was honored that anyone would think of me as a champion. But, on the other hand, I had mixed feelings about telling the world I had MS. Of all the scenarios I had imagined for going public with my illness, I had never dreamed of doing it in front of a bunch of industry bigwigs eating chicken."

He decided that he would discuss Sherak's request with his wife, Kathy, who brought her own valuable perspective to the discussion. That Sherak wanted to honor him proved that Lander's MS was no longer a secret, known only to a few friends. If the top executive running Twentieth Century Fox knew, then Lander had to assume that his illness was already fairly common knowledge in Hollywood.

The real question he still faced was how and when he should tell his fans. He asked Kathy about revealing his condition at the dinner; "Go for it," she told him. Like my own wife, Mary, who initially dealt with my struggle with cancer pretty much on her own, Kathy must have been exhausted from carrying this load for so long. "And a decision to go public was at least a decision toward some sort of resolution," Lander recalled.

There's something very liberating about revealing a major secret. Sometimes, what was thought to be so big and frightening ultimately proves not to be so terrifying.

Having been through it twice, I could relate to Lander's discussion with Kathy and his daughter, Natalie, now almost seventeen, who cried with relief because she wouldn't "have to make excuses for Dad anymore."

With months to get ready for the Dinner of Champions, Lander had time to decide exactly how he wanted to leak the story beforehand, so that attention from the media and the public, sure to be intense, wouldn't hit him all at once. He chose to speak to *People* magazine, granting them the exclusive right to break his secret to the public.

In making that decision, after his wife and daughter expressed their support for his decision to reveal his illness, Lander began to realize that he now had a far greater calling. He could reach out to thousands across the country who all had the same disease he did. His actions could help liberate them from their fears, while he worked to quell his own.

As soon as the *People* article was published, his phone began ringing off the hook. Every news organization sought him out for interviews, and he appeared on *Entertainment Tonight, Access Hollywood, 20/20,* and *Good Morning America.*

But, in sad contrast to the overwhelming outpouring of sympathy and support Lander received from the general public, "Hollywood welcomed me and my news with closed arms and a total silence," he said, which was the reaction he'd feared all along. "I received exactly zero calls or notes from the people I had worked with without revealing my disability. What did they think of me for deceiving them? Were they pissed off? I wondered if anyone who had ever fired me in the past felt any remorse now that they knew I was trying to hide MS."

If that response bothered Lander, he didn't show it then, and he doesn't now.

His big night at the Dinner of Champions was a huge success. Given his celebrity, the usual low-key event turned into something akin to a medical Oscars ceremony. As he and his family made their way into the Century Plaza Hotel in Los Angeles, he was peppered with questions from throngs of waiting reporters: "Aren't you glad you came out?" "What's it like hiding such a horrible disease?"

I respected Lander's honesty in telling me how stubborn he was in the beginning about answering those same questions, over and over, and I totally understood his reaction. It's too much explaining, trying again and again to describe the disease, every facet and symptom, every odd knock. For me, it wasn't worth it. I was having a tough enough time dealing with it myself.

For a while, he didn't even want to accept well-wishes from people. But the more he thought about his new, much greater responsibilities, the more he took on and grew into the most serious and challenging role of his life, that of a goodwill ambassador for the National MS Society.

It was a role he soon came to relish, and thousands with the disease appreciated his efforts. Now when Lander is peppered with questions by the media, sympathetic individuals, and fellow MS sufferers, Lander handles them all with dignity, and humor.

Rarely has the MS Society been blessed—and I think you almost have to call it that—with someone of such good humor and wit, who can joke about the disease and make those with and without the condition feel special. People understand him, like him, relate to him. And they want him at their dinners, functions, and events.

Given his talent for comedy, and desire to lighten the load for MS victims, their families and their friends, it's inspiring when Lander makes light of MS's more serious side effects. "My family will still say, 'you have to empty the garbage, you know, it's Tuesday night.' And I'll tell them, 'Oh, I can't, I have MS.' It's a good disease for the lazy man."

His audience always laughs. And those with MS, or who know the illness well, get his inside jokes, about hoping there aren't too many stairs to the stage (for fear he'll trip), or that the air conditioning is working that day. (MS patients generally avoid warmer places because heat tends to exacerbate their symptoms.)

With Lander though, it's not all jokes, and it's common for his audience to cry. He talks about being ostracized, and not knowing where MS will take him. He doesn't know if he'll end up in a wheelchair, or lose his vision, or maybe suffer some other serious setback. He wonders if the disease will affect his acting and ability to concentrate, and if it does, to what degree.

He tells his audiences the truth: He cannot control what has happened to his body. But for now, he can control what he has to say, and how to say it.

MS Society officials tell me that Lander remains one of their most sought-after spokespersons. You would think he'd be tired of his duties by now, but no matter how bad his condition, or how painful his symptoms, there he is, telling his story, admitting his regrets, sharing his mistakes and triumphs.

A friend of mine who also suffers from MS heard one of his speeches. Lander came to the stage after a neurologist told the audience about some of the medical progress being made against the disease.

"But Squiggy brought the house down," she told me. "He put it all in perspective for us. And we all figured, hey, here's this star who has this horrible thing I do. He was worth more than a hundred doctors talking about MS. He was living MS."

When I had my own chat with him, it was clear that he was as much on a mission to keep MS sufferers' spirits up as he was to promote sensitivity toward those with MS in the broader public, so that they'd interact better with those who had the disease.

When I disclosed on the air that I too had MS, he piped in, mid-introduction, "welcome to the club." It is a time-worn phrase among those with the condition, who know that members join in disease and name only.

Throughout the interview, Lander was gracious and funny, witty and irreverent.

When he was first diagnosed, MS was a little-known, barely understood disease. That's changed, fortunately, thanks to the continuing efforts of brave people like David Lander and Montel Williams. Now we know that this formerly obscure condition affects upwards of 350,000 people, and perhaps many more who have been misdiagnosed, and don't know yet that tragically, they're part of "the club."

Lander knows even better than I do, the unpredictable nature of MS: how some can walk one day, but be paralyzed the next. Of vision that's fine one minute, then suddenly blurred. Of strength that's with us one moment, easily allowing us to pick up a book, then deserting us in a flash, forcing us to put it back down.

He talks of treatments but no cures, of possibilities but no sure things.

But he also laughs, and he makes others laugh with him, just as he did more than a quarter century ago as an odd but enduringly lovable character named Squiggy.

Back then he made us laugh at the silly things. Today he makes us laugh our way through the tough times.

You always get the feeling with Lander that his good humor will take him through whatever he may encounter. Squiggy's done a lot of good. He's been on a remarkable journey, and as a fellow MS sufferer, I'm very happy he's on that journey with me. And I know tens of thousands of MS patients are as happy to have his company as I am.

CHAPTER 5

"THEN ALONG CAME BRANSON"

Among the tens of thousands of business executives who populate the world I've been reporting on for more than twenty years, there's an elite, fascinating, and too rare breed: *entrepreneurial visionaries.*

These are the leaders who create their own companies—from scratch.

These inspired people were not satisfied by just taking over and running a company someone else had founded and established, expanding existing success, having to play by the company's restrictive, conventional rules.

Taking on that kind of top management role would have bored and limited them, and would have left their potential mostly unfulfilled. Those positions were too easy, too traditional, and too hierarchical. They thought them about as exciting as memorizing a management-structure chart.

These executives dared to overcome the most trying challenges and the toughest odds, taking entrenched competition, and legions of doubters, because they *want* to risk everything by betting on the value of *their* vision. They want to find out how ingenious they really are, and how successful their ventures can become.

There are three gentlemen in particular whose careers I've studied with intense interest, because of what they did, and especially how they did it, and to this day I find them absolutely fascinating. What also makes them special is what they did outside the corporate world:

- There's the dyslexic billionaire who didn't understand the difference between gross profits and net profits, but knew precisely what to ask his executives: Were they making money or not?
- There's the political advisor who helped get three American presidents elected as a warm-up to his entry into a media industry in which he had no experience.
- Finally, there's the beloved CEO who handled his prostate cancer with more concern for his employees than himself.

Their stories, struggles, and careers are as epic as the companies they built and the obstacles they overcame, and too grand to fit into a single chapter. Therefore, I thought it was appropriate to their brilliant entrepreneurial spirit to create a separate chapter for each of them: A brash British visionary named Richard Branson, whose brand, Virgin, redefined all things cool; Roger Ailes, a political veteran with virtually no journalism experience, who reshaped the broadcasting world with a new television channel, Fox News, regarded as an oxymoron at the time; and Herb Kelleher, a lawyer who blazed a new trail in commercial air travel, building the first discount airline, Southwest Airlines.

However, before I begin the first tale of this extraordinary trio, I want to describe the very rare and essential qualities each of them share, and define them as *entrepreneurial visionaries*. And it's the subtle but very powerful, mutually reinforcing effect of all of these characteristics that made these men and their respective ventures into dominant, major forces in their various industries.

Studying their careers, I am increasingly appreciative of the attributes each has in common, and how central these attributes were to these future titans, all of whom launched new enterprises that most thought were sure to fail.

What's most fun in beginning to describe them is their remarkably sharp sense of humor. These men are boundlessly affable, bringing laughter to almost everything they do, and if that laughter happens to be at their expense, even better. They don't take things too seriously, and they certainly don't want themselves regarded solemnly. That shared sense of humor has lightened their battles against daunting impediments, massive competition, and apparently endless criticism.

They fought for their share in businesses thought closed to new entrants, but to a man, they didn't care then, and they don't care now. They welcome critical remarks, no matter how harsh, from the media and their rivals, because it gives them something to laugh about, and re-energizes their motivation.

They used that derision in other ways, too: When entrenched competition laughed at their visions for their new companies, they saw opportunities where no one else did. They found room to compete in sectors dominated by giant, established companies, flying under the radar as they built their "crazy" enterprises.

The fact that their competitors dismissed their initial efforts actually helped, when their rivals failed to take them seriously until it was too late.

The constant whining and carping from critics who thought these moguls wouldn't amount to much, and the sniping from the press, which never seemed to cut them any slack, were valuable distractions, because while so many others ran their businesses based on all that criticism, each entrepreneur was quietly gathering his troops and resources en route to stunning victories.

Their ambition, humor, decisiveness, and ability to see differences, potential, and overlooked opportunities, resulted in some very unorthodox, even "nutty" behavior. But those who dismissed them and their methods as kooks and blowhards were missing the point.

There was so much rugged competition in all of these industries that conventional approaches would have produced nothing. Only unconventional thinking and audaciously risky methods would be effective, as they built their companies into global leaders.

These three men are so unorthodox, with such colorful and distinctive personalities, and because they were starting new companies with business models and target audiences that didn't seem to make any sense, most run-of-the-mill chief executives paid them little mind. That neglect would quickly fail them, and their inability to compete on their own terms became quite apparent.

For traditional corporations, the question of success was almost rhetorical. How could these outrageous founders prosper, when not one of them subscribed to the notion of exhaustive studies or focus groups? They didn't care about, and even seemed to sneer at, the traditional trappings and social niceties of the leadership positions they occupied.

They had no formal corporate or academic training and, craziest of all, they had almost no experience in the industries they'd joined. Some business school professors thought their efforts to be the equivalent of miners digging for fool's gold.

That's the problem with most of the corporate world, as I see it. There is a persistent mentality holding that "everything goes back to the mean." They believe that unusual characters, improbable ventures, and out-of-left-field wonders cannot survive for long, so why bother? Why worry? Why spend so much time fretting over a company that's just going to burn up?

What they fail to see is that the really good ones don't burn up, and don't burn out.

They continue to build, and grow, and laugh, and joke, and stick it to competitors, who were prepared to stick a fork in them.

The traditional business types also don't see that these "characters" have interests and passions, personal lives that form the texture of their business enterprises. And they neglect the fact that these leaders are as smart as hell, specifically because they could give a damn about convention. While so many perceived the characteristics shared by Kelleher, Branson, and Ailes as liabilities, they were in fact invaluable assets.

What they lacked in classroom training and industry experienced, they more than made up for in observation of the real world. Each took his gut, and not his degrees, to his missions, driven by his uncanny instincts, upon which great enterprises were built.

They saw not only the forest through the trees, but I really believe they saw the whole mountain, and then some.

And because they laughed as they succeeded, they also *enjoyed* building their empires, and they made sure that those who worked for them were having as much fun as they were.

The companies these men created prize hard work, expecting a collective effort almost impossible to compete with, and they nurtured motivated, smiling employees who worked harder than almost anyone else because their bosses cared about their happiness.

Years and decades later, these funny, self-deprecating, unorthodox, instinctual leaders are *still* having a great time with their companies and workers. The CEOs and their employees joke, socialize, and enjoy the ride. Most important, they believe that getting a kick out of their bumpy journey is as important as finishing the ride and achieving their goals.

In much the same way that each man has a fresh, outsider's perspective on his industry, each has a gift for seeing talents in potential employees that other companies have overlooked or undervalued. As a result, they've filled their companies with people who, in these environments, prove that they are far better, far faster, and far surer than traditional company men and women.

These compassionate, motivating, insightful bosses get and keep loyalty from their troops, helping the companies through the inevitable hard times, as well as the good. That loyalty is returned as ardently as it is received.

Because these leaders are born risk-takers, they achieve long-term success by making big bets, and moving their companies in unpredictable new directions, and that means there's going to be repeated failures. But with committed, talented workers, unrelenting courage, and rock-steady reliance on their instincts, these CEOs keep driving their companies to greater heights, and are prepared to experiment again and again.

Each man has assembled what one chief executive fondly called his "renegade guerillas," capable of moving fast, and thinking faster. These renegade guerillas are not from your father's boardroom. They are not even remotely from your father's workforce. They are the closest thing to a corporate version of the "island of misfit toys." But they click, and they work. And as you'll see, they succeed.

As these men build their brands into global leaders, they are still redefining their industries—which they first charged into with little if any professional training—and breaking into new sectors as well.

I'll get around to Roger Ailes and Herb Kelleher a little later on. For now, though, I'll start with multibillionaire Richard Branson, whose Virgin empire consists of hundreds of different companies worldwide, because he always seems to be having more fun than anyone else.

In countless interviews with me, the maverick, British-born CEO always struck me as unflappable and ever gracious. It's as if he hasn't a care in the world. He's an entertainer who loves a little corporate shtick. He's pulled off dangerous, outrageous, and unforgettable publicity stunts all around the world.

He is an inspired, international, dyslexic visionary who saw something many American executives were blind to: Bored Americans were hungering for pizzazz in *everything*—from the airplanes they flew in, to the record shops they frequented.

There's nothing in Branson's background that even hinted at the fact that one of the world's richest men was in the making.

He was the oldest of three children born to Edward Branson, a lawyer, and his wife, Eve, a former dancer and flight attendant. Although far from poor, Branson remembers plenty of meals made up of bread and gravy.

Notoriously impatient, even as a child, the young Branson always was creating something, and even as a kid, Branson "thought" like an entrepreneur; while still a schoolboy, he hatched a scheme that saw him growing Christmas trees, a business that, sadly, if predictably, didn't work out. But despite that disappointment, he never gave up trying. Pointedly, Branson enjoyed the process more than the final results. As he grew into adolescence, he also began new businesses, learning lessons from each one, whether they succeeded or not.

His creativity and entrepreneurial spirit are among the few positive consequences of his dyslexia, which seriously impeded his reading and writing, and caused him enormous trouble both in school and out. It was even a struggle to speak properly and comprehend what was said to him.

People who suffer from this horribly misunderstood condition are viewed as slow or stupid, or even worse, unable or unwilling to learn. The very real physical condition with which they grapple is often complemented by emotional distress and attendant psychological woes.

Dyslexia results from neurological, maturational, and genetic causes that affect everything from reading simple text to grasping basic concepts and principles. The common notion is that dyslexics see everything backwards, that letters or words are reversed, making reading almost impossible, but the condition is actually much more complicated than that.

Eight out of ten individuals identified as dyslexic show an auditory language disorder that prevents the individual from linking the spoken form of a word to its written equivalent. It's not surprising that the more common forms of dyslexia make it difficult to pronounce new words or distinguish similarities and differences in words. And because dyslexics routinely reverse words and letters, comprehension suffers, and for students, their grades as well.

The ironic thing about dyslexics is that they aren't *dumb.* Far from it—in fact, most have normal to above-average intelligence. And many show strengths in other, more intangible areas, especially creativity, in its many forms.

Branson is one of the best examples of the extent to which dyslexics can not only triumph over their disabilities, but use their intelligence and highly developed creativity to succeed wildly.

A couple of years ago, when his Virgin empire consisted of hundreds of different companies, and Branson was a multibillionaire, I heard a story about how this business titan, who's considered notoriously scatter-brained by those who don't know he's dyslexic, still didn't know the difference between gross profits and net profits.

Not knowing that distinction didn't seem to matter at all; brilliant, creative, imaginative—and dyslexic—Branson keeps things simple, and leaves the details to others. He's the one who sees the big picture that's made Virgin what it is.

As a teenager, though, suffering the embarrassment and frustration of being a "slow" student, Branson dropped out of high school. His formal education may have ended, but he went on to start new ventures, learning business on the fly. By January 1968, Branson was working in journalism, a dyslexic high school dropout, working to help report the news, a job he approached with characteristically fierce determination. He published the first issue of *Student,* an alternative magazine, out of a friend's basement to the deafening strains of the Beatles, the Rolling Stones, and Bob Dylan. A self-proclaimed peacenik, Branson and his new magazine railed against America's involvement in Vietnam.

In October of that year, he took his entire staff to a student rally held outside the American embassy in London, featuring, among others, Vanessa Redgrave. As he later recalled in his autobiography, *Losing My Virginity:* "The mood of the crowd was exhilarating but at the same time slightly frightening. I felt that at any moment things could get out of control. And they did. When the police charged the crowd, I ran like hell. A photograph of the demonstration later appeared in *Paris Match*. It shows me, back arched, an inch away from the outstretched hand of a policeman who was trying to catch me as I sprinted across the square."

That period proved a seminal turning point for him. Although unabashedly liberal on some social issues, Branson had his limits. "While I opposed Vietnam," he wrote, "I didn't feel as passionately left-wing on other issues as most of my fellow demonstrators."

Later, after the United States left Vietnam in 1975, the rock-loving Branson noticed that records were consistently expensive no matter where you went.

He had an idea: He would sell cheap records by mail order. (His uncanny knack to divine business trends is another ability often found among very successful people who suffer from dyslexia.)

One friend suggested calling the company "Slipped Disc," but another had the idea that caught Branson's fancy and sense of humor: He suggested they call their project "Virgin."

It made sense. They were all virgins in the music business. The name stuck, and the Virgin empire began. Writing in his autobiography about Virgin's birth, Branson says, "The more diffuse the company becomes, the more frequently I am asked about my vision for Virgin." Branson answers that question by explaining that, "My vision . . . has never been rigid and changes constantly, like the company itself."

The first Virgin record store opened in 1971, and the first Virgin recording studio in 1972. Both gained a sort of cult following. The Sex Pistols, Phil Collins, and Culture Club were among the performers that Branson signed up for his record company, and suddenly Virgin was impossibly cool.

And Branson the even cooler guy behind it.

That was fun, but it only made Branson even more ambitious. He still wanted to build an unparalleled conglomerate, and he had

to make a big splash. He always looked for something to differentiate his company from the competition.

He focused as much on "how" to launch a product as he did on
the product itself. And he got headlines because he knows how to get
headlines; not with stuffy press releases but rather with stunts—
pure, unadulterated, guess-what-I'm-gonna-do-next stunts!

No media debut was too flashy or publicity stunt too over-
the-top, and Branson isn't happy unless he's making an outlandish
arrival, or taking on some new death-defying challenge. (An enthu-
siastic balloonist, he has survived some close calls on his many cross-
continental hot air balloon journeys.)

For the opening of a Virgin Megastore in New York, he wore a
silver jumpsuit and flew over Times Square; at another opening in
Las Vegas, he dressed up as a Roman emperor. On April Fools' Day
in 1989, he dressed up one of his hot air balloons to look like a UFO
hovering over London. The balloon landed in a park, and as policemen approached, the midget Branson hired for the prank popped
out of the gondola in an alien suit. As Branson later recalled,
"You've never seen anyone run so fast."

He has also climbed a London skyscraper in a Spiderman suit,
escaped off the island of Alcatraz, and, to make a big splash in
Miami, water-skied for the curious. After taking a spill, he emerged
from the water with a fish in his mouth and two air hostesses on
his arms. He is, as a friend once put it, the perpetual Peter Pan who
dumbfounds aging, clueless competitors at every turn.

Because his products were as good as his marketing, he was able
to sell Virgin Records for almost $2 billion, in 1992. He used some
of the profits from that deal to launch many other projects, and of
course continue his outrageous stunts, with no self-consciousness
to hold him back.

An episode involving a wedding dress is an effective example.

He had to get the word out that his new Virgin Bride chain of
stores was the place for young brides to find better deals, so how
else to draw attention then shave off his beard and mustache and

squeeze himself into a sexy bridal dress, throwing flowers to all he encountered. After that little stunt, he correctly surmised, "everyone knows we're in the bridal business now."

Branson's acts define him, his sense humor, and his ability to laugh at himself and the stoic, joyless business world around him.

Only Richard Branson could top a best-dressed poll conducted by a sweater company, keen on his stated preference for dress wear, and make a worst-dressed poll as well, and one sponsored by a suit company, no less.

Branson enjoyed having the world laugh at him, but he made sure they mentioned the brand. He knew that if his audience was laughing, they were buying, too. He hasn't stopped making them laugh, and they're still buying—all over the world, and at an expanding rate.

Branson posed for the front cover of his autobiography, dressed (scantily) as a pirate, and later appeared as a Zulu warrior. He went shopping with Pamela Anderson, looking for good bondage stores, shortly after signing her up as a spokesperson. He once confessed to me during a Fox appearance, "Sometimes I think, oh my God, am I going too far today? But we like to have fun, and we like to enjoy what we do and get headlines."

What I don't understand is why any of his competitors haven't mimicked his outrageous behavior. He has succeeded phenomenally, and the methods that propelled his company are often obvious. But his competition seems bound by convention, and their achievements are diminished by their unwillingness to be daring, imaginative, and risky.

Every so often you might find some guy who comes up with a new pricing wrinkle, or a way to recalculate the costs, but I don't see guys rushing to don wedding dresses and elaborate costumes, or launch themselves out of a cannon, or pose nearly naked on a best-selling cover. Not too many CEOs have the talent or confidence to do what Branson does, but more should at least try to climb out of their corporate box at least a little and take a chance now and then, especially as they lose ground to Virgin's great showman, who's made the Virgin brand click with every business he's started or acquired, from television to sperm banks and music.

I remember one marketing executive telling me years ago that Branson is among two or three corporate chieftains he knows who has made a name stand for something for so many years, and compared him to Donald Trump, whose ever-present name in the New York skyline is evidence of stature in the Big Apple, and far beyond.

Even Trump, though, doesn't have Branson's willingness, even eagerness, to take the most dignified events and turn them into curious affairs. But although he did experience Branson's style at close range: While attending an elegant banquet in London, Branson scooped Ivana Trump up by the waist and turned her upside down. Trump reportedly was not amused.

Branson leads people to believe he's all show and flash, but he's a lot more than a suave charmer with lady-killer looks. He's a very good businessman, whose flamboyance and flippancy about his dyslexia masks a keen business mind.

"Look," he said in a *Fortune* interview, "if I'd been good at math, I probably never would have started an airline."

The airline industry is one of the most conservative, competitive, deeply entrenched, and costly businesses in the world. The expense of running a major airline is so high that annual profits seem almost miraculous. But for a man who relishes the dangerous pleasures of flying hot air balloons, the idea of challenging the airline industry to make room for his new Virgin Airways was irresistible.

That enterprise nicely depicts what I've known from personal experience: Branson's amazing facility for comprehending details and trends that other business titans miss. He knew exactly what millions of weary, bored passengers wanted—and weren't getting.

"The original concept for Virgin was born out of the frustration of flying on other people's airlines. It was a miserable experience. I wanted to make it fun," he told me in one of our interviews. It was classic Branson, emphasizing fun. Virgin Atlantic Airways was and is that, and more.

It was the first airline to install video screens in seat backs, so people could watch movies or play games. It was the first to offer in-flight bars, lounges, masseuses, and manicurists; anything to break the everyday monotony of flying that Branson had described. Even his airport clubs became destinations in and of themselves; some passengers would thrill to delays, pampering themselves with Virgin hairstylists, libraries, even putting greens and swimming pools.

"The whole idea is to have *fun*," Branson underscored again. "And hopefully if you've had a good time, you'll come back." His attitude is as vital to employee morale as it is to the customers.

Branson has always made working at a Virgin company fun. He wants his employees to have as good a time as he does, because he cares—and knows that their attitude appeals to Virgin customers, who keep coming back, not just for the products or the service, but because they enjoy interacting with the cheerful Virgin employees.

Having successfully combined creativity and business since childhood, the charismatic Branson easily inspires his employees to employ the same daring mentality that he does.

As a result, happy, hard-working, and thoughtful Virgin employees are constantly coming up with new schemes and ventures, and their ideas over the years have helped Branson vastly expand the hundreds of companies and operations that are part of the Virgin brand.

Branson, who prefers to travel incessantly rather than sit in an office, is forever popping up in company locales to have a good laugh with employees. His speeches are improvised, and absolutely hysterical, and he can get the troops fired up even when business is suffering.

Sir Freddie Laker, who also challenged the established airlines some years earlier with his no-frills transatlantic Laker Sky Train, said of Branson in a June 26, 1996, *Washington Post* story that "He gives the impression of being much into fun, but right deep down he's got a razor-edge brain, a brain like a computer."

But it's this further insight from Laker that crystallizes the real Richard Branson, and how he overcame his dyslexia: "He can work out any deal in any currency, and by the time he's done, he's worked out a plan where he'll be able to take 5 percent for himself."

Most of Branson's competitors don't appreciate that side of his personality. They see most of his forays as foolish ventures at best, and costly boondoggles at worst. In reality, though, they're well thought-out business plans, because Branson acutely understands the risks of exceeding costs.

As one business associate told the *Australian Financial Review* in October 1998, "The way Branson sees it, with things like Virgin Atlantic and Virgin Cola is that if he takes on the big boys and loses, he is still a hero for trying. And if he wins, he is a genius. So long as the losses are not too heavy, it is another way of advertising himself and the business."

Even his balloon ventures are well-planned, sponsored, and executed, so that the accompanying wave of worldwide publicity more than makes up for the time and cost.

While his ballooning adventures may look like a billionaire's lark, to those who know him, it is vintage Branson. They understand his endeavors, and know that he's a guy that loves fun, risky propositions, especially those that give his business a boost in the process.

When he launched Virgin Airways, Branson made the flying experience fun, which was always an essential aspect of the Virgin experience in any business, but he made it sexy as well.

I remember asking Branson in one interview whether it was his intention to only hire beautiful people to work at his airline. (I defy you to ever find an ugly employee on board, because I truly believe if they get so much as a blemish, they're hauled off the plane mid-flight.)

Branson was typically coy in response: "Well, I'd love to take responsibility, but they are beautiful. They are bright, and they are glamorous. But flying should be glamorous. It used to be glamorous, you know. Virgin, I think, has brought the glamour back to it."

He also made it hip to fly, featuring everything from sleeper seats that offered a host of possibilities, to joke-cracking flight attendants who put even the most serious passenger at ease.

And then there was what I think is one of the greatest marketing tie-ins of all time: Branson's improbable, apparently ludicrous but typically inspired, link-up with Austin Powers.

When *Austin Powers: The Spy Who Shagged Me* was about to be released in 1999, Virgin launched an hilarious campaign featuring Mike Myers's sexy secret agent with bad teeth—one billboard captured the spirit of the link-up, featuring the velour-clad Powers's innuendo, "There's only one virgin on this billboard, baby!" Another offered, "Non-smoking flights. Unless I'm on board, baby." It proved a brilliant pairing, and passengers on both sides of the Atlantic ate it up.

They enjoyed the knowing humor, the unpretentiousness of stamping the Powers character on the nose of the aircraft, and even temporarily rechristening the airline "Virgin Shaglantic." (Virgin's web site adopted the leering Austin-ism as well.)

I don't think I've ever seen a campaign that so effectively put fannies in seats and smiles on faces. I know there are many staid executives, particularly in the airline industry, who'd wince at the notion of a "shagadelic" airline. But that was very much Austin Powers, and that was very much Virgin Atlantic. But most importantly of all, that was very much Richard Branson.

For him, it wasn't about taking risks, but rather it was about taking a shot at the drab and dreary world of flying, and having fun with it. Who says you can't have a great time on a plane? Or just make something so ordinary so extraordinary?

N ever one to miss an opportunity, Branson has appeared on my show many times. He was there to be interviewed, but more importantly to promote his latest media stunt or business undertaking.

But he has also revealed his more serious, deeply compassionate side. On November 1, 2001, Branson stopped by my studios to promote travel to a still reeling New York. While Branson hadn't been affected by September 11 in the ways John Duffy and Fred Alger so tragically had, he was significantly supporting and contributing in his own way.

Mindful that September 11 had made many people afraid to fly, he flew, at his expense, 400 contestants (from more than 25,000 entrants) to New York City as part of a campaign to help the city *and* Virgin Airways. This all-inclusive Branson treat, covered not only the flight and hotels, but food and sight-seeing costs as well. He even arranged for the whole bunch to meet New York Mayor Rudy Giuliani, which made the experience even more rewarding.

It was all a huge media event, and immediately impressed cynical and terror-worn New Yorkers as something special.

When I suggested the New York contest was a nice thing to do for New Yorkers, Branson was quick to point out it benefited both sides of the pond.

"Look, we needed to kick-start things again," Branson told me. "There's a business reason as well. I mean, people are not flying and we need to get them flying. In the past, we brought a million people a year to New York. They spent about a billion dollars a year in New York. And we need to get them back again," he explained. "We have to help people overcome their fears. . . . And so to benefit the airline industry, and New York, we thought this would be a good way to do it."

Branson used the media event to promote the fact Virgin was offering $199 fares from New York to London. People would fly, he reasoned, if they were given a compelling reason to do so. Cheap fares were a good start. That encapsulates his logic: Appeal to their heart; then appeal to their brain.

I remember Branson telling *Fortune* that he never pictured himself as a businessman; that he was more interested in creating things he could be proud of. Virgin Atlantic was an extension of that, a response to all those dreadful airlines that had made the experience so uninteresting.

Never did he expect any venture to be the best in its particular industry, or even make much money. That he'd become a multibillionaire with a vast global empire was a consequence of the sheer fun he had in starting new companies, competing in industries in which he had no experiences, and doing any stunt he could imagine to promote his companies.

Another example of Branson's daring was his unveiling of Virgin Wireless in the summer of 2002. It was a lousy period for the stock market, and an even lousier time for the wireless phone industry—after much promise and hype only two years earlier, the industry was rapidly losing money and key players were quickly consolidating as well.

Not only was the American economy slowing, mobile phone penetration wasn't nearly as high in the United States as abroad. Forget about expanding business; most players were desperately hanging on to the business they had, which wasn't much.

Then along came Branson, convinced that it was the best moment to offer a flashy Virgin-stamped model of his own for the industry. This swashbuckling confidence in being able to triumph in very well-established industries in which he has no experience, even in the worst economies, typifies Branson.

As was so often the case with his new ventures, his concept was evolutionary, defying past strategies and taking the industry in different directions. Risky the way new, untested business models usually are, the state of the American market that Branson was charging into made the prospect riskier still. But it was precisely because things looked so bad here that Branson wanted to leap into the business in 2002.

Explaining his reasoning, Branson said, "Well, I know some people will think that we need our heads examined. But what we did is we looked at the American market and we found that only 45 percent of people had mobile phones. So, we asked the question . . . why?"

The answer to that question intrigued him deeply. It seems that young Americans, in particular, simply couldn't afford the expense or the hassle of having a mobile phone; that the elaborate contracts required by most cell-phone companies precluded many younger consumers from signing on to the cell-phone craze.

Now the man who had inaugurated enormous record stores and apex-of-cool airplanes was offering hip wireless, using naked models to advertise his new service, emphasizing his new mobile phone company motto, "What you see is what you get."

In his typically tongue-in-cheek fashion, Branson was making a very serious point. With many wireless phone contracts, what you see isn't what you get. "When we launched in the UK," Branson recalled in our chat, "we noticed that with mobile phones, there were all these hidden charges. You know, people think they're only paying $30 a month, but they end up paying $90 a month. And so the whole idea of our mobile phone company is an honest, open contract. It's no contract, really, so you know where you stand."

Then there was the issue of a brand name for young Americans to aspire to.

Branson, who'd spent thirty years making Virgin a global brand synonymous with cool, understood that excellent brand names had enormous marketing value.

"Virgin had a strong brand name," and pursuing another partner that had done a similarly impressive job at branding, he "sat down with MTV," and they agreed to join the project. When he had finished talking to MTV, "they agreed to let me have their brand as well. And we agreed to work together to let music from MTV flow into the mobile phone." As soon as Branson added MTV to Virgin Wireless, huge distributors such as Blockbuster and Target began marketing and selling his phone service. "They got very excited about it," Branson remembered.

Every retailer craves younger customers, and Virgin, despite its fifty-something CEO, attracts young customers, just as it had in the early seventies when Branson started Virgin Records.

That Branson was able to maintain his brand's cachet, even as he moved into middle age, reflects the enduring adventurousness of his spirit, the value of his ongoing stunts, as much for his own entertainment as for marketing, and his youthful eagerness to keep trying new things.

Musing on his own empire, which spans the globe, he freely admits even he can't accurately tally the full scope of the company he created and shepherds, but Branson keeps the scale and the mission in perspective. He appreciates the airline, and clothing line, and soft-drink company, and the countless specialty stores pegged to his, eclectic interests, but he remains very much the same curious child he once was, always looking for ways to turn a new deal, or discover a new product, or take a stab at a new venture.

He needn't dominate a business, he once told me, as long as he can "just have fun doing it." The rest, he said, should take care of itself.

CHAPTER 6

IN THE BLOOD,
AND NEAR THE HEART

Cancer can be treated but it is incurable, and for many it is deadly, as it was for my mother and father. Even massive, prolonged treatment only delays the inevitable.

The odds are automatically against you, and the treatments—everything from chemotherapy, to repetitive, often painful blood transfusions—can make you wonder whether the chance at a longer life is worth it.

These are some of the hard facts of this disease, even today, after decades of medical research. That makes the following group of people all the more special.

I very deeply admire cancer survivors. Having been one myself for seventeen years, I have some insight into the toughness of spirit, stubborn determination, and passionate desire to keep enjoying life, a fortitude that has a lot to do with why these victims survived after the initial diagnosis, often agonizing treatment, and slow recovery, and have a special appreciation for living.

Survival, like cancer, takes many different forms. Joe Torre and Mel Sottlemyre battled the disease in the glare of the media spotlight, watched carefully by millions of concerned baseball fans. The three cancer survivors I'm profiling in this chapter are as different from one another as they are from the two baseball legends.

Evelyn Lauder has spent most of her life making her mark in the cosmetics world, her name synonymous with good looks; Harry Pearce, a top-ranking, highly regarded General Motors executive, is a terse lawyer who embodies integrity; Geraldine Ferraro was a former congresswoman and well-known vice presidential candidate, who dedicated her life to public service.

But they're all united and defined by how they survived—by maintaining a positive attitude as they battled their respective illnesses. More importantly, they're linked by how they changed the lives they'd fought to keep, choosing to dedicate their lives to helping fellow cancer victims and those at risk.

They continue to wage personal and corporate campaigns to increase the public awareness of cancer, to educate people about the many insidious forms of the disease, and to motivate people to become more involved in the battle, for others and for themselves.

These crusaders could have decided to indulge only themselves, because they had experienced enough anguish just dealing with their own misery. Also, every survivor, including me, fears the return of cancer, and we can't be sure how much longer we'll have to live. Why not live for ourselves, while we can?

What they decided was to indulge themselves, but *not* by focusing on themselves alone, their suffering and their fears—even when for one of these survivors, the nightmare came true, and cancer did return. That they put aside their own pain and worked to help everyone stricken with cancer plainly demonstrates their honor and their courage.

BEAUTIFUL ON THE INSIDE

A Vienna-born socialite, Evelyn always lived according to her own values, which often broke from those common in the wealthy circle she'd been born into. She met her husband, Leonard Lauder, on a blind date while she was a student at Hunter College, working at a Barnes & Noble store. They were married in 1959, and throughout their marriage they have celebrated their anniversaries not with galas or parties or elaborate gifts, but rather with contributions to their communities. For instance, she led her Manhattan neighbors in a fund-raising drive to plant and care for trees on their street.

Although her husband was the son of cosmetics legend Estée Lauder, Evelyn at first continued with her own life, including teaching, instead of taking the easier path and joining the family business. She had to be persuaded to join the cosmetics giant by Estée Lauder herself, who perceived Evelyn as the ideal choice to initiate and guide Estée Lauder training programs. Estée was right, as legends so often are, and under Evelyn's leadership and direction, the Estée Lauder training programs became almost as famous as Estée herself.

When Evelyn was diagnosed with breast cancer in 1989, her thoughts, as always, turned almost at once to helping others. She told the *Cleveland Plain Dealer* that "My own situation doesn't really matter. The fact that I'm an activist is what's important."

For more than thirty years, she'd been engaged in philanthropy and the energetic support of causes she believed in. Now, she began the most important effort of her life.

She knew she had a very famous name, and she wanted to leverage the marketing value of that name into helping those who might not be able to help themselves. Evelyn Lauder understood that the cause of fighting cancer could be marketed as effectively as any product. The difference would be that she'd stress communication, information, and specific descriptions of potential therapies that people might not be aware of. She made her marketing campaign a holy, life-saving mission, dedicated to stamping out breast cancer, and more importantly, raising awareness of, and treatment for, the disease.

In October 1992 (not coincidentally, October is National Breast Cancer Month), Evelyn marketed a campaign to heighten awareness of the disease. She distributed hundreds of thousands of pink ribbons and "Breast Self-Exam" instruction cards, and used a built-in base, involving all the Estée Lauder counters across the United States.

Evelyn knew the value of person-to-person contact, and she used all her retail connections to help spread the word. She dismissed those cynics and skeptics who thought a simple ribbon campaign to raise breast cancer awareness would prove a waste of time. Suddenly the pink ribbon was an internationally recognized symbol for a disease that, at best, had only surface recognition.

In short order, she established the Estée Lauder Global Landmarks Illumination Initiative, which periodically bathed historic landmarks in pink lights to focus global attention on breast cancer. In another fund-raising effort, she assembled *An Eye for Beauty,* a book of her own photographs, and all of its proceeds were donated to her effort to combat breast cancer. She also founded the Breast Cancer Research Foundation in 1993, which worked to provide funding for clinical research on causes and treatments of the disease. The animating principle behind her efforts, based in part on her experience as a teacher, was that with knowledge came power, and a way to overcome the initial shock of the disease. Arming patients with that kind of power, and that level of information, was crucial to Evelyn.

The more people knew about their disease, her thinking went, the less they would be intimidated by it. She was right, just as Estée Lauder had been all those years ago in asking Evelyn to join her at the company, which her daughter-in-law would later use as an essential means of communication, marketing, and education.

By October 2001, only nine years after Lauder launched her pink-ribbon, breast cancer-awareness campaign, more than 200 landmarks in more than forty countries around the world were given the pink treatment. Niagara Falls, the Leaning Tower of Pisa, and the Tokyo Tower were all bathed in pink. Every year, the number of landmarks taking part in the program has doubled, and world attention soars.

In 2002, celebrating a decade of heightened understanding, increased funding, more effective prevention, and a greater emphasis on early treatment, Evelyn wrapped up a Breast Cancer Awareness

Tour, where she barnstormed through eight cities during a month-long tour to support *An Eye for Beauty,* and greater awareness of the disease she had worked for so long to combat.

A host of retailers, including Bergdorf Goodman, Blooming-dale's, Macy's West, Nordstrom, Marshall Field's, Lord and Taylor, and Saks Fifth Avenue, all donated funds to the foundation. Macy's alone gave $100,000, based on sales of a Macy's-inspired pink breast cancer keychain. That same year, the Estée Lauder Companies do-nated $2 million to the Breast Cancer Research Foundation. (Since the Foundation's inception, Evelyn has helped raise nearly $50 mil-lion to help find a cure for the disease.)

What started out as something small within the cosmetics com-pany has now grown to include scores of organizations, especially retailers, from around the globe.

While she worked to stamp out the disease, Evelyn kept her own pain to herself, never mentioning her own suffering. In no in-terview, press conference, or media event did she ever talk about her own battle with the disease, her own difficulties, or her own fears. This intensely private and dignified woman opted instead to focus on others.

E velyn Lauder, Harry Pearce, and Geraldine Ferraro are unified by surviving cancer. Pearce and Ferraro have even more in com-mon, both suffering from cancers that affected their blood.

Pearce was burdened with Leukemia, a from of cancer charac-terized by an abnormal increase in the number of white blood cells, specifically leukocytes, whose primary purpose is to destroy dis-ease-causing organisms. Left unchecked, this leukocyte-spurt can turn lethal, turning on the cells that they were meant to protect.

Although the survival rate for various forms and stages of leukemia has improved since Pearce's initial diagnosis in 1998, especially with early detection, it is still deadly to the majority of people who suffer it.

Later that year, Ferraro was diagnosed with multiple myeloma, the same incurable blood cancer that ravaged Mel Stottlemyre almost two years later. More than 40,000 Americans currently have multiple myeloma. For them and the estimated 14,000 new patients diagnosed each year, the odds are daunting. Even today, the median lifespan after the diagnosis is only three to four years.

For Ferraro's form of blood cancer, the standard treatment was chemotherapy, which has its own dizzying array of side effects, and a bone marrow transplant, which is how Stottlemyre was treated. His multiple myeloma was put into remission.

That Pearce would return to work as vice chairman of General Motors during his grueling two-year treatment and battle with leukemia, and that Ferraro would emerge from retirement and become publicly active again after suffering through a second series of experimental, brutal series of treatments, is awe-inspiring.

What they did after that, however, can only be described as true heroism.

THE BIG ENGINE THAT COULD

After being told that he had a potentially lethal form of cancer, Harry Pearce quickly decided that he would make his battle with leukemia public. Speaking to the *Los Angeles Times* in 1998: "It changes your attitude toward life in general. When you're facing your own mortality that directly, it causes you to reassess in a very broad way what's important in life."

He then began what would become a two-year sequence of treatments, first having a bone marrow transplant, and then undergoing follow-up chemotherapy.

He also continued working, as much to let people know he could, as to offer encouragement for many others who could not.

Even as he was going through treatment, Pearce committed corporate resources to a life-saving mission, just as Evelyn Lauder had, to help people who found themselves in his position. For example, he launched an organ, bone-marrow, and stem-cell donor drive and registry among GM's 395,000 employees. Pearce had gotten the idea for the drive after his own combination treatment of transplant and chemotherapy, when he started wondering why more patients weren't benefiting from those available therapies.

"You'd see the other patients and pretty soon you'd see empty rooms and know that somebody didn't make it," he told AP. "That's the tough part of going through this process—the ones who don't make it. And I just kept thinking about them and what I could do."

Bone marrow transplants are the best hope for curing leukemia and many other blood diseases, and can increase the chance of survival by up to 60 percent. The problem with the procedure is finding the right sort of cell types for the patient, which can be far more difficult to match than blood types. Pearce found his match in his brother.

One out of three patients that receive tissue matches find them in relatives, but many die before an appropriate donor can be found. What's worse, minority patients seeking donors have an even tougher time; few minorities are on donor lists, so African American and Hispanic patients are harder to match, and sadly, more likely to die.

Pearce thought that by expanding the pool, he'd be improving the chances for others to find a match. Something this vast and expensive—$1 million to launch a donor drive and registry involving nearly 400,000 workers—had never been tried before. But no one so senior at one of America's preeminent companies had ever led the charge.

"This is a big deal," Dr. Jill McGovern, chief executive of the Washington-based Marrow Foundation, told the Associated Press at the time. "There's nothing that's been done on the scale that GM is considering." The scope of their effort was staggering then, and remains so now.

　　　　　　　　　　　　　　　　〰〰

Pearce, an attorney, has defended GM in product-liability suits since 1970. His expertise on crash dynamics, fuel cells, and myriad other complex industry issues made Pearce an early dynamo at the company.

Environmentalists and consumer advocates who've taken Pearce on in court grudgingly acknowledge he does his homework—and he usually wins. His reputation soared in 1993 when he revealed that GM pickup trucks had been rigged by NBC's *Dateline* to show how the trucks can explode in side-impact crash tests: Unbeknownst to viewers at the time, NBC had taped model rocket engines near the gas tanks to deliberately ignite the fires. Pearce heard about the rigging from an inside tip, and advised General Motors to fight NBC, in court, head-on, regardless of the bad publicity that would probably be generated in the short-run. The GM leadership agreed.

Pearce stated and personalized his case at a packed news conference, saying: "I will not allow the good men and women of General Motors, and the thousands of independent businesses who sell our products and whose livelihood depends on our reputation and the reputation of our products to suffer the consequences of NBC's irresponsible conduct. GM has been irreparably damaged, and we are going to defend ourselves." *Dateline* issued an on-air apology, and the story was fully retracted.

General Motors survived what easily could have been a company-crushing blow, and Pearce became a legal legend. He had proven both his and GM's mettle by responding to charges that up to that point were routinely settled out of court, at great expense, even when proven to be without legal merit.

Pearce is tough, guided by his values, and gifted in many ways. For example, industry analysts are always struck by his

"Rainman-like" memory of arcane industry facts and figures, and his unusual gift for speaking without notes or scripts has made him something of a marvel.

In my own discussions and interviews with him, he always strikes me as a guy who wastes few words, who knows that the best argument is often the shortest one. That's why in discussing anything from advanced hybrid cars to some far-flung litigation, Pearce is terse and always to the point. From a journalist's standpoint that can be difficult, but at least with Pearce, you know you're getting something concise.

His legal mind, decades of experience in preparing court cases, and long tenure as a high-ranking executive at one of the largest companies in the world combined to make Pearce's sweeping, methodical push for tissue database research efforts at GM successful.

When the donor drive and registry initiative was first introduced in the spring of 2000, it had two objectives: to educate workers about the benefits of organ donation of any sort, initially with videotapes; and to expand blood drives to match bone-marrow and stem-cell donors to the people who needed them, especially inside the African American and Hispanic populations, where tissue shortages were particularly acute.

Having finished his own two years of treatment at around the same time, and with the initiative organized, Pearce was finally free to travel to GM factories around the country, on what one insider called "Harry's good health missions."

At each factory, each shop, each corporate town hall meeting, Pearce urged workers to participate in a bone-marrow registry, or sign on to be an organ donor. He knew that such registries and organ banks would help cancer victims improve their odds, and give them a fighting shot at survival.

He visited hundreds of patients, personally cheering them on, reportedly spending hours with some patients, many of whom were eager for a kind word, or any show of support from someone who had made it. Every patient's phone call was returned, every letter answered. Because he remembered so much of his pain, he had a greater sympathy for theirs.

Pearce is a folk hero to employees of GM. They see in him someone who suffered greatly, and in response, committed himself and his company to doing everything possible to help others avoid the same fate—and he's still helping as many people as he can.

In addition to sitting on the board of cancer organizations and the National Marrow Foundation, Pearce has expanded his mission to include the expansion of research and development spending on cancer. He still speaks to patients, employees, and the broader public, reminding cancer victims that their attitude is as important as their treatment.

"If you come to the conclusion . . . that you're not going to make it," he told the *Los Angeles Times*. "I personally believe that it can become a self-fulfilling prophecy."

Because he is not one to blow his own horn, much of what Pearce has done doesn't get recognized. You don't hear stories about people like GM's Debbie Sobol, who had leukemia and has undergone two stem-cell transplants made possible by Pearce's work. You don't hear about the employee who was afraid he would lose his job when he became ill, only to have Pearce offer him comfort and support every step of the way. You don't hear about Pearce's speeches before scores of union workers at plants across the country, urging them to join up and help each other.

You don't hear about all the people Pearce has helped, or whose lives have been saved because of his donor drive and registry, but the substance, results, and undying gratitude are there, and that's all Pearce wants.

Cancer experts today say it's hard to estimate how many lives Pearce's campaign has helped save, how many tissue matches have been found, or the number of organs donated as a result, but it is certainly in the thousands.

And all because an executive with a heart decided to commit more than his good name to a cause. He decided to commit his life to one.

THE CAMPAIGN OF HER LIFE

Geraldine Ferraro had retired from a long, admirable, and well-known political career, and was enjoying her new life when she was first diagnosed with multiple myeloma after a routine physical in December 1998.

She was told that this particular type of blood cancer kills half of its victims in five years or less. However, it was currently in an inactive state in her bone marrow, a state doctors called "smoldering myeloma." Not a very comforting term. The cancer hadn't yet started to spread, but it could burst into "flames," and begin to grow rapidly at any time.

After overcoming her shock, Ferraro told only her immediate family. After decades of public service, she was now a private citizen, and she wanted to keep her privacy and protect her family from invasive media attention (a subject about which she knew a great deal), which would inevitably follow any announcement that she had cancer.

As the first woman on a presidential ticket, she had seen more than her share of journalistic probing, of her family's finances, her children, their friends, backgrounds, and education; whatever the subject, Ferraro had had enough of it.

In addition, she was and is one of the few political types I know who has absolutely no interest in the limelight. Indeed, part of her incredible political longevity was due to her never seeking out public attention in the first place.

She's a woman I had grown to admire from afar and, after her numerous appearances on my show, have come to know fondly. She is passionate in her beliefs and never wavers, vacillates, or amends them to make them consistent with the results of some focus-group or the latest litmus test. I've told her on the air that she could teach many both in and outside her party the meaning of "core" beliefs. You didn't have to agree with her, but you knew that what she said and what she believed meant a great deal to her.

Ferraro and I are not exactly on the same political page; her traditional liberalism doesn't always fit comfortably with my own convictions. We've been known to rib each other, always in good nature, on our shared Fox News broadcasts, and she remains a favorite of mine because of her passion and her commitment. I told her one day on my show, "Geraldine, you've got a no-BS way about you," and I held her then, as I do now, in the highest regard.

We differ mightily on how best to govern, but let there be no doubt, she remains a conscience in her party, and one of my favorite political figures. Those in her party continue to debate their policies and their role in society, but Ferraro always made it clear that their platform should be about compassion, honor, and dignity, and she has never failed to attack her fellow Democrats if they fail to act in a way that reflects that compassion, honor, and dignity.

As a congresswoman, she was deeply passionate about leveling the playing field for all Americans, and building a country that saw its greatest strength in helping its weakest members. She fought to end pension discrimination against women and provide them better job options. She fought to open IRAs and hold corporate crooks accountable, long before they became front page issues.

That's what I like most about Ferraro: the ardor she brings to all of her causes. She doesn't just spout popular rhetoric—she's real.

As I've pointed out many times on my show, I don't care if you're liberal or conservative, Democrat or Republican, Marxist or Maoist, but be true to your beliefs. Even those who disagree with you will admire you for your guts.

I recall one pundit who said of Ferraro that if he was in a foxhole, he'd much prefer Ferraro to any other Democrat, because she'd always be there, as opposed to others in her party, who to his mind, likely would abandon him when he needed them most.

I suspect much of Ferraro's appeal is that she takes life in stride, big political setbacks included. Even when criticism became deeply personal, she never responded in kind. As a good practicing Catholic, she was taken aback when no less an authority than New York's John Cardinal O'Connor took on her pro-choice views during the 1984 presidential campaign.

In what some considered at the time to be an unusually harsh rebuke, Cardinal O'Connor essentially questioned whether Ferraro could be a good Catholic when she espoused views that went so overtly against those held by the Church. The issue seemed to take on a life of its own, with Ferraro's religious beliefs suddenly a divisive campaign issue. Yet she never shot back at the Cardinal or even attempted to question the Vatican's doctrine. It almost seemed as if the Church itself was itching for a fight, but Ferraro wasn't taking their bait.

I later asked her about reports that relations with the Cardinal had become so strained that he refused to talk to her. Quite the opposite, she told me—the two spoke and wrote each other often, even kidding each other about the political heat of the moment. Moreover, Ferraro was granted an audience with O'Connor only days before his death from cancer, and such privileges are not granted freely or often.

Her strength helped her and her family after her diagnosis, while the disease remained inactive for more than two and a half years, and Ferraro kept it private.

Then her life changed dramatically, as new tests showed that the "smoldering myeloma" had begun to metastasize. As I've said, that's my worst nightmare and that of any cancer survivor, because the disease is still incurable.

Now she would have to begin intensive, excruciating treatments, with only a few options to choose from, and all miserable. Additionally, she'd have to go public. It would be almost impossible to keep her procedures secret, and even trying to do so, would make the media attention even worse.

When Ferraro first told the world in July 2001 about her form of blood cancer, little was known about it, and most people had a tough time even pronouncing the name of the disease. However, Ferraro's announcement hit me very hard. My good friend was battling something terribly serious, and all too familiar.

Ferraro understood that few Americans knew about the disease, and even fewer knew about potential treatments. Surviving would not be easy for any victim, but they needed to know they weren't facing an automatic death sentence.

She decided, before going public, that once the news was out she could move on even while she was being treated, and like Harry Pearce and Evelyn Lauder, engage in her own campaign. Like she did during her long tenure in Congress, she'd work to help the American people directly. She'd commit her time, energy, and political stature to getting attention for multiple myeloma, so more people would know about it and understand it better.

She engaged in a focused effort to educate Americans in general as well as Congress, with all the important information she could assemble about multiple myeloma: the importance of early detection, and the range of available treatments that could be used to fight this strange, mercurial disease. She knew was that 11,000 people were dying each year from multiple myeloma. Surely some stood better odds?

When she appeared on July 19, 2001, on my show, she was in true Ferraro form. No sympathy, no tears; all she wanted was the viewers' understanding, and to spread the word.

"I don't want anybody to treat me differently," she told me. "I may not win this race, but I've lost races before, so it's not the end of the world." Leave it to Ferraro to find humor in what had to be medical horror.

She looked great and flashed the same old smile. She recounted how old friends, and even those who were not always so friendly, had called and written to offer their support. She had spoken just the day before with her former running mate Walter Mondale, and had heard from Bill Clinton, George W. Bush, George H. W. Bush, and hundreds of others. Some she could talk to, others she could not, but all wished her well. She told me she never saw that kind of reaction coming, even as she saw a similar emotional outpouring at Fox that day.

I was a bit surprised myself. That kind of intense empathy was unusual, even for our tight-knit broadcast family. Commentators, editors, producers, interns, everyone approached her; some people hugged her, most just looked her up and down and in the words of one associate producer of mine, said simply: "We're with you, Gerry!" When I saw the expression on the sixty-seven-year-old Ferraro's face, I asked her, "Why are you so stunned?" "I just didn't expect any of this," she replied.

Leave it to Fox viewers to conclude the same about Ferraro. They're a tough crowd, but it was this very same crowd that e-mailed my show by the thousands after she appeared, with the same compassion and admiration that those at the studio had shown.

They appreciated her personal courage, and her selflessness, as she broadcast to the world, and testified on Capitol Hill, about the urgent need for more research to combat this unusual disease. As a retired politician, as she once put it, she has no axe to grind, no political cause to glom onto. She wants only to help, and she had the cachet—in a town that responds to it—to accomplish exactly that.

This cause was clearly personal for Ferraro, and the fight was different. Multiple myeloma doesn't choose political sides. It affects men and women, rich and poor, black and white. It cuts across all boundaries.

While she was continuing her drive to educate the public, she had to make decisions about her medical options, none of which were great.

The standard treatment was chemotherapy, with its own dizzying array of side effects, and a stem cell transplant. This combination of therapies was what Harry Pearce had endured from 1998 to 2000, and Mel Stottlemyre had suffered from the Yankees' 2000 spring training through the World Series and beyond.

But in the late summer of 2001, Ferraro was told there was another option. But it was still untested and considered by many to be risky. Doctors at Boston's Farber Cancer Institute were having some success with daily doses of thalidomide, a drug approved only two years earlier for use in treating leprosy.

But thalidomide didn't come without very serious side effects. It had been banned years earlier after it was linked to birth defects; pregnant mothers had commonly used thalidomide for morning sickness, but after the report that it endangered the health of babies, prescriptions and sales tumbled.

Still, thalidomide had some promising properties. Doctors found it could inhibit the blood that feeds tumors, a process known as *antiangiogenesis*. In arresting a cancer like Ferraro's, thalidomide had a more curious and direct use: For some reason, the drug interrupted the ability of the myeloma cell to bind to bone marrow. In other words, it somehow stopped the cancer from progressing or spreading.

But thalidomide itself has limitations. The body can take only so much of it before the drug loses its interruptive power—or, worse, becomes harmful.

With Ferraro, doctors thought they'd detected the reactivated multiple myeloma in its early stages. Her cancer had not taken hold outside the bloodstream, and hadn't gotten into her bones. Once that happened, the bones would quickly become brittle, and treatment of any sort would be very limited.

For the seemingly fearless Ferraro, thalidomide's potential to stop the disease was more important than all the associated risks, and she was immediately put on the drug.

Doctors told her they'd carefully watch the progress. What neither they nor Ferraro could predict was how quickly and well her battered body would respond.

The results were even better than hoped for. The cancer was prevented from spreading, and as of this writing it's still in remission. It's a welcome development, though as I know from my own bout with Hodgkin's disease, doctors will not use the term "cured" with regard to cancer.

Ferraro's case exemplifies this. Her cancer was dormant when it was diagnosed, and remained that way for almost three years before becoming active once again. Thalidomide worked—as she took on cancer a second time—and she'd be the first to say that at any moment the disease could return a third time. Cancer survivors never have the comfort of certainty, only the anxiety that the disease may resume.

It was encouraging that thalidomide worked so well for Ferraro. Doctors reported that her case had best demonstrated thalidomide's role in helping those with early stages of multiple myeloma. The symptoms had to be caught early, but only a few might be that lucky. Ferraro therefore urgently wanted to get the word out about the potential thalidomide might offer to many other people suffering from this cancer.

As advocates go, she's not just a make-a-speech-and-go crusader; she's a missionary. Every day she spins out the frightening details of a disease the nation is only now grasping, informing people that her sort of cancer is twice as common in males as females, that it affects more African Americans and Native Pacific Islanders than any other ethnic groups, and among African Americans, in particular, multiple myeloma is one of the top ten forms of cancer.

Ferraro has spoken in cities around the country, to small groups and large, to let them know about the great strides being made against multiple myeloma. From city to city, state to state, even country to country, anywhere there's an audience, there's Ferraro, preaching, warning, and quietly reminding anyone who'll listen that the sum of our resources is greater than the sum of our illnesses.

And she's spoken with and encouraged hundreds with the disease, some whose prospects look positive, and others who were losing the fight against their diseases.

"Sometimes I feel guilty," she told me in a later appearance on my show, about her own remarkable success with thalidomide. "It doesn't work for everybody. But other great things will come along."

Raising awareness of multiple myeloma, and raising money to fight that strain of cancer and a host of others continues to be her most important mission.

"It might not happen in my lifetime," she said, but she clearly wants to help stamp out cancer for the benefit of those that the disease will afflict in the future.

"That's what I'm out here for, too," she says of her TV appearances. She uses them to inspire everyone with cancer and her supporters, by letting them know that day by day, hour by hour, she's fighting for them, and for herself, so she can continue to help them. And she tries to be a role model, indicating through her own actions that you can go on if you have enough determination.

"I don't know where this disease will take me," she said. "But I'm going to fight it every step of the way, and that's what I want others to do, too. . . . I just take every day one day at a time," she told me. "I can't do much more than that."

She enjoys her family, promotes awareness of her disease, and quietly prepares for the unthinkable. Ferraro tells me that she and her husband, John Zaccaro, who have seen and been through so much together, carry on through this together as well.

She explains that she's moving from their Queens home to an apartment in Manhattan, because soon she won't be able to climb the stairs in their four-story home, especially if she gets weaker, or the cancer invades her bones.

"You always anticipate in a marriage that the wife is going to survive the husband," she says. "I've taught him how to make breakfast now, and he's not bad at making sandwiches, but I don't expect that will happen for a while." As of this writing John Zaccaro hasn't progressed much beyond sandwiches, "but he's learned enough to get by," Ferraro tells me.

As a frequent panelist on Fox, including my shows, Ferraro lives her life, continues to raise awareness of this most insidious of cancers, and never uses her public appearances to focus attention on herself.

In addition to her mission, she talks about the liberal causes she holds dear and the conservative positions she rejects. Republicans like to take her on, but she's fast with the facts and even faster with the quips. She's good on TV. As one Republican party operative once put it to me, "Geraldine is the liberal you can't help but love."

She's also the one liberal that conservatives better not take lightly. Cancer certainly hasn't diminished her intelligence, and her passion for her causes has made her even more knowledgeable and current. She knows her stuff and if anyone is under the impression they can filibuster with emotion, Ferraro is there to surgically strike back with facts.

I find myself doing extra homework ahead of one of her visits!

She freely talks about not knowing how much time she has left, but you get the distinct impression she's sure as hell going to make the most of whatever time she's got, razzing Republicans and rousing Democrats.

She is the political conscience of the left that loves to tweak and loves to challenge. It drove her political career, and now that moral conviction and her continued commitment her vision of America— one that sees its greatest strength in helping its weakest members— drives her personal mission as well.

CHAPTER 7

OVER THE EDGE

It's a tragedy to lose your child. It's even worse to lose your child to suicide. Having this happen to you as a parent, when you're very much a public figure, can be even worse.

The Royal Bank of Canada's Michael Wilson lost his eldest son, Cameron, when he killed himself in 1995 at the age of twenty-nine, jumping in front of a train in Toronto.

Cameron, who had been diagnosed with severe depression, told few people about his condition. He feared if they knew just how tormented he was he would lose his job and almost certainly lose his friends. It's likely that the same anxieties prevented him from telling his father about his depression as well.

How do you make sense of something like that?

Wilson responded to his son's suicide by changing the direction of his career, and devoted his life to raising awareness of clinical depression, in all its forms, and alerting people about the everyday, tell-tale signs that he himself never noticed until it was too late.

What made Wilson's life story fascinating to me then and now is that, in the years after Cameron's death, he courageously broke an all too conventional mold: Most business and political titans are tight-lipped about their personal lives. The understanding in their world is that you do not bring details about your family into the office with you.

Wilson changed that. He is convinced that secrecy only added to his son's anguish, and made matters worse.

He vowed to try and make things better, and not just in Canada. His willingness to bring the issue of depression to the fore changed ideas about the illness not only in his country but in the United States as well.

I have always prized executives and politicians who aren't stoics. Perhaps because of my reputedly volatile Irish-Italian heritage, I value emotional, passionate people, who aren't afraid to show their feelings.

What really impressed me about Wilson's efforts was his profound, heartfelt ardor. He turned a deeply intense personal crisis into a platform for change, initiating a very public campaign to raise awareness of and money for treating depression as an illness, not a stigma.

After privately wrestling with his son's death, Wilson started to talk publicly about Cameron's suicide, and the damage done by his unwillingness to discuss the issue earlier.

"I myself was guilty," he told the Canadian Club in May 1998. "I grew up believing that depression was a sign of some personal weakness."

Then he really opened up. He spoke more of how Cameron, the eldest of his three children, had been treated for acute depression; he discussed Cameron's hallucinations, psychosis, and excessive anger; he touched on some of the other signs as well, noting the persistent sadness, in particular.

"It's an illness that affects the biological, the psychological, the interpersonal, and the spiritual components of any person," he told the Club. "It's an illness that can strike any of us, because it is the product of a tragic interplay of genetic, constitutional, and experiential factors."

With his passion came cachet. Wilson was a major media figure in his country, with impressive credentials in politics and banking. Early in his tenure as Canada's finance minister, Wilson led the charge to reduce the country's federal deficit. He never won that battle, but before almost anyone else, he signaled the importance of the issue, and the imperative to dismantle much of the Canadian welfare state.

In 1983, he lost another battle when he campaigned to become Canada's next prime minister, winning only 155 votes on the first ballot. But he threw his support behind Brian Mulroney, leader of the conservative Tory Party, who went on to win the election.

In his post as finance minister, Wilson began chopping everything from baby bonuses to old age security payments. He replaced the manufacturers' sales tax with a more logical one, even though such moves created a political firestorm.

While critics said his tough-love governmental efforts were long overdue, they cost him politically, and in 1993, when Wilson thought about running a new campaign and replacing Mulroney as Tory Party leader, he ultimately decided to retire from politics instead. He went on to become a senior executive with the Royal Bank of Canada, one of the country's largest corporations.

It was because of his history as an aggressive cost-fighter and one not prone to waste government money that Wilson's call for funding a psychological well-being program took on an added sense of urgency. Also, in the competitive world of fund-raising, Wilson had connections, and he was ready to use them.

The greatest asset among hard-charging executives and politicians with a cause and a passion is their clout, and they carry much of it in their respective business communities. Harry Pearce used his connections and reputation to bring attention and funding to leukemia, managing to raise millions of dollars for specialized research centers.

In her own way, so did Evelyn Lauder, whose pink ribbon campaign promoted global awareness and understanding of breast cancer, as she maximized the various resources of the Estée Lauder company and its prestigious brand name.

Geraldine Ferraro returned to the political world to encourage public attention of her mission to educate people about multiple myeloma, and she used her prominence and long-established record of fighting tirelessly for Americans who had it hardest, to spread her message everywhere.

Michael Wilson recognized early on that depression cannot be lumped with diseases like leukemia or prostate cancer. Those are recognized medical illnesses, whereas depression is vastly misunderstood. Moods are a murkier subject, and Wilson fought hard to show even the most high-powered executives that they too could fall prey to dark moments.

Wilson tried every approach he could to clarify and educate people and employers about the true nature of depression: He headed up the Business and Economic Roundtable on Mental Health, and used that position to collate extensive data on the cost of mental illness, something he felt the business community would respond to if its leaders saw those costs in black and white.

He reported that 31 percent of short-term absenteeism is related to mental illness and addiction, and explored the questions raised by the statistic, including: How many of employees exhibit telltale signs of the illness; how many of them are quiet, passive, distant, or remote; do they commonly fail to enjoy the people they work with and lighter moments on the job; and to what degree are they still productive but missing that extra spark? Those were the employees Wilson wanted to get to know and better understand.

Many executives, however, had little interest in depression. In the business world, weaknesses of any sort are not looked upon favorably. There's the story of one official telling him, "I don't have stress, I give stress." It was almost taken as a badge of honor. That sentiment was a mighty obstacle to overcome.

But Wilson was not deterred, and as a result he was the first person since Rosalynn Carter to put depression on the table as a legitimate issue that needed real, effective therapies and answers.

Wilson began to prove that depression was not isolated to only a few random workers; in fact, he demonstrated the possibility that the illness was common to a plurality of Canadians in the workforce, offering some uniquely startling facts to reinforce his claims.

When Wilson presented his roundtable case in the summer of 2000, he reported that an estimated three million Canadians suffered from some form of depression, yet only six percent were properly diagnosed and treated. And the condition was growing, mainly because pressures in the workplace were mounting as well. Office politics, tight job competition, too much work, and too little control—they were all combining to create hostile environments that overwhelmed workers, in Canada and elsewhere.

Wilson repeatedly pointed out that we are living in an information economy, that it's a thought-based economy, and that a "healthy mind is very important to the successful workings of this economy." Left unchecked, depression could lead to a number of dangerous problems, including absenteeism, alcoholism, injury, and even physical illness.

The roundtable wasted little time showing depression was becoming a hemispheric problem, and that between the United States and Canada, depression costs nearly $100 billion per year, mostly in lost productivity. Wilson calculated that Canadian businesses alone could save up to $7 billion in five years in prescription drugs and wage replacement costs, if only half of their employees who needed treatment for depression got that help.

He brought his case home again and again, consistently in dollars and cents, not just heart and mind. He recruited dozens of doctors, medical experts, and people suffering from depression to speak out on the matter. Among those who joined Wilson's drive was the distinguished Dr. Russell Joffe, Dean of Health Sciences at McMaster University. Dr. Joffe, with his considerable medical expertise, confirmed the very real physical risks, such as heart attacks, that can result from mental illnesses, including depression.

A celebrity who was very open to discussing the disease was Ron Ellis, the former Toronto Maple Leafs' star, who spoke out about his own experiences with depression.

In a country where hockey is as much a religion as it is a sport, enlisting a major athlete to describe candidly his own difficulties with depression helped many Canadians better understand the random, you-could-have-this-too nature of the disease.

Wilson continued to get the word out. He led a massive public service campaign that included ads in newspapers and magazines, as well as a web site, and a province-wide speakers' bureau to augment well-established community education forums and workplace programs. But Wilson was his own biggest draw: He was the one Canadians would always remember and listen to. Because he had taken a personal tragedy and turned it into an international public service campaign, Cameron was helping more people after his death than people had ever helped him in life.

Wilson encouraged people to see Cameron as any kid, any young man, and by describing his eldest son, his experiences, and the emotional turmoil that led to his suicide, as openly and emotionally as he did, Wilson opened people's eyes to the stark realization that what happened to Cameron could also happen to their sons, their brothers, their friends.

A gifted athlete—he was a superb rugby, hockey, tennis, and football player—Cameron also worked on election campaigns, and had started to build a good career in business. His life seemed to plot a normal course, curving in the usual pattern. His professional advances seemed to show him as a young man growing and maturing in the world (he worked at a merchant bank in London before moving back to Toronto, to land a job on the trading desk at National Trust Bank).

Everything seemed normal—and then, as Wilson tells his audiences, Cameron suddenly changed. In the final months of his life, he became aggressive and angry. He was fired from his job after repeated clashes with his boss. He had to be institutionalized by his father, when neither of them had ever been inside a psychiatric hospital before.

Wilson spoke of the pain that caused them both, and how Cameron never wanted to have his friends see him there, or have any visits.

Wilson movingly described how in those last months Cameron was so angry, sad, and lost, and that his father did nothing to help him emotionally. These haunting stories registered with Canadians more than any statistic.

On average, he explained, 20 percent of the Canadian population suffers from a mental disorder or is abusing drugs, and Cameron had been one of them. It was estimated that depression cost the Canadian economy more than $12 billion a year, but Cameron was a person behind that cost. And one quarter of the 34 million hospital days used in Canada each year were for the treatment of people with mental illness, but Cameron was treated—and he'd still committed suicide. By personalizing those statistics, in stark, often heartbreaking, personal stories, Wilson humanized mental illness in his country as few had ever done before.

He also woke people up to the inherent prejudices against those suffering from depression in business and in society at large. He described how unthinkable it would be for an employer to fire an employee recovering from cancer or heart bypass surgery, but dumping someone afflicted by mental illness often isn't given a second thought.

He reminded still skeptical employers that whether they knew it or not, some of their best and brightest workers likely suffered from some form of depression. He told them that it was in their own financial interest to reach out to those workers.

The more he talked about depression, the more he reminded his listeners about its enormity: Depression was and is the leading cause of disability in the world, and it affects one in five women, and one in ten men, at some point in their lives. Yet three out of four people who need psychiatric care don't get it, even in a country like Canada, long recognized as having one of the best-funded public health systems in the world.

Wilson would constantly mention the great potential of new medicine and research, reminding anyone who would listen that 80 to 90 percent of the time, major depression can be successfully treated. As he told *The Globe and Mail* of Toronto in September 2000: "Mental illness is a hidden tragedy. There is a lot of it, and it isn't getting attention. I have been quite open about Cameron's depression because that is what took him from us. Mental illness is not a weakness. It is an illness, and we must treat it as an illness."

During his speeches, he repeatedly asked the same questions to different business audiences: Are you noticing changes in some of your key employees? Is a once talkative worker now suddenly quieter? Is he or she withdrawn or irritable, inexplicably late or short-tempered? He also offered suggestions as well, saying that it is cheaper in the long run to suggest to that person to see a doctor early.

Employee assistance plans were out there, but they were severely underutilized. For example, only 7 percent of eligible workers used them, and most didn't even know about them. In a taped statement to an October 2000 gathering of the Center for Addiction and Mental Health, as it was launching its depression campaign, Wilson talked about his son, saying, "Our son had depression, and we saw when he was ill, that he was worried about talking to anybody about his depression. And because of that, he didn't get the proper treatment at an early enough stage, and when he was ill, he didn't have [that support] from friends, from people that he was working with, who are so important when you are sick." His message hit home, and the timing, coinciding with Mental Illness Awareness Week and World Mental Health Day, doubled the impact.

By December 2000, The Business and Economic Roundtable on Mental Health, moving swiftly, began to offer all Canadian businesses an explicit twelve-point plan to combat depression, laying out the following steps, which were picked up and reprinted verbatim in scores of newspapers and business magazines throughout Canada:

1. Brief the CEO on the impact of depression at work, and empower the CEO to set detection and financial targets associated with reducing the effects of depression inside the organization.

2. Set annual targets to reduce the effects of depression at work through early detection. Target per-employee annual savings of $10,000 through prescription drug and wage replacement costs. Additional gains would be realized through productivity improvements.

3. Train management in the early identification of depression's symptoms. Create written policies to help managers to deal with such matters. Redesign current employee assistance plans and group health plans to target and reduce the effects of depression at work by providing state-of-the-art information on depression.

4. Survey employees to identify stress, which threatens individual health. Interrupt the treadmill effect plaguing employees with too many priorities and too much to do at once. Combat distrust, disrespect, autocratic management styles, and too-repetitive tasks—all of which contribute to stress-related health problems.

5. Look for ways to reduce the "overload" of frustration and aggravation associated with the exaggerated and random use of e-mail. Develop e-mail and voice mail culture training to reduce stress and overuse of this technology at the expense of human contact.

6. Create disability management and return-to-work strategies that address recovery issues associated with depression.

7. Educate managers and human resource executives on connections between depression and heart disease, stroke, immune system problems, and other chronic physical disorders.

8. Create an inventory of emotional work hazards that put employee and organizational health at risk. Develop an organizational action plan.

9. Create policies to protect the balance of work and social lives among employees. Establish an incentive program based on the fact that absences due to employee eldercare obligations run into the hundreds of millions of dollars a year. Enact specific policies, including flexible work hours, home care services, workplace daycare, and eldercare services.

10. Deploy a process to be offered by the Business and Economic Roundtable on Mental Health to differentiate between employee-performance problems stemming from depression and those attributable to standard work deterioration or failure.

11. Create a health index to monitor the status of organizational health in the company.

12. Aim to reduce disability rates by 15 to 25 percent a year by targeting mental health issues.

The twelve-point plan represented a dramatic and financially valuable opportunity to the business community, by listing and describing essential and specific measures that could be implemented, without incurring prohibitive costs or significant additions to company payrolls, to combat mental illness in Canada.

The opportunity was there—now it was up to individual businesses and the broader community to take action. Some companies began to introduce the program, but Wilson could see that he still had a lot of work to do.

Nearly two years later, in late 2002, speaking as part of Canada's Homewood Health Center's Lett Lecture Series, Wilson talked again about the lessons that could be learned from cases of untreated depression, and how they could apply those lessons and help those in the workforce that are afflicted.

"It's people who make the sales, who build the product and who generate the profit," he said. "It's people who make the machinery run."

After the Lett Lecture Series, Wilson once again went on to speak directly to businessmen and women. He expounded on the tough times businesses had gone through, which had promoted a "cold-blooded culture, where downsizing became the norm and employees became expendable."

It is no surprise then, he said, that in this kind of impersonal environment, employees fear for their jobs. They know well that mental illness is still seen as a character weakness, by businesses and society as a whole.

He also touched on lessons gleaned from the aftermath of September 11. "We watched CEO's grieve not for the computers and offices lost, but for the people. This is different from the perception of the hard-nosed businessman—[in] sharp contrast to the slash-and-burn corporate environment."

Michael Wilson didn't mention them by name, but he could have been talking about Fred Alger and John Duffy, and less directly, Richard Branson. Duffy, Alger, and Branson modeled what Wilson was trying to persuade Canadian employers to do—help their employees, because then everyone gains.

Now in his third year of leading the charge, for Cameron and for Canada, Wilson kept speaking in terms that everyone could understand, saying that "Depression is public enemy number one, with a 15 percent mortality rate and the leading cause of suicide."

As he's continued his work against depression, he's described disturbing new trends, explaining how anti-depressants are replacing antibiotics as the leading medication prescribed by doctors, how younger workers, those between twenty-five and forty-four years old, were the ones most inclined to suffer from the condition, and that collectively they made up half of the hospitalizations for mental illness.

And he still discusses Cameron, his demons, hopes, fears, and Wilson's fatherly desire to imbue the memory of his lost son's life with meaning and hope. Wilson has dedicated his days to constant effort, and has spent years advocating greater awareness of the disease that claimed his son, presenting figures and facts, statistics, and supporting medical documentation.

He's organized major business leaders and groups to help him in his battle to educate employers and the public about depression, and to create a new perception of the condition, and to move companies to act.

He's still fighting, despite so much inaction, doubt, and unwillingness in the corporate world to commit resources to help their employees combat a mental illness the symptoms of which their bosses can't easily grasp, and too often attribute to other causes.

He has finally made important progress in some areas, but there's so much more that's possible, and to date relatively little is being done, as beneficial programs have gone unimplemented.

The fact that Wilson to this day commits his time, energy, and vast financial and political connections to encouraging a nation and its businesses to focus on the misunderstood disease that claimed the life of his eldest child says a great deal about *real* passion, commitment, and love.

As Wilson often says in public campaigns and speeches, to small groups and in panel discussions, he cannot bring Cameron back. But he can keep alive the hope that his son's life—*and his death*—meant a great deal.

CHAPTER 8

ADDING IT UP!

Those born with dyslexia have to struggle with and compensate for the misunderstood and often embarrassing medical disorder throughout their entire lives, even when they go on to remarkably successful careers. Richard Branson has, even as a multibillionaire.

This condition is probably hardest though when dyslexics are young: Imagine being a teenager, already faced with the ample challenges inherent to that period, and having to overcome learning disabilities that carry heavy emotional baggage for good measure.

This complexity of this sort of learning disability makes school a permanent struggle, both educationally and socially. Three special people, though—Diane Swonk, Paul Orfalea, and Barbara Corcoran—responded to these obstacles by becoming stronger, more determined, and intensely focused on somehow succeeding.

Paul Orfalea describes well the problems he experienced growing up and the painful consequences of difficulties at school for young dyslexics. As he explained, it's hard enough to just keep your head above water.

A severe dyslexic, Orfalea graduated eighth from the bottom of his high school class of 1,500. ("To be honest," he once said, "I don't know how seven people got below me.") He relied on humor to combat his anxieties, and maintained a healthy sense of optimism as well. In a revealing interview with *First Person,* a collection of essays by those with learning disabilities, Orfalea offered hope for those who suffer from learning disabilities.

"In second grade," he says, "I was in a Catholic school with 40 or 50 kids in my class. We were supposed to learn to read prayers and match letter blocks to the letters in the prayers. By April or May, I still didn't know the alphabet and couldn't read. I memorized the prayers so the nun thought I was reading. Finally, she figured out that I didn't even know my alphabet, and I can remember her expression of total shock that I had gotten all the way through the second grade without her knowing this."

He went on to explain how his parents offered his brother and sister $50 to teach him the alphabet, "But that didn't work. So I flunked second grade. I had the same nun again, and she was mean. She paddled me for two years, but I still didn't learn the alphabet or how to read."

Orfalea explained how years later, his mother found a remedial reading teacher who understood his dyslexia and helped him work with phonetics to work around it. "By seventh and eight grade, I still had barely learned how to read," he told *First Person*. With characteristic self-effacing humor, he added, "I wasn't too worried about it then because I somehow knew I'd have my own business one day, and I figured I'd hire someone to read to me."

The interview with *First Person* reads like a casual, very humble, "if-I-can-get-through-you-can-get-through" life lesson; in remarkably few words and with great humor and wit, Orfalea described how even against enormous odds, you can succeed.

He remembered the embarrassment of being thought stupid, of working at his Dad's factory and overhearing a fellow laborer say, "Don't let him do that, he can't even read."

He admitted a 1.2 grade point average, reading Cliff Notes, and watching great plays on TV instead of reading books, and recalls overcoming spelling errors and dismissive teachers.

I remember a kid in college who dealt with dyslexia challenges, saying only that he got used to working twice as hard to get half the grades. That image stuck with me.

Orfalea explained that he got so many little things wrong, but got a few big things right—and how important *that* was, in creating copy giant Kinko's.

Diane Swonk said her dyslexia affected almost every facet of her life. "I didn't know my left from my right, couldn't tie my shoes, or dial a telephone number without mixing up the order." But Swonk now describes her dyslexia as a gift, and says it "helped me think outside the box when it came to the economy."

As much a visionary as Orfalea, Swonk, because she loved economics, decided to use her gifts, imagination, and ability to overcome her limitations by working within an established company, rather than starting up a new one. She joined one of the country's largest banks, Bank One, as an economist, and is now the corporation's chief economist.

Barbara Corcoran remembers a time when she was a D student because of undiagnosed dyslexia. But she found other ways to compensate. Most dyslexics are of above-average intelligence, and most important, extremely creative, and even visionary. The enormous educational obstacles that they can't get *through,* they learn to circle *around.*

They are very resourceful in finding clever and inventive ways around handicaps inhibiting their ability to read that almost assuredly would stymie more "traditional" minds.

As Corcoran writes in her bestseller, *Use What You've Got,* "I've since learned that children who struggle with written information and facts almost always have great imaginations. They can see the big picture, think outside the box, and with just a little encouragement, can learn to use their fertile imaginations to fill in the blanks."

Corcoran herself "had a very good imagination," and, she would point out, "a very good mother." It was her mother who encouraged her when she was young to play to her vivacious personality and vivid imagination. Years later, Barbara Corcoran would go on to found and lead one of the largest residential real estate agencies in the country.

In her book, Corcoran reveals the great value of her mother's approval. Since her mother never judged her problems at school, she expected Barbara to succeed in other arenas. That support, early on, was crucial to Barbara's own sense of self, and her drive to succeed.

Orfalea and Corcoran became entrepreneurial visionaries, founders, leaders, and CEOs of their own companies in very different businesses, as did Roger Ailes, Herb Kelleher, and Richard Branson. They battled as many doubters and skeptics, fought with tough, well-established competitors for market share, and like Branson, conquered their own dyslexia at the same time.

Swonk, Corcoran, and Orfalea have had to be at least as tough and determined as their competitors in order to succeed, but what sets them apart is that each has the characteristic empathy common among dyslexics for the suffering of others. They *know* pain.

They know the feeling of being ostracized, of being called dumb, of being dismissed or disregarded. They know that the world will pay them little heed unless they make the world notice them and their outsized achievements. They are deeply sensitive individuals who have been treated insensitively, and what's remarkable is that despite all they've had to endure, they work extremely hard always to respect those with whom they come into contact.

Their special effort to help others began when they were very young, when they were first ostracized and made to feel different, because their parents (and others) taught them how to rise above their hurt, and think about what was best for others instead.

Swonk, meanwhile, uses her vision and passion, inside and outside her company, through meetings, interviews, and reports, to get out her message to Bank One's leadership, other economists, the media, and the public, that they should think beyond the abstract numbers of finance and economics. They should ascribe as much importance to the people affected, often negatively, by those bloodless facts and figures, and who are usually ignored when companies are making their decisions.

She continues to make her case, as Michael Wilson does, that compassion is not just a public service, but good business as well. As Wilson has discovered, persuading business leaders and employers that depression was costing their enterprises real dollars, and that they'd be better off ameliorating those losses through affordable treatment, will take a considerably long time, but he hasn't quit and neither has Swonk. That deep determination, toughness, and passion to proceed, despite the many impediments, requires strong belief and the support from others who care about the cause as well.

That combination of leadership and empathy characterizes all of the heroes I've profiled in this book. They have what I like to call "confidence without arrogance," or in the case of Orfalea, Swonk, and Corcoran, who each had incredible hills to climb, "visionaries without vendettas." Each of these three people has the ability to see the big picture that so often eludes others without their distinctive imaginations.

Paul Orfalea may have flunked second and ninth grades, but he had an amazing grasp of societal trends and needs that far smarter people, who weren't "disabled," failed to appreciate; Corcoran was a D student who had an unconventional understanding of what needed to be changed in the impersonal buy-and-sell routine of the real estate world; and even though Diane Swonk cannot grasp numbers as easily as most people can, she understands economics, and saw a new, more human dimension to the traditional staid and academic approach to finance.

What they lacked in traditional reading skills, they more than made up for in moxie, intense hard work, and perseverance. They simply never quit. Something made them keep believing in themselves, despite all the setbacks, ridicule, and the fact that they had to work twice as hard as everyone else just to keep from getting further behind. It would have been tempting to live down to the taunts they were subjected to, but where others saw only weakness, they saw strength.

Corcoran, Swonk, and Orfalea clearly were aware of their learning disabilities, but they certainly didn't see themselves as idiots, and that confidence and self-realization is common among truly successful people who persevere despite dyslexia.

They see themselves not as the sum of their disabilities, but the whole of their possibilities. They correctly conclude that just because something in their learning methodology doesn't work, that doesn't mean that their ability to process information is irretrievably broken, and that's an important distinction. They have an appreciation not for what *separates* them from society, but what sets them *apart* from society. The artist Robert Rauschenberg, brokerage founder Charles Schwab, and actor Tom Cruise, are all dyslexic, and inspiring examples of the value of this particular ability to see past their own disabilities, and succeed beyond measure.

One thing is certain: For each of these people, dyslexia didn't just make them compensate. In the end, it made them dominate.

GOOD HUMOR, GOOD COPY

The son of Lebanese immigrants, the confident but self-effacing Orfalea knew from an early age that his true calling was in business. And, as he said in the *First Person* interview, if he couldn't read and write clearly, he'd hire someone who could.

As a student at the University of California at Santa Barbara in 1970, he was already figuring out trends, another positive side effect of his learning disabilities, which stimulate creativity and imagination. Considering his college campus, he noticed immediately what college students needed: notebooks and supplies. There was a school bookstore, but many found it inconvenient, and its hours of operation weren't practical for the typical college student, notorious procrastinators.

He began selling school supplies on campus, charging low prices, in a convenient location, and operating during hours that fit the students' last-minute needs. It wasn't long before he had a steady stream of customers, and he was ready to expand operations.

He opened a store in an 80-square-foot, former hamburger stand, near the university, with little more than a big Xerox copier. Friends pointed out that the university library already had a copier, and wondered how he would attract customers.

Orfalea, as he had always done, shrugged off their doubts and followed his reliable gut, charging four cents a page to the university's ten cents, and soon his business was booming.

Next, for $100 a month, he rented a small garage near a taco stand, selling both school supplies and copies from the new location. The gawky kid with the curly red hair used his nickname for his new business: Kinko's.

The fact that Orfalea understood the market before anyone else meant that he was able to swiftly move his operations from a small hamburger stand, to a rented garage, to his first Kinko's store near the University of California (opened on the wings of five thousand borrowed dollars). He was continuously willing to gamble on what seemed to be little more than good hunches. Orfalea sensed early on that if he could appeal to rushed college students as an all-inclusive, last minute resource of sorts, he could build on that—and he was right.

He recruited student scouts to drive up and down the West Coast, seeking ideal college locations, usually near schools with over 20,000 students. He'd then set up shops close by, and to announce each location, they would stuff flyers in mailboxes and under residence hall doors. It was very low-tech, but earned very high profits. Clearly Orfalea was onto something, and just-budding competitors like Sir Speedy and Pip Printing proved that fact.

〜〜〜

Orfalea rarely gives interviews—he once flatly refused a reporter's request by quipping, "my mom said, 'your friends don't need to hear it, and your enemies won't believe it anyway.'"

When he does grant an interview, it's usually pegged to a product launch. For example, in the summer of 1995, Orfalea reluctantly agreed to talk to a *Forbes* reporter, if only because it gave him a chance to show off his newest service. *Forbes* described Orfalea's uncommon wisdom, gleaned more from conversations with his immigrant grandparents, who prized common sense, than any college textbook.

The magazine also pointed out that Orfalea "felt deep in his bones that he could never work for anyone else. As he puts it: 'I sort of thought, halfway through it, you know, I'm sort of unemployable. I'm basically a peddler.'"

But he has proved a talented peddler with a keen sense of marketing.

Just as Pip Printing and Sir Speedy were taking Kinko's on in the student market, Orfalea was looking elsewhere. He saw the rapidly expanding and evolving small business owner as his next beachhead, and Kinko's grew from service centers catering to college kids to "branch offices" for entrepreneurs and mom-and-pop businesses.

Kinko's would do the work others didn't want to. It would provide the resources so that far-flung independent operations could focus on the things they were good at. Orfalea would administrate their stuff so that customers could get on with their ventures. And what's more, he would do it reliably and conveniently, twenty-four hours a day.

Eventually, other companies would offer the same services, but Kinko's had a dramatic head start. It had the trust of communities where it set up shop, and a fanatically devoted following that grew as a result.

His clients would grow to include telecommuters and traveling business people. They were lured to Kinko's to take care of the personal tasks they couldn't or wouldn't do on their own. It would prove the "in" place for outsourcing, a one-shop Mecca for copying papers, collating reports, creating and mailing invitations, and enlarging photos and mounting them.

To this growing, demanding group of customers, Orfalea marketed his business as "your branch office." The fact that so many of those branch offices were open around the clock, and were able to handle large, last-minute copying and collating jobs with little if any notice, only cemented the customers' trust, who by now, had other choices.

With each competitive onslaught, Orfalea managed to stay one step ahead: When Orfalea agreed to talk to *Forbes* in 1995 it was only because Kinko's was breaking into the teleconferencing business. Several partners had suggested the market didn't exist yet for such technology. His response: "God hates a coward."

None of this is to suggest that Orfalea and Kinko's haven't seen their share of setbacks, only that he's found ways to overcome them. For example, when laser printers and copiers were thought to be his undoing, he just found bigger and better printers and copiers, and stayed ahead.

The democratization of technology, making the same equipment Kinko's offered broadly available for reasonable prices, similarly was thought to number the copying giant's days. But most of the company's entrepreneurial customers had more elaborate needs. They wanted more sophisticated graphics, and more original-looking reproductions, collated and organized in ways most people hadn't heard of or asked for.

Orfalea simply found greater efficiencies and conveniences to keep his outsourcing post secure.

Kinko's again proved to its devoted customers that it offered far more than copying and enlarging; it had grown to incorporate the most technologically advanced services, including videoconferencing and high-tech computer work, previously thought to be available only from bigger or more technically minded competitors.

In this regard too Orfalea was on top of huge demographic shifts in America.

By the early 1990s, nearly 30 million Americans were working from home. The number of Americans working at home would double by 1996. "Everyone has good machines," he told *Fast Company* in December 1997, and he understood that sophisticated customers using advanced systems would require document processing that a home printer simply cannot offer, and he knew to cater to their high-end needs.

But for all his inspiration and prescience, Orfalea is rare among corporate bosses who make light of their own success. In that same *Fast Company* interview, he low-keyed his own approach to the job: "People think I'm busier than I am," he joked. "Basically, I've got this job down to about six hours a week. The rest of the time, I'm wandering."

He goes to great lengths to tell the world that he's no great genius. Yet his consistency in picking the right strategy for the right moment and the right customers seems to clearly prove otherwise. But perhaps that is the man's genius—his ability to see both the humor and great potential in his position.

"I thought that anybody who worked for me could do the job better," he said. "I wanted to make sure my employees were happy and that they would continue working for me. I felt that if my coworkers were happy, they'd work harder." And they do indeed, which is why, as Orfalea said, Kinko's employees are the major factor in keeping the company ahead of their competition.

There is an innate modesty to Orfalea. He mentions how much he'd love to read, but that it is still hard. "I would like to enjoy reading and books, I regret not having that ability. The newspapers are the only thing I read, which I love because I am a current events junkie. . . . When I talk to college students about all of this, I tell them to work with their strengths, not their weaknesses," he adds.

"If you're not good in reading, do something else. Go where you are strong."

The most enjoyable and revealing part of this remarkable "pep talk" with *First Person,* is his closing comments: "Trust what you see, rather than what you hear. And don't take life so seriously. Just enjoy it."

Some would see Orfalea being labeled a dyslexic burden. He chose to use that label as a badge—something that has stayed with him all his life, and something he uses to offer hope and inspiration to others similarly afflicted with any significant illness in their life.

When he exited the job as chairman of Kinko's in March 2000, Orfalea refused to elaborate to the press. "He's just not for one interviews," said Kinko's spokeswoman Laura McCormick at the time. Orfalea would only say in a statement that he was proud of what the company had accomplished. "We've humanized technology for millions of customers and enabled one of the greatest economic transformations of the 1990s: the emergence of small and home office businesses," read part of the statement.

Other successful individuals seem to chart their lives from the moment when they first knew they'd made it; Orfalea charts his up until the time he first became successful, selling notebooks and school supplies. The rest, you get the feeling, is just gravy.

MAKING THE NUMBERS DANCE

After more than twenty years of reporting financial news, I've probably talked to thousands of economists. After a while, they all begin to blur.

Most are pretty smart, and unsurprisingly, they know it too. They waste little time before unleashing big words and confusing jargon. I think it's an ironic insecurity—for some reason, *they* feel they have to impress *me*.

Most of the time in my days as a street reporter, I just wanted a quick sound bite on why this economic number was up or down. I wasn't looking for *War and Peace,* just a comment, and the quicker and tighter the better. I usually got something more like the novel.

Economists were all the rage in the 1980s. Ronald Reagan had just come into office, promising sweeping tax cuts and huge military expenditures. I've always loved history, and I had discovered that well-respected economic intelligentsia throughout America's history had laughed at tax cuts, and sometimes even pounded them.

The early 1980s were no different. Reagan's tax cuts were pure folly, economists said.

But as a cub financial reporter, just getting my journalistic feet wet with the new administration, I learned something about economists: Most of them don't have a clue. Oh, they can sound very smart, but often they're plain wrong.

I guess because they sound so damn impressive, we don't dare counter them. Probably the only reason I did was because they were all so maddeningly dull. Just to break up the monotony, I had to challenge them during interviews, or at least offer an opposing view. It made for more entertaining news but the predictions remained as bleak as they were boring.

What still amazes me is how dire economists are as a group. I think they're so focused on data that they become oblivious to reality. There was a point during my tenure as a reporter on Wall Street when I received no less than 145 economic reports a month, and most of them predicted doom.

The deficits they feared did come to pass, but so did an economic turnaround and a bull market unprecedented in American history, both of which triggered a tidal wave of foreign investment in the United States, which also was without precedent.

Why didn't economists see that? Why did they only see the problems, and not the possibilities?

One of my theories is that economists who aren't dyslexic can sometimes fail to grasp the bigger picture. They get so caught up in the intellectual moment that they refuse to consider the emotional possibilities. But common sense, maybe a typical dyslexic's sense, tells you that when you give someone more money, they're going to spend it. And the more they spend, the better things go for the economy.

Some economists did get it, but there were just too few of them, and their analyses were so overwhelmed by the cascade of negativity that they went unheard.

I mention all this because it says a great deal about the predilection among supposedly very smart people for saying very stupid things. They're too often numbers people who are all statistics, and no soul.

I'm leery of people who act like they were the smartest kid in the class. Maybe they were, but I didn't like them when I was in school, and I trust them even less now that I'm many years removed from the classroom.

That's why I value those who look beyond the facts and figures of the business world, and economists who see more than the statistics of their gray universe. Bigger minds do see the bigger picture.

Dyslexics get a bad rap for missing the little things. But Corcoran, Swonk, and Orfalea more than make up for this shortcoming by appreciating the bigger, more important things. They get it without overanalyzing, they appreciate it without writing endlessly about it, and they see the trend without getting tied up in the tedious.

In economics, it is rare to find such people, given their inherent fascination with all sorts of mind-numbing data, but there are a very special few who crunch numbers using common sense. One of them is Diane Swonk, chief economist at Bank One.

Most economists would think it crazy to admit a condition like dyslexia, but not Swonk. In her book, *The Passionate Economist,* she wrote, "I think the dyslexia helped me to think outside the box when it came to the economy." While all her colleagues were looking at statistics, Swonk was looking at people and huge societal trends, and correctly anticipating where those trends would lead.

One of the very significant trends that she was able to apprehend and study far into the future was the effect of corporate downsizing on consumer spending. It would be years before her colleagues finally began making the same correlation.

Back in 1995, Swonk was a favorite of mine on *Power Lunch,* a CNBC show I hosted at the time, and she predicted major changes to come in the manufacturing sector, long before anyone else was saying anything remotely similar. Her analysis would later prove to be correct.

I liked her because she cut through a lot of the academic nonsense economists traffic in. Because of the nature of television, you don't have much time to waste. And I preferred not to waste it on economists of any sort. I felt most of them just parroted the same thing anyway, so viewers weren't missing much.

But Swonk was different. She spoke in a language all of those viewers could understand. She understood all the jargon and nuances of her business. She just refused to spout it. She also had a great sense of humor. I remember one time hitting her with some gossip I had picked up that indicated her name had been floated as a potential replacement for a departing governor on the Federal Reserve. I'll never forget her reply: "I don't comment on rumors, Neil, especially your rumors." It was classic Swonk: a rare economist who gave as good as she got.

Swonk learned her excellent debating skills early on, from a father who encouraged it, and later from a boyfriend who put up with it. And that gave her the advantage of mastering crisp and clear delivery of often complex and arcane economic points. She would put those oratorical skills to excellent use in college.

In that regard, rather than working against her, dyslexia actually helped her. Years later, when *Fortune* magazine did a cover story on dyslexia featuring Swonk, among others, the condition by then was being described as an ability as much as a disability. "It has certainly forced me to do what I do differently than others," she said, "and in some ways it set me apart from the pack."

As a college student, to help her keep her wandering mind focused, during study sessions she would routinely argue her points versus the subject matter—a sort of running commentary with her notes. It kept her stimulated, sharp, and attuned, and when it came time for a class debate, well prepared to argue her points.

As she later wrote in *The Passionate Economist,* "This theory on speaking is probably rooted in my dyslexia. I don't write my speeches, I speak from a handwritten outline that I rarely use. It is more of a safety net than a script."

She would also battle her dyslexia by making notes so detailed that even her professors were floored. But what truly set Swonk apart was her passion for the subject of economics, and not simply the numbers that make up the balance of the science.

She was among the few students at the University of Michigan who subscribed to business magazines, and she devoured the *Wall Street Journal* and *New York Times* daily. She joined the Michigan Economics Club, and even debated social change over beer. She was that deeply into her work, into her calling.

She might have seen some things backwards, as she once did during one visit to the Clinton White House when she walked through the entrance exactly opposite to the one she was supposed to use en route to a crucial economic forum, but that didn't stop her from ravenously taking in all sorts of information.

As her rejoinder to my report about the Federal Reserve rumor indicates, she has as much good humor as she does passion for her science. I remember chatting with her shortly after a White House economic summit she attended with the likes of Bill Gates and Alan Greenspan.

My first question, which she would later address in her book, was about her interaction with Bill Clinton. "No, he did not make a pass. . . . I am not his type; my hair and the rest of me are just not big enough."

But you got the impression that this incredibly smart and savvy woman regretted what had become of this paradox of a president— a man clearly gifted in discussing often intricate financial policies, who presided over the longest economic expansion in history, but who would be best remembered for getting impeached by the House of Representatives, and managing narrowly to avoid the same fate in the Senate.

As I've said, dyslexics seem to have a great empathy for people.

Perhaps because they're so often slighted, they feel a deep responsibility in life to avoid ever treating people the same way. They care deeply, and freely wear it on their sleeves.

Swonk exemplifies that trait, as her heart and compassion set her apart from so many others in her field. She is one of the few economists I know who feels deeply about displaced workers, the ravaging long-term effects of protectionist trade policies, and other policies harmful to people in this country, and she has railed against both Democrats and Republicans who prefer to take the easy way out.

In 1999, long before the stock market began its inexorable slide from its lofty position in early 2000, Swonk was among the first economists to predict—and *care about*—the wrenching readjustment of scores of workers to the new-new economy that would correct the unfounded enthusiasm surrounding technology issues, thought for so long to be fast ways to make piles of money.

I remember that when Alan Greenspan was raising interest rates in early 2000 to respond to what he perceived to be an overheating economy, Swonk feared the effects of the fallout on the average investor.

She discussed first-time home buyers, who would likely be priced out of the market for a mortgage just as things were looking up. She mentioned the risks of acting too soon to head off an inflationary bubble that might not be there; of careers that could be lost and opportunities that could be dashed. These were not the musings of a typical economist.

What other person in her field addressed the need to retrain workers in order to prevent a flight of skilled workers and financial capital? What other economist focused entirely on the loss of human capital after the horrifying events of September 11, and not just the financial ramifications?

Before others did, she described how firms and markets would come back, but that there had to be an appreciation of the great emotional loss in the aftermath of the attacks, and how it would affect people as they first got back to work, and how they'd react to remaining in their downtown New York offices. She accurately predicted that the toll would be immense. She understood that the wounds would heal, but that the emotional and economic recoveries would take time.

In New York particularly, Swonk saw the acceleration of economy's downward spiral, and she sensed that Mayor Rudy Giuliani's successor, Michael Bloomberg, who was elected in November 2001, would bear the brunt of the financial fallout.

Other economists had relayed these opinions through statistics, but Swonk expressed them in words, easily understood and sympathetic, and made her forecasts as much about people as they were about stark, impersonal numbers.

Characteristically, in early 2003, when the prospect of war with Iraq was being debated, Swonk was one of the few who talked about the economic dislocation for people who would be directly affected by war: "What's left for them?" she asked. "Will the new government be better than the old government?"

She thought beyond the traditional economic arguments about the immediate consequences of the war, and focused on the long-term ramifications of attacking Iraq for the nations involved, and those on the periphery of the fight. To dismiss global uncertainties "would be foolish," she told me. "It's not the war. It's the life *after* the war."

Economists generally don't talk like that. But Diane Swonk does. And more should.

THE REALTY MCCOY

When I think of real estate agents, *pleasant* isn't the first adjective that comes to mind. Given the dog-eat-dog nature of their business, perhaps it's inevitable that most good realtors are relentless and domineering.

Maybe realtors who enter the business think that if they're courteous and nice, they'll be considered "weak," and eaten alive— better then to make the sale, close the deal, and be on your way.

The few agents I've encountered in my own real estate forays have not been particularly helpful or knowledgeable, but they were definitely pushy. It's enough to make you completely cynical about the entire business, but then there's Barbara Corcoran, who by herself can change your whole perspective.

When I hosted *Power Lunch* in 1995, Corcoran was an early favorite to talk to about real estate. She was a rarity because she genuinely cared about her customers first, and her passion for the job second.

She valued professional relationships, and made them personal, knowing that a satisfied first customer more often than not will happily use her service again. But her concern for her clients extends beyond encouraging their repeat business.

She *connects* with people, listens to them, takes the time to get to know them, and does it all before the people she meets become actual customers. She was brilliant about real estate and she *cared.* What a dynamic combination, especially as she made her competitors look like robots and sharks, without even trying.

In a cutthroat world seemingly dominated by men, she stood out. And for me, as a broadcaster desperately trying to widen my audience beyond the middle age and older, white, male stereotypical business titan, Corcoran was a breath of fresh air. Viewers responded to her instantly, and her appearances brought considerably more women to my audience.

The viewers and I also appreciated Corcoran's honesty about her dyslexia. Being publicly candid about a learning disorder while working in a business where every competitor is looking for an exploitable weakness took courage, but that was the Corcoran way. Displaying equal measures of courage, toughness, and compassion was how she'd lived her whole life.

Knowing about her dyslexia, and the sensitivities it so often entails, helped me understand why Corcoran's emphasis on her relationships with customers wasn't just a shrewd and calculated way of doing business. Because of her reputation for employing an unusually personal approach, legions of clients came to her agency, and marveled at her attention to details, and her willingness to go the extra mile to answer their questions, allay their concerns, and ultimately, of course, close the deal.

These are enormous assets in the subjective world of real estate, where a customer's emotions can dominate and sentimental feelings for a property can and do make a difference.

Lots of realtors know the facts and figures of the business, but Corcoran knows her customers. She understands both the buyer's and the seller's mind-set. She didn't gain that knowledge from a book or text. It came directly from her attention to her customers. It was that passion, imagination, and empathy that made the difference, and resulted in her legendary career.

She'd learned a lot from her tough school days, and all the social and educational difficulties that come with dyslexia. She grew up in a three-family house in New Jersey with her parents and nine brothers and sisters, and it was Corcoran's mother who saw solutions to her daughter's problem before anyone else.

Watching Barbara struggle with dyslexia, her mother taught her important life lessons that helped her then and are still guiding her now. Barbara was told that to succeed in life, you have to learn how to turn a liability into an asset. The other kids might call her stupid because of her learning difficulties, but that label and her disability didn't have to hold her back. She had other gifts, especially creativity and imagination, which she could develop in ways that could put her far ahead of the regular kids who relied on their basic intelligence and tended to think conventionally.

Because of her mother's constant prodding, Corcoran came to realize that she might have bad grades but a good "gut," with special instincts and a natural intuition that allowed her to envision ideas, trends, and opportunities long before anyone else did.

And the shame of being thought "stupid," could give her insights into other people's own insecurities, which all of us have, and most others might be blind to.

Corcoran has always given credit to her mother, and shared some of her mother's amusing and imaginative expressions because they may help others, too. For example, in her book *Use What You've Got,* Corcoran offers a series of "Mom's Lessons." Not lessons from Wharton, or insights from Harvard. Just hints from Mom.

Among the most memorable:

Mᴏᴍ's Lᴇssᴏɴ #1: If you don't have big breasts, put ribbons on your pigtails.

Mᴏᴍ's Lᴇssᴏɴ #2: Paint the rocks white and the whole yard will look lovely.

Mᴏᴍ's Lᴇssᴏɴ #3: If the sofa is ripped, cover it with laughter.

Mᴏᴍ's Lᴇssᴏɴ #4: Use your imagination and fill in the blanks.

Mᴏᴍ's Lᴇssᴏɴ #5: Offer that bigger piece and yours will taste even better.

Corcoran would later gain considerably from her innate understanding, and as her mother had predicted, see opportunities that others didn't, and move on them immediately. But it would take years and failed tenures at twenty-two other jobs before Corcoran finally found her calling. In 1973, Corcoran finally found the arena where she could best apply her talents.

She quit her job as a waitress, and borrowed $1,000 from a boyfriend to start a tiny realty firm. She was only twenty-three years old, but she had a gift for marketing. Corcoran's early forte was high-end properties. She knew them and marketed them like no other.

Also, in the staid world of real estate, Corcoran was among the first to sell an image of herself as much as a firm. She didn't just create the brand—she was the brand.

Her name alone elevated the importance of a property. Sellers had to have her; buyers had to deal with her. She became the "real estate lady," and quite literally became the face of Corcoran. Her picture graced billboards, newspaper ads, subways, and buses.

Those who followed the industry had to talk to her. The image-conscious media saw in her someone who could put a sprawling, exclusive industry in perspective. She was telegenic, funny, irreverent, and quick—and she was attractive. The media gave her exposure, and she entertained their audiences and gave them a reason to follow what was happening in the world of real estate when they hadn't much cared to before.

~~~

B
ut even with a loving and supportive mother, stigmas and insecurities are hard to overcome, and Corcoran has often spoken to reporters and others in her business about how, to this day, she still fights those demons that make her feel dumb, still tries to prove to the world that she's not stupid.

It is sad but understandable that many dyslexics work overtime trying to prove they're smart, or that they matter, even after they've achieved what few people ever have. Despite her anxieties and sometimes shaky self-esteem, Corcoran is incredibly insightful.

You cannot succeed in New York real estate if you're just passionate. You have to be pretty savvy, too. You have to know the ebbs and flows of the market and the subtle trends within that market. And Corcoran's firm has regularly been on the cusp of key demographic trends in New York, including the migration from apartment rentals to actual ownership.

Adding to the Corcoran brand and that pretty face was *The Corcoran Report,* her unique compilation of sales statistics and market trends that was sent out to reporters.

It quickly became an industry bible, akin to the retail industry's Johnson Redbook surveys, or the University of Michigan's Consumer Confidence Reports. Corcoran became the authority on trends affecting New York real estate. Others could have introduced the same service, but Corcoran did it first.

Just as Paul Orfalea saw early on the need to make Kinko's synonymous with one-stop printing, copying, and business needs, and Diane Swonk sagely anticipated one major economic change after another, Corcoran kept moving forward, leaving the competition behind.

She made the Corcoran firm a one-stop for everything: the Kinko's of real estate, and a growing global media brand that emphasizes image in its marketing as much as it does real estate. Also, her firm was recession-proof. Properties can come and go, and their values may rise and fall, but Corcoran discovered before many that good research and market timing never goes out of style—when Manhattan real estate prices plummeted in the years after the 1987 stock market crash, Corcoran registered some of her best years.

Her trend analysis became more valued and her predictions more scrutinized. The fact that she accurately predicted the rebound in prices after that October debacle, and the high-end trends that would once again emerge, says as much about her intellect and "good gut" as it does her passion.

And she uses every technology at her disposal. An early devotee of the Internet, The Corcoran Group launched Corcoran.com in 1995, making it one of the first real estate web sites anywhere. The site showcased luxury properties around the world, and the rapid increase in sales proved once again the value of Corcoran's prescience.

Moreover, her genuine, enduring gift for relationships kept her and the firm going through bad times, and made them recover faster when the good times started to return.

Like her fellow dyslexics, Corcoran not only greatly values personal relationships at work, she rewards the hard-working employees that populate her company. Corcoran is legendary in the business for her kindness to her workers, and her efforts to make them feel appreciated.

Norma Hirsh, an executive vice president at Insignia/Douglas Elliman, described her time at Corcoran's firm with the *New York Times:* "Barbara always made you feel you were very important to her, and because of that you wanted to do well for her. She really wanted to hear what you had to say, and she actually incorporated it into the business."

All of this isn't meant to imply that Corcoran's a pushover. She can be a tough taskmaster, but even her critics acknowledge that she is a fair one. She demands of her staff what she demands of herself: hard work and a certain edge.

The Corcoran Group is now New York City's number one residential real estate firm. It has more than 700 agents scattered throughout eleven offices, and generates sales north of $4 billion. Corcoran would say that a lot of her success is because of "Mom's Lessons," but I think "Mom" would agree with me when I say that it's Corcoran's own efforts that took her to the top of her world.

It's what Corcoran learned from her mother, and everything she did to discount the notion that she was "stupid," that transformed a group of learning disabilities into creative abilities, which, combined with her innate intelligence, makes her one of New York's greatest real estate assets.

Diane Swonk, Barbara Corcoran, and Paul Orfalea have little time for money maxims. They have all the time for basic truths.

Life gave each of them more than their share of misfortune. Theirs are lives struck early on by doubt and the gnawing sense they didn't fit in.

Dyslexia prevented much in their early days, but it opened much more to them later in their lives. It gave them something they could turn into an opportunity, an edge, which, as *Fortune* magazine put it, provides them a different view of the world that makes them appreciate the weakest, the neediest, and those most in need of understanding.

What's inspiring about them is how much value they place in the little things—making workers feel wanted and appreciated, and their audiences involved and intrigued.

Orfalea is now regarded as among the most successful entrepreneurs in recent American history; Corcoran a standout in a male-dominated profession; Swonk is a number cruncher who never fails to include emotions in her gray science. They've made their professional lives testaments to looking after the people they supervised, and in Swonk's case, the people they reported on. Far from torpedoing their careers, dyslexia helped make their careers—and even now defines their careers, for their own good and the good of the world around them.

Lesson learned for those similarly afflicted: You are worth more than teachers tell you and a lot more than cynics handicap you.

No wonder *Fortune* called it a gift. Not for those who suffer it, but for the thousands more who mentally and emotionally profit from it.

CHAPTER 9

THE ARTFUL ROGER

There are famous business titans who founded and built great companies because of their obsessive, hard-driving entrepreneurial spirit, and their special ability to see business opportunities in industries that most business executives thought were already so competitive that a new, start-up company didn't have a chance of surviving for very long.

They too belong to that special breed I call *entrepreneurial visionaries.*

I respect them and what they accomplished but I don't admire and enjoy them, their companies and their success the way I do those even more elite visionaries, whose stories I'm telling in this book.

The major difference, for me, between the hard-driving titans, and Richard Branson, Herb Kelleher, and Roger Ailes, is that they always had *fun,* and they made sure that everyone who worked for them enjoyed the ride as much as they did.

Because they shared their pleasure in what they were doing so broadly and enthusiastically, everybody, from customers to the national and global public, could enjoy the company-building process and the subsequent, growing success, about as much as they did.

As you know from the Branson story, he was Peter Pan with a screw loose. He built a worldwide Virgin empire of hundreds of

companies while acting like a crazy playboy, who was as happy risk-
ing his life in a hot air balloon as he was wearing a white bridal
gown and walking down a runway.

Ailes at Fox, and Kelleher at Southwest, had just as much fun,
but each did it *their* way, and with equal success and similar results:
establishing major companies in businesses in which they had no
experience, and industries where the competition was considered
an immovable force, and doing so with intensely loyal workforces,
who worked and laughed at the same time.

The more fun their leaders had, the happier and more productive their employees were. I'm grateful for CEOs like Ailes, Kelleher,
and Branson. They set an example for how to achieve extraordinary
success and have a good time doing it, but there aren't enough chief
executives who have the guts or sense of humor to do what they do.
I'm hoping that will change.

I have a special appreciation for these three gentlemen who have
no trouble talking about having fun, and then *having* it. There is
something enticing about a chief executive who doesn't act like one,
who dares to be different, and funny, and irreverent. Lack of fear of
violating convention, that absence of self-consciousness, that allows
them to act impulsively and do whatever crazy thing will make them
and their workers laugh, is a major factor in a CEO's eccentric but
inspired triumphs.

To me, those factors explain why Kelleher, Ailes, and Branson
ultimately, thrived, in businesses they were not expected to even
have a good shot of surviving.

As these guys kept making work fun for their employees, they
motivated them to take up their crazy cause against the crazy odds
at the crazy times. They made them crazy, too.

They encouraged their employees to become a little stranger, a
little more offbeat. They *wanted* their workers thinking not only
outside the planet, but well into other solar systems. Because
that's where the new, potentially breakthrough ideas and opportunities were.

Some of us grow out of the restlessness of childhood. It seems a pity, because we lose much in the process. We forget what it was like to be young, very young, and very inquisitive, and very impatient, and very unruly.

These are not the qualities of cookie-cutter corporate kings. But not having any or all of these qualities makes them fleeting kings.

The enduring kings who reign and succeed for so long that they become legends, even beyond the business world, have retained those qualities of childhood, even into middle age and older.

How could Ailes, Kelleher, and Branson keep having so much fun, if they hadn't kept their childhood directly joined with their adulthood? How could they go on seeing new wonders around them, instead of being numbed by the numbers, if they didn't keep their eyes wide-open to the world, like children?

The good minds, the facile minds, even the crazy minds, see what's expected in life, and venture precisely toward what is not.

They see the world around them, not in a conventional way, looking for the predictable, but in other-solar-system ways, where they hope to see, discover, and use, what others have said can't happen, or have never been thought of before.

They aim for the unlikely and impossible, and make us laugh—with them, and at them. The more we laugh, even if it's at their expense, the happier they are, because they know that the sense of fun that's such a treasure to them, is enriching the lives of others.

And if the joy of the ride and the laughter make their stellar companies even more successful and profitable, well . . . that's just part of the fun.

Let me say this again, emphatically, for full disclosure: Roger Ailes is my boss. But he is also my friend. I've known him for more than a decade, and his wife, Beth, for nearly five years longer than that.

You might think it odd that an author would take the literary risk of including his own chief executive in a book like this. But given this kind of book, how could I not include this kind of guy?

I've always joked with Roger that I am best equipped to someday write the definitive biography on him. While I've personally known him more than a decade, I've known of him for decades more.

I'm a political junkie. As a kid, I closely followed presidential campaigns and was well schooled in every race, every primary, and every contest going back to 1968, when I was ten years old.

That was about the same time a guy in his late twenties named Roger Ailes was making waves in the political world.

As an advisor to then Republican presidential candidate Richard Nixon, the Ohio-born media consultant was helping to repackage the man who only six years earlier was considered through with politics, after losing his bid to become governor of California.

Nixon seemed to sum up his political demise himself, stating simply to reporters, "You won't have Dick Nixon to kick around anymore."

Ailes knew that the problem wasn't Nixon himself. Many people, those who knew him personally and millions of others who didn't, liked and admired the former vice president.

It's just that people never felt comfortable with him, and for good reason: Nixon didn't feel comfortable with them. A very private man—ironically for such a public figure—Nixon didn't relax easily when talking to or interacting with people.

He was stiff, and on television that stiffness came through. Nixon was not good TV, but that medium was a vital aspect of his presidential campaign.

Ailes had recognized early on the tremendous power of television.

Eight years earlier, as a college student, in 1960, he had seen how a restless, fidgeting, and sweating Nixon squandered his lead to a tanned and relaxed younger challenger named John Kennedy in their historic debates.

Ailes saw and understood how, from that campaign on, television would define who was elected president in this country. It would break or make a candidate.

As a young producer out of Ohio (of all places), working for a talk show host named Mike Douglas, Ailes fine-tuned his communications craft.

He learned the essential aspects of how and why a candidate or show's message, delivered and broadcast on television, mattered a lot more than the particular candidate or message.

Substance and meaning were important, but if they could be made appealing, the viewers and public would respond much more positively.

Nixon was not appealing, and Ailes knew that he'd have to work hardest on that. Nixon was willing to listen and change, in accordance with the young Ailes's advice—and this time, he won the presidency.

As I watched and studied him through the succeeding years, I saw Ailes help Ronald Reagan get elected, and re-elected. Later, as the brains behind electing George Bush Sr. president in 1988, Ailes once again proved himself a marvel: a major force in getting three presidents into the White House, and winning four presidential campaigns.

I still believe that had Ailes not retired from his political advising after the Bush victory, and re-upped with Bush later for his re-election bid in 1992, Bill Clinton would have never won the presidency, and history would be different.

So many bad decisions during the Bush re-election campaign were made in so short a time, that Ailes's enormous advisory importance in presidential elections was defined almost more by the disasters that happened in his absence, than by his incredible string of victories.

By 1993, a few years after retiring from politics, Ailes was a powerful corporate consultant. His Ailes Communications was a pivotal player in training major Fortune 500 company executives and countless others in the ways of getting out the message, and staying out of trouble.

That same year, the business news channel CNBC was looking for a new chief executive, who had exactly the abilities, qualities, and experience that Ailes did.

CNBC was floundering. Within the NBC organization, it was still considered the bastard stepchild . . . valuable but not necessarily valued.

The fact that it was based not in the treasured canyons of Manhattan, but the Siberian outpost of Fort Lee, New Jersey, further cemented CNBC's image of being "out there."

The odd thing, and what few executives at NBC understood or appreciated, was that CNBC was a broadcast diamond in the rough.

I should know. I worked there.

I was there when the channel first started up in April 1989. In fact, I have the distinction of being the first anchor to kick off the channel with a morning show called *World Business.* I was pretty rough at the start, perhaps a metaphor for the channel's other ills.

Getting distribution was tough. Getting industry respect even tougher.

Still, some good things had happened along the way, including General Electric's prescient decision to buy out financially hurting competitor Financial News Network.

What's more, CNBC did have good people overseeing it. Under its first CEO, Michael Eskridge, and later, Al Barber, this Fort Lee outpost was clicking with investors. They were just getting onboard with this phenomenal new stock market boom, and CNBC was the electronic window on that world.

The trouble was, the network was struggling. As some said at the time, it was a white elephant—lots of potential, but lots of problems, too.

It was growing, but for GE's purposes it wasn't growing fast enough.

Barber, the current CEO, wanted to step down, but who would step in?

Taking on CNBC wasn't exactly an up-and-coming broadcaster's vision of a good career move. In fact, to many it seemed a dead end.

For NBC, it was a kind of stalemate. No qualified broadcast CEO wanted the job, and the television executives who were interested didn't have the qualities NBC was wanted for their new CNBC leader.

Then, in an outstanding example of unconventional executive thinking, NBC President Bob Wright looked outside the insular world of television executives, even far beyond the borders of the TV industry, and thought of a fellow named Roger Ailes.

Wright had tracked Ailes's political and then corporate career, much as I had already been doing for decades. He was impressed with Ailes, his connections, the work he and his Ailes Communications firm were doing, and his political and communications background.

Perhaps this was the guy who could right the wayward CNBC broadcast ship, even though he'd never worked directly in broadcast television.

I wasn't privy to the details at the time of those initial discussions, which led to contract negotiations, and I didn't understand why Ailes would risk so much by even bothering with this kind of nonsense.

Why would a man who had helped elect three presidents, and scores of governors, senators, and congressmen, who had helped turn around so many troubled companies, want to give any thought to an executive position like this?

Knowing Ailes as I do now, it was almost certainly because of the challenge: Roger loves challenges.

Perhaps turning around CNBC was the equivalent of his turning a 22-point deficit in the polls for George Bush Sr. into a surprisingly comfortable election victory.

Because I knew Ailes's work and past so well, I frequently was peppered with questions by CNBC colleagues, all wanting to know who this guy was, and what he might have in store for us.

Some would ask the obvious questions: What's this guy know about cable? What's a political veteran doing slugging it out in the business news world? And on and on.

My response was always the same: "Roger Ailes is just what CNBC needs right now."

And CNBC got him. Ailes became the new CEO, and my colleagues and I suddenly had a new leader and, in my opinion at least, a more certain future.

I had signed a contract with the channel a few months earlier, with plenty of doubts about where it was going. After I heard the Ailes news, I told my wife, "we're in good shape now."

Roger Ailes was just what this fledgling business news channel desperately needed.

He immediately established an unusual *esprit de corps,* first in group meetings with the staff, then in individual one-on-one sessions with all anchors and reporters.

I remember well my first face-to-face meeting with Ailes.

"People say you're arrogant and a little too tough in your interviews," he said within moments of my sitting down in his office.

"Yes, I guess that's right," I answered.

"Good," he said. "I like your stuff."

And then he spelled out his vision for CNBC . . . how we had a lot of great pieces, presumably mine included, but that it was poorly marketed, and poorly focused.

In short order, Ailes turned the place upside down. He crafted a two-fold strategy for the network: business during the day, talk at night.

He instituted a new show, called *Talk All Stars,* at night, to showcase a friendlier, less wonky version of the hard business news channel of the day.

I can remember some of my colleagues laughing. But once the ratings started improving, they weren't laughing anymore.

And then Ailes set his sights on what CNBC was doing during the day. A programmer at heart, he wanted to market the daytime shows—to treat the hours of business coverage not as monotony, but as distinct shows.

He wanted to jazz up the coverage, make it more engaging and compelling. He also wanted something a little irreverent and fun to start off the broadcast day, so *Squawk Box* became his first business show creation.

Clever and focused banter, not dry scripts, would rule the day. Anchors and correspondents were encouraged to challenge their guests and conventional wisdom.

Ailes kept picking just the right guys who could forward that kind of message. Mark Haines, Joe Kernen, and David Faber were all quick on their feet, and more than versatile enough to wing it, for hours if need be. In fact, they were better without script . . . and a hell of a lot more fun to watch.

The show was an instant hit. Ratings soared, and suddenly Ailes wasn't being so summarily dismissed. Maybe this Ohio guy knew a thing or two about what these Wall Street brainiacs would watch.

Ailes was like lightning, making the same changes throughout the broadcast day for CNBC, compartmentalizing the day into themed shows to keep the momentum going.

There was *Power Lunch,* a midday show I was given, to help broaden the traditional view of business news beyond simple market coverage to more stories on marketing, sports, the media, and more.

Then there was a revamped and refocused *Market Wrap,* and later a day-closing show, *Business Center,* each with its own distinct personality and personalities, and each signing on to the Ailes mantra that just because it's business news, it needn't be dull.

My daytime colleagues were positively giddy at the results. Suddenly CNBC was becoming a force, and Roger Ailes an even bigger force. He was Mr. Brand. . . .

And then suddenly, NBC decided they wanted him to become Mr. Brand Extension. NBC higher-ups wanted him to create a brand new channel, called *America's Talking,* whose aim would be to build, in a general news and feature sense, what CNBC had built in a business sense.

My old friend Beth Tilson, who had been so helpful to me starting out at CNBC (on my first day, she even helped move a desk for me!) would be put in charge, along with Ailes's old pal from his Mike Douglas days, Chet Collier.

Ailes decided to give NBC what they wanted, and to take on the new challenge that *he* wanted. He'd revitalized CNBC but it was already established. With *America's Talking,* he'd have the thrill of starting an entirely new channel, that would build on CNBC but be different from it in important ways so that AT could draw its own audiences.

Once again, he proved to be a dynamo at creating programming that more than stood the test of time. Shows like *Pork,* which he created for AT, would miraculously appear reincarnated, on NBC years later, as something called *The Fleecing of America.* There are a number of other examples like that.

And Ailes was doing brilliant programming, providing inspiring leadership, and making work enjoyable for his employees at *two* channels simultaneously. There seemed to be no ceiling to what he might achieve in the TV industry that he'd been completely new to, not so long ago.

But amid all the success, what Ailes didn't realize, or at least failed to fully appreciate at the time, was the Herculean internal political struggle going on at NBC.

The network was having second thoughts about *America's Talking.* NBC higher ups were talking with Microsoft—something about a joint venture, in which NBC and Microsoft would co-create a news channel for the future.

The best way to start it was to simply replace *America's Talking.*

Not surprisingly, Ailes wasn't too keen on the idea, but not for the reasons you'd think. He just felt the synergies weren't there, and that NBC might be losing its senses.

"I just thought it was a horrendous mistake," he said, as we recently discussed those days.

"Everybody was talking convergence, and this was the latest big thing . . . that the computer was going to take over the television screen. And I never believed that. Maybe in ten years or twenty years, but not now."

Ailes feared everybody at NBC and Microsoft were getting way ahead of themselves. Worse, he was the only kid in the class asking the legitimate questions.

"I remember saying to somebody at NBC at the time, 'Look, as long as there are fat guys like me, who want to go home and watch the guy catch the pass, and not look up his stats during the game, television is going to rule, and computers are going to be just a mechanism.' "

What's more, Ailes didn't think the 50/50 partnership with Microsoft would work. "They thought it was just because I didn't know how to run my computer," he recalled.

"I just believed in the power of television over the power of the content that would be the Internet. People had a fifty-year history of buying ads on television. They didn't have a fifty-year history of buying ads on the computer."

He knew Bill Gates would come out okay. After all, the world's richest man wasn't in this for synergies as much as he was for content. And NBC had a lot of that, in the form of film and video that dated back years, and this stockpile would be added to under this arrangement.

That was video that Gates would be free to use elsewhere in all sorts of venues, more than justifying what Ailes called the "relative pocket change" cost for Gates. So Microsoft didn't do too shabby with such an arrangement, Ailes figured.

It was NBC that he thought was getting the short end of the stick, but he also realized how stubborn and excessively skeptical he was sounding to a company hell-bent on making this gargantuan of convergences work.

He knew that some at NBC would figure it was just "Ailes resisting this because he wants to maintain control of AT."

"Well, I can see there probably was some truth in that," he explained. "But I didn't think convergence like they were talking about, was any way near." That for Ailes was the real problem. And he had a better idea.

Go ahead and do the Microsoft thing, but keep AT. This way NBC would have three different cable channels.

There had already been talk that Rupert Murdoch was considering buying his way into the news business, by paying cable operators to carry whatever he might come up with.

It was all speculation at the time, but Ailes thought NBC, which was way ahead in the cable game at that point, could get into the cable news business in a substantial way that was a variation of Murdoch's approach: keep AT and build MSNBC.

But NBC had other plans, and increasingly it looked like Ailes was blocking them.

Soon, NBC started blocking Ailes, in subtle but significant ways.

For example, the company wanted someone else to handle distribution issues for CNBC.

Ailes could see where this was going. Whoever controls distribution, he surmised, essentially controls programming. He or she could argue that a cable operator didn't like a show or talent, effectively squelch the idea, and further reduce Ailes's control.

"I always told everybody that I worked with, that if I didn't control the income streams, I wouldn't do the job. I had to have ad sales and cable fees. Having run my own business for 20 years, whoever runs the income side, runs the business."

Increasingly, Ailes was realizing he wasn't going to get that control. Any other executive who had just signed a fat new employment contract would have grimaced and dealt with it.

Not Roger.

Not then. Not ever.

He had decided he wanted out, that he wouldn't just accept this cockamamie scheme. He wanted to be done with it. But anyone who thought he would go off quietly into the night was seriously mistaken.

"The end of the story is this," Ailes remembered. "I said, 'Look, you guys don't want me running all this. You guys want to do it. And clearly, I am not going to be allowed to run it the way I have been running it up until now.'"

He pointed to all the progress made at CNBC, largely because they had left him alone. He had made CNBC a name brand and its anchors all marketable and marquee names. They had all become richer and much sought after during his stewardship, and didn't I know it!

He concluded by saying to them, "And now you're going to try to help me. No, I need to move on."

NBC was surprised, but they had no choice. Ailes wasn't changing his mind, especially since they hadn't changed theirs.

The next step was working out the contractual particulars, finding a comfortable way for NBC and Ailes to part company and move on. However, when companies are parting with you, they want you to sign a noncompete clause that effectively thwarts you from ever competing with or threatening them in any way ever again.

Ailes was initially told that the noncompete clause would include not only new business news ventures, but regular news and entertainment enterprises as well. That proved a big sticking point, and for good reason.

"Well, they tried to block me out of all news, entertainment, and running a Dairy Queen," Ailes joked. "I guess what they wanted was a complete noncompete. I could never work again, as long as I lived, and I would have to be a dog."

Ailes is coy as to why he pushed so hard to exclude future news ventures in that noncompete, but the fact is he got that concession.

I think it was the biggest blunder NBC made.

Consider this: Had NBC succeeded in keeping Ailes out of news, Fox News Channel might never have gotten off the ground. And MSNBC might have had more than a fighting chance.

CNBC itself might have fared better through the market doldrums that cost it so many viewers, rather than fall to being a distant also ran, to no less than five Fox business shows, which are also the top five business news shows in the country.

I think I'm being conservative when I say that that single oversight about what a departing Ailes was capable of doing with what appeared to be such a narrow opportunity, cost NBC $3 billion!

And as time goes on, probably billions more.

And all because this underappreciated Ohio kid was smart enough to leave his best options open.

Myself? For reasons I still don't quite understand, I was the only CNBC anchor who had not agreed to a recent generous contract extension by management, even though Ailes was still CEO. My contract was expiring a few months later, which afforded me the rare opportunity to rejoin my friend on his biggest and most bodacious project to date.

But as Ailes was leaving, all those other things seemed so way off.

He had money and success, and more than enough contacts and prestige to restart his Ailes Communications. So he would be fine, no matter what he chose.

I wish the same could have been said of the workers he was forced to leave behind. So many were shocked by Ailes's leaving, that they were visibly shaken. I recall more than a few of them crying.

Ailes had established an unusual esprit de corps. His employees, particularly those higher up, were intensely loyal, and now intensely depressed.

Who would follow? What would happen? Who would make all the jokes and those famous, amusing digs? And those memorable little barbs with the infectious laugh? People were worried, and many more were sad, too.

In a short time, Ailes had become a commanding leader, with a reputation for respect and affection from his employees, that was rare indeed in the broadcast industry.

Within a week of his departure from NBC, Ailes dropped a huge bombshell. He was joining Rupert Murdoch to launch an all-news channel.

The *New York Times* put the story on the front page the next day. The drama was set: Conservative forces united to tackle the established names at their own game.

"Crazy" was the first word that came to some competitors' minds. After all, CNN was still going strong. And now MSNBC was in the works, and there was talk that ABC and Disney were set to do the same.

For some who had seen Ailes in near mythic proportions, this seemed a tragic ending. What could he be thinking? Fox had virtually no news infrastructure, and save some promising bureaus here and there, no means to tackle on a national scale what its competitors could easily do on a daily basis.

But it's precisely because the odds were so daunting, that Ailes was so intrigued. Remember, this is a guy who *loves* challenges: running presidential campaigns, guiding CNBC with no broadcast experience, and now helping to launch a new all-news channel against tough competition.

He also knew that Murdoch meant business, was putting cash up for distribution, and making a strong commitment.

In Murdoch, Ailes found a natural soul mate, someone else who was a risk-taker, and a risk-taker of far more dramatic proportions at that. Murdoch was a man who staked much on a hunch and an incredibly good gut.

"Rupert had the guts to go forward," Ailes recalled. "He doesn't get intimidated by odds either. I think frankly Rupert bluffed them out. He said, 'I am going, hell or high water, despite the odds.'" It was a good thing, because those odds couldn't be more daunting or the prospect of success more remote.

However, these two entrepreneurial visionaries realized something that their competitors did not: American news was slanted. "I felt the American people were under-served," Ailes recalled. Murdoch had been saying the same for years.

Polls that Ailes later commissioned, by a Democratic pollster no less, showed that by a three-to-one margin Americans felt the media tipped to the left.

"CNN had 4,000 people and Bob Novak, and they thought that was balanced," he said.

Murdoch agreed that conservative viewpoints weren't heard, and if they were, it was only with disdain. He had seen and triumphed over the same imbalance in various countries around the world through his media empire of newspapers and broadcast stations. He would do the same with an American national news channel.

Ailes was the guy to make it happen. And this time, Ailes had a boss who thought as he did and put his money in to back him up. The only thing Ailes had to do was deliver—fast.

Because people in this country were sick and tired of the way news was being presented to them, Ailes had to give them news that was fresh, different, conservative but balanced—and, especially, appealing. And that meant creating enough new programming to make a cable channel a real operation.

He committed to getting Fox News up and running in six months—an apparently insane goal, considering there was no news structure in place at all. But Ailes was comfortable with "crazy." He'd been characterized like that for most of his professional life and various careers.

Ailes was absolutely convinced he would succeed, even in the face of daunting odds, even through the laughter and derision of some old NBC colleagues who thought he was embarking on the biggest disaster of his career.

Ailes recalls reporters actually snickering when he laid out his news channel plans in early 1996 with News Corporation Chief Executive Rupert Murdoch.

He told me how he studied CNN. "I sat down, and watched CNN for a week. And I kept having to wake myself up. And I knew that if you are going to have to keep waking yourself up, this is probably bad. But I figured in the end, I ought to be able to take these guys because they just weren't watchable."

Ailes had studied the landscape well. Having decided his competitors were ripe for the taking, he knew he could move fast. It's also why he moved so quickly on his now famous "fair and balanced" marketing campaign.

What about the soon-to-be-launched MSNBC?

Ailes said he sensed early on it wouldn't go anywhere. "You get to watch a close-up of a guy punching a computer keyboard. I kept thinking, 'There may be some miracle here I am not getting. But if this is it, it's not going to win. These guys are off track.'"

A classic visionary, Ailes saw beyond and through his competitors. He realized the NBC news organization, so vaunted in the press, likely would prove to be its own undoing with MSNBC, which they'd make too much like network TV, not cable-centric enough.

"I learned at CNBC that they always disrespected CNBC. I could never get any cross promotion. I could never get anybody at 30 Rockefeller Plaza [NBC News headquarters] to give us anything. And the same people who should have been able to turn CNBC into something were going to be in charge of MSNBC."

Ailes wasn't worried. But in 1996, the dimensions of this seemingly impossible Fox undertaking seemed enormous to others.

This channel-to-come had only one marketing strategy: fair and balanced news.

No talk of global bureaus or fancy news equipment. No puffed up seasoned news executives or shelves stuffed with Dupont and Emmy Awards.

None of that. Only a credo that promised something different. And the guy leading that crazy charge was Ailes.

As insurmountable as the odds seemed, he was having no trouble recruiting soldiers for this all but suicidal mission. By the dozens, they were coming from NBC, and CNBC, and AT.

His old colleagues at 30 Rock were not impressed, but they did try to stop the flood-loss of employees by attempting to intimidate Ailes.

"Well, they called me and threatened me," Ailes remembered. "Somebody called and said, 'You realize there are legal remedies to recruiting our people.'"

"And I said, 'You don't know the difference between recruiting and a jailbreak. People are throwing out bed sheets over there. They are dying to get out of there. So you guys aren't treating your people too good. This is people seeing opportunity. This is like a race to freedom. Guys are willing to jump over the Berlin Wall, and make a mad dash through 100 yards of barbed wire.'"

I'd have loved to have heard the other end of that phone conversation.

Clearly, competitors were beginning to sense there was something to this Ailes guy that was worth watching and noting, but for many, at least not at the time, not worth fearing.

Out-manned, technically out-gunned, and decidedly out-spent, Ailes kept his troops committed.

He knew he owed it to them to make Fox work. Their careers depended on it.

"I had a great loyalty to them and what they sacrificed," he told me. "I couldn't let them down, and I wasn't planning to."

That he took all the pressure easily in stride inspired confidence in his troops. And to keep them relaxed, he'd regularly inject a little levity in even the most serious executive staff meeting. He'd become well-known for these qualities at CNBC, and because they worked, he was continuing them now at Fox.

He was playful then, when the pressure was greatest, but then that's how he always is.

In so many ways, Ailes changes the rules by simplifying them, and touching chords on clearly emotional levels. I've seen him reduce Wharton grads to fits of laughter as a result!

He encouraged executives to act and be the same way.

As he put it to me one day: "If you don't have any fun coming to work here, sell insurance, or do something else. You have to enjoy going to work every day." It was as much psychological as it was business advice.

"Look," Ailes explained. "I knew people had to play over their heads. They had to go in, being not just a couple of times better or three times better or four times better than the other guy.

"You cannot do that if you don't have good morale, if you don't have a positive attitude and if you're not having fun."

Ailes also knew that by contrast, his competitors were too serious and way too uptight. They might have the resources but they didn't have the heart or that very tangible thing called "fun" going for them.

Given the nature of the cutthroat news business, it's easy for Ailes's competitors and others to look at him, and see a worse reflection of their own ambitious selves: a nasty menace who wants to conquer the world.

But it's because they can't have, experience, or see true *fun* that they misunderstand, misinterpret, or miss completely, how truly fun is at the core of Ailes's being, and always has been, motivating and relaxing him, and making him the natural, charismatic leader and cheerleader that he is.

And he's not obsessed with his work, as so many executives are, perhaps because they fear for their jobs. Ailes has a personal life, and a range of interests that keep him informed and entertained. For example, he's a huge Civil War buff.

And he relishes tweaking people, from his big Fox News billboards directly across from CNN's Atlanta headquarters, to his full-page newspaper ads touting the latest Fox victory, and no doubt making his competitors foam a bit at the mouth.

I know some have said it was Rupert Murdoch's money that paved the way for Ailes, but the truth is best expressed by what Ailes's assistant Judy Laterza said of her boss: He thinks like a child, as a seven-year-old would . . . with laughter and curiosity and devil-may-care, and it's with a child's refreshing and humorous self-confidence that he leads his troops into business battles as easily and often as into mirth-provoking antics and comments.

I can attest, as a member of Fox News management, that Ailes's executive staff meetings are hilarious, fun, and looked forward to, which is an attitude of anticipation that's almost never found among business executives, who instead have to endure the seemingly endless grind of one tedious meeting after another.

As Ailes's self-imposed six-month deadline rushed ever closer, even his less confident executives and employees started getting what I call that "George Foreman feeling." It's the eighth round against Muhammad Ali and suddenly the tide's turning. You just know it's turning.

I remember being one of those early guerilla soldiers at Fox, and talking to a colleague of mine, who knew well the risk of failing.

"I can lose this job," he said. "But, man, I know I'll never have anything like it again!"

I could just as easily have been talking about Herb Kelleher's troops at Southwest Airlines or Branson's dozens of brigades throughout his global Virgin empire.

Ailes saw and felt the turning tide, as his troops did, and was excited about it, especially because when he set the deadline with full confidence in what he and his workforce could do, he didn't or couldn't have predicted how quickly the Fox News operation would come together, or how convincingly and enthusiastically.

And all with talent, me included, largely unknown, untested, and unappreciated by those outside the company.

Ailes, who'd been joined by Chet Collier, reactivating an old friendship and working relationship that had begun during their Mike Douglas days, were similar in their uncanny ability to get a read of good people and good shows.

The Fox workforce they put together was their own version of a broadcasting island of misfit toys. People like Bill O'Reilly and Sean Hannity, who would, years later, both become superstars.

And Ailes and Collier were patient with shows they knew would succeed. O'Reilly languished for years after Fox started up, but Ailes knew he had a good thing going in as the contentious populist, and he never stopped supporting him.

The same with Fox's morning show, *Fox and Friends,* blasted by some in his own company as going nowhere fast. Today it's the most watched morning show on cable, period. Often, it even beats the CBS show that's broadcast at the same hour.

"Frankly, I thought it would take me nine to twelve months longer than it did," Ailes said. But he knew it would happen. He knew that Fox and its fast-paced, "fair and balanced" news strategy, often maligned by liberals as being too conservative, would pay off.

And when it did, so fast, it started creating heat and in so doing, connecting with legions of disaffected viewers, who found with Fox, a voice they hadn't heard before and a news outlet they didn't have before.

Certainly, breaks now and then did come his way.

Disney later blinked in the face of Murdoch's offer to pay for distribution and effectively took itself out of the news channel running.

With Disney no longer a factor, Ailes's Fox News effort was a three-way race, with CNN already on, MSNBC soon to come on, and Fox not due to go on the air until the fall of 1996, a couple of months after MSNBC.

Cable executives who were interviewed in some trade publications concluded that CNN had little to worry about, but that if there was a threat it was MSNBC. In their expert opinion, Fox was at best, a lark. . . . "Murdoch's bombastic boondoggle," as one writer put it.

During our recent conversation, I asked Ailes how all this negative press had affected him, whether he'd been bothered by its unending carping, condescending tone. Not at all, was his response. Instead, like Kelleher and Branson, he made that criticism a further motivating factor, and a useful way to disguise how effective his new news operation was rapidly becoming.

Ailes wanted his critics and competitors to find out the hard way, when it was too late to readjust to the presence of a powerful new opponent, just how popular Fox News would become, and continue to be.

I also asked whether he'd like to go back and wipe the smirks off so many faces. "Well," he answered, "I don't think they're smirking any more."

To this day, though, Ailes does bristle at criticism and allegations that Fox is a tool of and for conservatives. "People have a real problem hearing both sides," he recently told me. "I don't. And I don't think our viewers do."

He's right, and it's amazing how it's all played out, pretty much exactly the way this crazy guy Ailes thought it would, with CNN stumbling, and MSNBC relegated to a cable also-ran position.

The simple fact is that MSNBC in 80 million homes is getting about the same ratings Ailes's AT was getting in 17 million homes. So much for NBC, the self-regarded greatest news organization on earth.

Still, Ailes's detractors are hardly admitting that they're wowed by Fox's success. Many are the journalists and journalism professors who scoff at this loud upstart channel.

Count Ailes unimpressed. "I don't give a rat's ass about the journalism professors," he snapped. "You need a certificate to be a hairdresser. You don't need it to be a journalist. The truth of the matter is I will not be taking over the Columbia University Journalism Department.

"And there is one very good reason. They don't even want to hear what I have to say. They don't believe any of this stuff."

To Ailes, that "stuff" includes patriotism, love of country, and realizing that journalists can do what they do because of this country, not despite it.

"All I'm asking is whether it would kill some of these guys to say there are a few things about America that are not so bad," he said. "But you'll never hear it."

Ailes remains as feisty now as when he embarked on this reportedly hopeless mission back in 1996. And he's still lamenting the state of the industry he has singlehandedly revolutionized.

Of journalists, he says: "America gives them the freedom to do what they want, but they don't mind attacking it every day. And yet, if somebody attacks journalism, they get their nose out of joint."

Ailes knows he might be on top of them all, but he is still not liked by them all. "Well, you know, I am a target, because I am not politically correct, because I say what I mean, because I didn't come out of the profession, because I won't go to the meetings, because I won't wear the rings or kiss the right ass.

"You know, I don't care about that. That's not really important. They are getting their rear ends kicked, that's number one."

I asked him whether he's concerned that people may finally have stopped underestimating him, learned to respect his success, even if they don't admire it or him, and become tougher competitors as a result.

He says, "No. The arrogance level just goes up, and it goes up faster." And he thinks that the more arrogant they become, the less willing they are to change—to their detriment, as they'll someday be forced to realize.

"And it's fine," he continued. "I mean, I have built a career on being underestimated. The best thing that can ever happen to you, if you are looking for success, is to have people underestimate your ability."

And they continue to underestimate.

"They still attribute it to, 'Oh, it's about politics' or 'Oh, he got lucky' or 'Oh, it's Rupert's money' or 'Oh, it's the weather' or 'Oh, it's Tuesday' . . . it all just becomes what drives me."

Ailes doesn't see things changing now. The people who dismissed him when he was a mediocre student in Ohio, or later just starting out with that guy Mike Douglas, or that other guy Richard Nixon, or that other guy Ronald Reagan, or George Bush, or that business channel CNBC, or now, Fox, will just keep doing so.

They've been blind to his remarkable abilities and triumphs for decades, and they'll be equally blind to any new success.

But the appreciation of all those people who don't "get" the real Roger Ailes, is meaningless to him. What matters most is that he *knows* that Fox has helped change this country for the better.

"Fox has given hope to those who believe that democracy and freedom depend on character," he explained, adding, Fox isn't just a news channel.

For many, it's a way of life.

Even on breaking news stories, long thought to be CNN's last broadcast bastion, Fox now dominates as well.

During the 2003 Iraq War, for example, Fox trounced CNN in all day-parts on all days among all demographic groups.

So the network that was defined by the first Gulf War was, in a very real sense, dismissed by the second Gulf War.

"My entire success is probably because I have enormous respect for average working men," Ailes said. "I think they're pretty smart, and certainly know what's in the best interests of their family and themselves. They have a great belief in our system, and that has provided them with something that their ancestors didn't have."

Fox is for them, he says proudly. It is not a channel for elitists or journalists or journalism professors.

Ailes is unimpressed with news awards, news parties, and socializing, and the clubby nature of the communications business.

Fox, as its early ads stated, is news, "for the rest of us."

Ailes refuses to relinquish that perch.

He knows well his competitors clamor for it, but they don't feel it in their broadcast bones.

Ailes does.

Even with all his wealth and accompanying fame, he is more prone to enjoy a burger with friends from the old days, than attend some gala media function in these vastly changed new days.

It's a success Ailes thinks of in terms of his own ancestors, his own family. "You know something," he told me one chilly March morning at his home. "I'd trade it all for one Sunday dinner at my family's house, with all those guys around the table.

"Just one moment to be with them, and to hear from relatives now long gone, 'Hey, so little Roger actually made something of himself.' I wish they were around to enjoy it."

CHAPTER 10

WHAT DO YOU DO WHEN THEY'RE GONE?

In telling the life stories of my heroes, I have now shared the tragic, triumphant, and inspirational experiences of five people who were diagnosed with various forms of incurable cancer.

Through their courage and commitment, Joe Torre, Geraldine Ferraro, Harry Pearce, Mel Stottlemyre, and Evelyn Lauder became cancer survivors, and more importantly, crusaders who have dedicated their lives to helping improve the lives and odds of survival of fellow and potential victims.

I have featured these stories of cancer survivors, most importantly because cancer is still incurable, and one of the major scourges of our society.

Because there are millions of cancer victims and survivors, and millions more who are at risk, it is my hope and goal that the inspirational power and potential lessons learned from these stories will help some of you, and the people you love and care about.

I also shared the tales of these heroes because as a cancer survivor myself, I can understand and describe their experiences as only a fellow survivor can. In this way, I hope the story of my bout with cancer will help others.

The three CEOs that I'm profiling in this chapter—Foote, Walsh, and Mead—have also had their lives devastated by cancer, but none of them is a cancer survivor. Their experiences are different, in some ways almost as painful, and in one case, even worse.

These stories are about two cancer deaths—including that of a CEO's young wife—profound losses, and wrenching adjustments to the new circumstances. And for two of them, dealing with such horrendous losses without their mentor or wife, and somehow making a better life, for their workers, their companies, and their families.

My personal experiences give me a deep empathy for what these people had to endure. As I've described, I lost my mother to brain cancer, seven months before my own cancer diagnosis, and my father died a few years later of prostate cancer, while my own cancer was in remission.

I'll never forget the aching, growing loneliness I felt and will always feel, as I lost both of my parents to cancer, when I and they were young enough that we'd planned on spending decades more of our lives together.

Every life, every tragedy, is different, in the small details and large elements, but there are also unifying emotions that bring us together in understanding, regardless of how many variables there are.

Terror, pain, fear of death, the loss of loved ones, giving love and then more love, becoming more selfless, more oriented toward what's best for others, survival, triumph, failure, determination, belief—and hope. Many or all of these emotions and actions are part of the stories I'm about to tell, and they have been an integral aspect of the life stories you've read this far.

I think you'll feel the emotion in these stories as deeply as I do, and that you'll give the lives and deaths of these people more meaning because of what you'll newly or better understand—about life, and everything else.

THE SUM IS GREATER . . .

William Foote was what they call a fast-tracker. A Harvard MBA and former McKinsey consultant, in 1994 Foote was a rising star at the giant Chicago building-products maker USG Corp., preparing for his appointment as USG's new CEO the following year. People knew him. They liked him. And even his competitors marveled at him.

By all appearances, Foote was your typical, hard-charging, top executive, controlling his life and career, and being richly rewarded for his intense efforts. That was the outside image, anyway.

What people didn't know was that even as Foote was moving fast toward being the chief executive, he was suffering through a private tragedy: His wife, Andrea Foote, had been diagnosed with breast cancer.

At the same time he was brilliantly executing his responsibilities at USG, he was caring for his wife, and increasingly helping her with their three young daughters.

At first, doctors seemed hopeful they could successfully treat Andrea's cancer, and as she started going through the brutal treatment, Bill was sharing what was going on at home with only a few close friends.

Soon, though, he decided that more people needed to be informed about what he, his wife, and daughters were going through, and little more than a month after Andrea's initial diagnosis, he informed his managers that his family was facing one of their biggest challenges ever.

He later told the *Minneapolis-St. Paul Star-Tribune* that he'd said to his colleagues back then, that he was "going to need some help." He'd get it from them then, and a lot more later.

As the months wore on, the treatments were not successful, and Andrea's disease worsened. The pressure on him at USG and on him personally intensified as he tried to balance his corporate and family responsibilities, prepare for an ever-closer appointment to CEO, and spend more time with Andrea and his daughters.

Realistically, Foote knew that time was running out for his beloved wife, and he was with her in the hospital and at home as often as he could get away from the job. By now, he was almost the sole caretaker of his daughters, and in addition to the usual parental duties, he had to help them understand and endure what they knew was their mother's approaching death.

Andrea died in 1995, ending her painful fourteen-month battle.

Foote was now a grieving, widowed father. Only a month later, he took over USG Corp., the culmination of his young life's work and his now-deceased wife's dream for him.

As the new CEO, Foote was in the biggest pressure-cooker job of his career. And that was only on the corporate side.

He realized that between his new position, the death of his wife, and his having to raise his three daughters, ages eleven, nine, and eight, he couldn't possibly do it all by himself and do any of it well. He needed help.

It's what Foote did next that makes him such a rarity among CEOs or any executives: He *asked* for help, openly, publicly, and from everybody.

After Andrea died, Foote opened his first big speech as CEO to 150 USG managers by talking about his wife, and the help his family received, even the spiritual lessons he had learned.

He talked of life being precious and fleeting, that it was important to live in the moment; that what really matters isn't work, but kids and self and family. He told his audience that he loved USG, but "my No. 1 priority is my family."

By all accounts, Foote's speech was mesmerizing.

One press report said "you could have heard a pin drop." Another mentioned that there "wasn't a dry eye in the house."

One senior executive told the *Tribune* there was a collective response, a determination that "if we have to go through a few walls for this guy, we're going to do it."

And they did. Within days, managers volunteered to take on extra business trips, even some of Foote's executive duties; anything to ease his burden and allow him more time with his family.

It was as if the entire organization had been sensitized to the rigors of the real world and real life.

I've been the surprised and grateful recipient of this kind of outpouring of support from my colleagues, twice. First at PBS, when my fellow workers heard that I had advanced Hodgkin's disease, and secretly helped me for months and sacrificed a lot of their own time so that I could leave the office as I needed to for chemotherapy. Later, at Fox, when I was diagnosed with MS—because I told the truth right away—the support was just as strong, but I knew about it, and could appreciate it while my colleagues were offering it.

Based on my experiences of overwhelming support, I can easily imagine how much it must have meant to Bill Foote and his daughters to have the entire population of USG executive and employees rally to his support as they did. You never forget, and you never feel you can give enough back—even when no one wants any "reward" at all. For them, the helping was its own reward.

Foote's grief, sense of loss, and great pressure must have been eased, and feelings of relief and gratitude added, as employees of all stripes and rank began to seek Foote out, to offer their support, even if it meant little more than a kind word.

Foote continued to talk about and share his loss. He talked to everyone. He wanted to be upfront. He talked openly at work about his loss and about being a single parent. He also talked of the challenges, how difficult it was for a now single forty-four-year-old guy to raise three young girls.

Because of the courageous actions of Bill Foote and other gutsy CEOs like him, the business world has changed today, and top executives feel more comfortable talking about personal problems and issues.

But at the time, in 1995, Foote was taking what was considered a significant professional risk. In those days, CEOs projected power, invincibility, and dominance. They dominated their companies, and they wanted that power to be seen by and possibly intimidate competitors. If a CEO showed any sign of weakness or vulnerability, there was the risk that a competitor might see an opportunity for attack, for some form of action that would exploit that weakness.

Foote was more concerned about his family, his company, and his employees than he was about his career. The benefits to all of his publicly asking for help outweighed the risks, which he chose to disregard.

Foote's family situation was hardly unusual. Some four million workers are bereaved each year, and I'm reminded of what Canada's Michael Wilson said about depression: "At any time for any reason, it can catch you. You are at once vulnerable and helpless. In the corporate sense, you can often appear useless as well."

The trip mechanism for this sudden bout of sadness can be anything, a demotion at work, a personal matter at home, or something worse, like the death of a loved one.

But most employees and executives keep their grieving secret. Many fear they'll look weak, or that their bosses or coworkers will deem them vulnerable or less than equal to the job.

Most choose to suffer privately, hoping the world won't notice, and that it's no one else's business anyway. There's a sense of my pain is my pain, and nobody else's pain.

But it's a risky strategy, because, as with depression, the loss of a spouse or loved one takes an immeasurable toll on a worker, especially *at* work.

Absenteeism, moodiness, and declining productivity are just some of the more obvious symptoms, but there are more.

An emotionally distraught worker invariably draws inward, handicapping his own ability to climb out of his pit, and preventing others from helping him dig out.

Fortunately, especially because a great CEO is so often a role model, Foote took a different approach. He had lost his wife but not his kids, and now it was more important than ever for him, as the only parent, to keep his daughters strong—and at the same time, not letting down his company, and his tremendously loyal employees.

As he talked, he kept making one aspect of his situation very clear, just as he had with the USG managers: He had priorities at work, but he had even greater priorities at home.

He was convinced both could be met, but he was venturing into largely uncharted waters on the job front, so over and over again, he thanked everyone for their guidance, understanding, and support, and told them that he would continue to need them and all they provided, just as much.

Foote's first priority were his girls. He needed to be there for them, so with typical executive flare, he drew a giant family calendar. Everything was color-coded: yellow for days he had to work late, blue for days he was traveling.

As often as possible, evenings were set aside for stories.

He'd sit by his daughters' beds and regale them for hours with loving reflections about their mother or their grandparents.

He wanted to keep their memory alive, and nearly each and every night he was home, he did, no matter how tired, or rushed.

Nighttime was the girls' time, and no crucial meeting or sales target deadline would change that.

His coworkers understood, and more, they admired Foote as the truly loving father he was. Unexpectedly, they also thought that his attention to his girls made him a better CEO, because if he was capable of prioritizing his daughters, with such corporate risk and additional burden of work, then at those times when his *employees* needed him, he'd be there for them in the same, dedicated way.

That's part of the reason those workers kept standing by Foote even through the corporate tough times that the company would encounter in the years ahead. Another reason was that, as they'd expected, Foote stood by *them.*

When a Virginia plant was closed in 1996, it was only done after employees got ample warning and even more than ample outplacement help. Everyone was and is in the loop, for good or ill.

Downsizings are usually done with much corporate and employee venting and publicizing. But typical worker-management tensions, so commonplace in corporate America today, are decidedly less so at USG.

Deluged by a wave of asbestos-liability claims that was walloping the entire building products industry, USG filed for chapter 11 bankruptcy protection twice in the next eight years, under Foote's leadership.

USG was hardly alone in this regard. Since January 2000, massive claims have pushed at least twenty companies that sold or used asbestos products into bankruptcy. At least forty other companies have filed asbestos-related bankruptcies over the past thirty years.

The difference with USG, though—and the reason it's still in business even after two bankruptcy filings—is that it has an emotionally strong chief executive and executive staff, with emotional bonds that extend into every office, and into the working life of every employee.

USG survives because from top to bottom, there's a shared feeling that's stood the tough tests of eight years in a devastated industry: that they're *all* in this, the times and the company, together.

USG continues to struggle with the difficult economic problems that plague many in industrial America today, but it is seeing some promising signs.

The building market itself remained strong, and some of the company's other products, including new ceiling-tile products and ready-mix join compounds, offer USG watchers hopeful reminders that the company's underlying business actually is quite strong.

One man particularly convinced of that is Warren Buffett, a big investor in USG, and when the finest investor in the world has confidence in a company and its CEO, that's encouraging indeed.

Bill Foote has survived his personal bad times, and while he'll always grieve for Andrea, he's remarried and remains a dedicated father. He continues to clamp down on what he calls "extraneous activities," including nonfamily socializing, so he can spend as much time as possible with his daughters and new wife.

This still young, hard-charging chief executive and father has proven something very important by the way he's lived and led, something that many more executives and workers should learn, re-member, and put into practice in their own lives and jobs: It's okay to be human, and it's even more okay to show it. The benefits, both emotionally and professional, are striking.

You can't show the value of these actions on a corporate spread-sheet, or its annual report to stockholders, but that value is there in a corporation's heart . . . as real and as valid as any statistical mile-stone by which a company, any company, should be judged.

STEPPING UP . . . STEPPING DOWN

By 1992, Michael Walsh, CEO of the Tenneco Corporation, a manu-facturing conglomerate, had long been a legend, a Wall Street hero, universally praised as a corporate visionary.

And he was a dynamo. Within twenty-four hours of being named president of the company at only forty-eight years of age, he hacked the dividend 40 percent and initiated sweeping layoffs and asset sales.

Later, he singlehandedly masterminded a $3 billion restructur-ing that took Tenneco from the brink and turned it into a profitable global powerhouse.

After losses of more than $2 billion in 1991 and 1992, including nearly $1.5 billion in restructuring charges, Tenneco was begin-ning to hum.

So many people associated him with Tenneco that few could see Tenneco without him. Much the same was said of Coca Cola Chair-man Roberto Goizueta, after he died of lung cancer, or Jack Welch, after he retired from General Electric, or Walter Wriston, after he left the top job at the old Citicorp to John Reed.

However, Walsh was an extremely rare and corporately self-less CEO with enormous power, who was not only willing to transfer his power, but was farsighted enough to plan his retire-ment and the training and preparation of his successor years be-fore he actually retired.

When he was only forty-nine, Walsh made Dana Mead his first big hire in March 1992, plucking him from a top executive post at International Paper.

Mead was now Tenneco's president and chief operating officer, and Walsh had appointed him as what corporate America likes to call his "handpicked successor."

Any smart CEO can make his first major hire, a gifted and experienced executive who can contribute to the company at a variety of high levels. But for Walsh to make his first such hire his own successor is remarkable indeed.

The value to Tenneco was obvious and huge. The legendary Walsh could spend perhaps ten years or more training and educating his successor, gradually increasing Mead's responsibilities, so that when the succession actually occurred, Mead would be about as perfect a CEO as could be imagined.

In turn, Mead—having the patience to be in the number two position for such a long time, when he could probably have become CEO much sooner at some other company—would be taught to run Tenneco by the legend himself, an extraordinary education and preparation.

However, Mead was being asked to make great professional sacrifices. To think long-term about what was best for Tenneco, rather than what would best advance his own career.

Walsh had made the perfect choice though. Mead was willing to wait through the long years of preparation, realizing the value of that extended succession plan, for Tenneco, himself, and Walsh, as almost no other ambitious executive would have.

The understanding was that Mead was the heir apparent, and that he would spend the necessary years waiting.

He would have a strong and prominent role at the company but it was very much Walsh's company and given the notoriously well-known workaholic's schedule, it would likely remain that way for some time to come.

Mead didn't have a problem with that, and neither did the Tenneco board.

Walsh, who was not yet fifty, appeared to be the picture of vigor and good health—and with no specific retirement date set, Mead settled in for the long haul, with admirable maturity and respect.

With so much understanding between them, and the exact nature of their evolving working relationship clarified before Mead even joined the company, he and Walsh made an outstanding executive team.

The next year, in 1993, Tenneco had net income of $426 million and operating income of $1.1 billion on revenue of more than $13 billion. Walsh was given most of the credit for that, but he and Mead both knew how much Mead had contributed in his characteristically quiet way.

Everything was going even better than expected—until, less than a year after bringing Mead on board, Walsh began feeling ill. He was getting increasingly fatigued, suffering from bouts of headaches and other puzzling neurological symptoms.

I'm still not sure of the order of events, or who Walsh told and when, but I do know Walsh was smart enough to tell Mead first that *something* was going on.

After doctors suggested a biopsy, Walsh reportedly informed Mead again, as well as another senior board member, Dr. Peter Flawn.

But it wasn't until the biopsy showed brain cancer that both Walsh and Mead told the rest of the world.

They also worked together with unusual harmony, to swiftly prepare Mead to be president *and* acting CEO, and then after Walsh's departure, the sole CEO.

Throughout this unexpectedly agonizing and truncated CEO succession, as Walsh prepared to step down, and Mead did everything possible to be ready to step up, the vast Tenneco workforce gave their struggling leaders their full support. There wasn't much they could do directly to help, but what they could they did.

The employees' sympathy, helping out in small but spiritually significant ways, and their trying to keep company operations running as smoothly as possible, made it much easier for Walsh and Mead to concentrate on what was most important for the company and the transfer of power.

Grief and a deep sense of loss were felt by everyone, especially Mead and Walsh. Mead was heartbroken by the possibly imminent loss of his friend and mentor—though ambitious, as good executives are, Mead would much rather have remained the heir apparent for several years more until Walsh retired as planned, than become one of the youngest CEOs at one of America's largest companies.

Walsh knew that he was dying, and thinking of his family, Mead, and Tenneco, he mourned the loss of everything that he and his deputy could have done together to make Tenneco that much better, and fully prepare Mead for his ascendancy.

Both men went to great lengths to keep others informed about what was going on with Walsh's illness. They truly valued communication, and as a result were very much in synch. Both would appear together at countless interviews and analysts' meetings.

That Walsh and Mead could jointly communicate to so many different people about the same excruciating issues, as well as their plans for the company and the inevitable, unexpectedly swift change of power, says a lot about both men. As Mead would later relate to me, it was as if the two of them were on the same wavelength, thinking the same thoughts.

Their goal at each joint appearance was to prove that Walsh was still on top of things and that Mead was there, ready to step in. I can only imagine what both men were going through, particularly Walsh, a revered chief executive, who exuded youth and optimism, debilitated by one of cancer's most fatal strands. Then, as now, very few people survive brain cancer; a tumor of any sort in the brain is notoriously difficult to target.

When my mom was dealing with her brain tumor, I remember, it wasn't the tumor itself that was the gravest concern, but rather the swelling it triggered. The brain is such a sensitive and vulnerable organ that any slight swelling, any artery pinched, pressed, cut off, or choked can put the patient in a vegetative state, sometimes in little more than weeks.

My mom was a very strong, vibrant, and keenly aware person. Realizing what was going on and how it was slowly compromising her capacity to think, act, and move had to have been hellish.

At the time she never let on to me or my siblings just how gruesome the condition was, but knowing that her faculties were waning and deteriorating must have been terrifying beyond my imagination.

For intellectually astute individuals like my mom and Mike Walsh, that had to be the most chilling and painful aspect of all—watching themselves slip away slowly, piece by piece.

A *Fortune* cover story at the time described Walsh's brave new battle to defeat his greatest challenge yet.

Like my mother, he tried new technologies and laser-guided tumor treatments that offered much hope. There were reasons for optimism: signs suggesting that maybe radiation, pinpointed right to the tumor itself, could shrink the mass and reduce the damage.

Eventually, though, hope turned to despair for my mom and everyone in our family, as none of the treatments worked. I can only imagine the similar grief that hit the Walsh family as they too realized that the treatments would be unsuccessful.

Dana Mead, meanwhile, assumed the weight of leading Tenneco, but had no one to share the burden with; seeing his good friend's accelerating illness and diminishing odds, without any ability to help him, only made his new position that much more difficult. He occupied Tenneco's highest office and was all alone. It was an almost impossible situation.

After Walsh began his medical regimen, it was Mead who took on more of the day-to-day duties of running Tenneco, but he never got much attention or publicity for his efforts.

A Vietnam veteran, graduate from West Point (where he'd later become a professor), and proud recipient of a doctorate from MIT, Mead had also served in the U.S. Army for twenty-one years, was a White House fellow and a top executive at International Paper. He was widely known as a disciplined, accomplished figure in the corporate world, but nothing could have prepared him for the prospect of having to assume Walsh's duties only months after arriving at the company.

I know firsthand the wrenching effects of watching someone being ravaged by a disease that cannot be stopped; and I think I can appreciate the extra workload that was passed on to Mead as Walsh's illness progressed. It's astonishing how Mead just assumed the additional pressure, increased responsibilities, and enormous workload, functioning, essentially, as an acting CEO, while standing by his boss as his health deteriorated.

He never sought attention or sympathy and always advanced the notion that the office of CEO still belonged to Walsh. That's not the kind of man he is, and that's why Walsh's choice of Mead to be his successor was quite simply brilliant, even though it was mostly unappreciated at the time.

In looking back at Mead's stewardship while Walsh fought his illness, what impresses me still is his quiet strength, discipline, serene affect, and his ability to take the demands of the very high profile job in without saying much in public. Mead was as forthright and strong as any executive I've seen thrust into such an intense situation. Other executives with bigger egos and less patience would have chafed at the arrangement.

Mead waited to be named CEO officially, although he already had the acting CEO's responsibilities. He looked every inch the corporate boss. Tall and commanding up to his neatly cropped white hair, Mead *breathed* gravitas. (Years later, after he'd left Tenneco, I used to joke with Mead that he looked like he'd been sent by central casting to play the role of CEO!) No doubt his appearance eased one of the most difficult transitions I've ever seen in business.

Although he never publicly showed how taxing his ascension was, Mead would later tell me, "It was a very difficult period." As succession programs go, "it was pretty intense."

Part of that intensity was due to the commitment on the part of both men to make the succession seamless, and almost flawless. Under the circumstances, living up to those goals required almost superhuman effort, particularly on Walsh's part.

In February 1994, Walsh stepped down as chief executive. Mead became Tenneco's sole leader. He would say of Walsh, the man he was replacing, that "he is fighting a very tough battle right now."

When asked whether Walsh's condition had improved, Mead would simply answer, "no, it hasn't." He would say no more, and no less.

Part of their understanding was that Mead would maintain what had been their mutual commitment to change and willingness to take huge chances. Mead proceeded to focus on the big projects that were still of paramount concern to Tenneco shareholders, including the planned restructuring and sale of the company's 35 percent stake in its Case Corporation farm and construction equipment unit. Walsh and Mead had agreed when they first discussed the situation nearly a year earlier that restructuring Case was a top priority for Tenneco.

The difference now, with Walsh almost certainly dying, was that it was up to Mead to quietly win the biggest corporate battle of his life.

Also, with Walsh so intimately identified with Tenneco, there were persistent questions regarding Mead's ability to replace a man so widely praised. Mead's year-long tenure as Tenneco president—during which he was very much in Mead's shadow—hadn't definitively answered that concern.

Mead's fitness to occupy a position last held by a legend was not merely a question of competence, but of history: Walsh was Tenneco's Babe Ruth, and no one remembers who took Babe Ruth's spot in the Yankee lineup. Indisputably, for all of his mentoring and public praise for the man who would replace him, Walsh was a tough act to follow.

I don't think the corporate pundits ever really counted on a guy like Dana Mead to carry on Tenneco's mission. The fact that he did, flawlessly executing the Case restructuring only three months after Walsh lost his fight with cancer, had turned Tenneco completely over to Mead's leadership, belying the age-old corporate truism that it's tough for the guy who replaces a legend. Mead, in fact, surpassed Walsh in many respects.

The fact that the company's stock held its own, and that investors stuck with Tenneco through the whole ordeal of Walsh's illness and eventual death, says much about both men.

The problem too often with executives who follow legends is that they try not to rock the boat or alter what their predecessor has created. What they fail to understand is that what won the former CEO acclaim was a willingness to reshape and recharge a company. As Jack Welch himself has reminded me often, "You have to be willing to tear something down completely to build it up at all." It's rare, however, that people taking over for great corporate executives realize that fact, particularly early in their tenures.

Mead had already made the same huge commitment to change, and proved his willingness to take great risks, even before he joined Tenneco. Those shared qualities were part of why they came together, and then functioned so well. After Walsh's death, Mead proved that he could do on his own what he and Walsh had begun to do together.

As Mead moved Tenneco through the mid-nineties, he was an active player; by the end of the decade, he was pushing information technology as his next big campaign at Tenneco. This is where Mead's military experience came in handy. He appreciated the value of information of almost any sort. It was under Mead's leadership that Tenneco pursued information technology initiatives that would have made Werner Van Braun blush.

It's obvious why Mead was the overwhelming choice to head the National Association of Manufacturers in 1997. He took a largely staid, traditional group and, as one reporter stated a few months later, "rocketed them into the next century."

Mead spoke about staying on top of technology, and making sure that employees always have access to new advances. Early on he realized that the best workforce was technologically literate, bringing new efficiencies to the factory floor and beyond, and he set out to excite manufacturers about the possibilities.

Mead also focused on the basics, including cutting material and operating costs as Tenneco expanded abroad. Following Walsh's lead as it did, there was nothing timid about Mead's strategy. He knew that in order to stay strong and true to his predecessor's vision, he had to constantly innovate, and sometimes destroy.

While other companies pegged their hopes to their ballooning stocks, Mead used his market currency wisely: He consolidated eleven data centers into one, and overhauled and ultimately divested Tenneco's shipbuilding, energy-equipment, and agricultural subsidiaries, all while scooping up more than two dozen companies worth a staggering $3 billion.

There is much to admire about Mead's career, and especially his innovative leadership of Tenneco, but to me his handling of Walsh's illness represents his greatest achievement, one both corporate and personal. His communication, obvious discretion, and compassion helped pave the way for one of the best transfers of corporate power in American history.

Michael Walsh was already Wall Street royalty when Mead joined him, but he added to that legend by his own approach to the succession, his openness, and his effective collaboration with his deputy when tragedy changed their lives. Walsh deserves all the credit and admiration he's been given.

Mead's achievements are different because they're so little known and unheralded. That's always been fine with him because his actions were motivated by passion and belief, not glory. He did it all with a smile and steadfast determination.

He deserves the highest accolades for this unsung part of his career, but he'll never ask for them, and doesn't consider them important. His life is guided by higher values.

He's the shadow CEO who quietly assumed more duties and headaches, and never boasted, never shouted, never sought out headlines and fawning press accounts.

Dana Mead performed without looking like a performer. Some call that stature; I call it *gravitas*.

CHAPTER 11

"UP IN SMOKE"

Imagine working your whole life to get a business up and running, and suddenly in one devastating moment, it's gone. Everything you worked for; everything you built; everything you devoted your life to . . . all of it up in smoke, just like that.

Imagine being Aaron Feuerstein, whose family-owned Malden Mills textile company was lost after a fire destroyed its main factory in Lawrence, Massachusetts.

Or Milton Cole, whose own Logansport, Indiana, hardwood company similarly went up in flames, wiping out 190,000 square feet of warehouse and half of Cole's lumber handling equipment.

Or Jack and Suren Avedisian, the father and son owners of Massachusetts-based Omni Foods, an eclectic grocer that prides itself on personal service and fosters intense customer loyalty, who lost their premier store when fire in a neighboring four-story building in Newton, Massachusetts, spread to their facility.

Fire demolished what each family had worked sometimes several generations to build.

Each of these owners could have cashed out, depositing insurance checks that would have kept them and their families well taken care of for years to come. That would have been the easy way out—but none of them chose to take it. So committed were they to their customers, their employees, and their businesses that they found ways to keep going. But even that's not the whole story.

Normally when businesses rebuild, they lay off people, and if those let go are lucky, some are rehired when the business is back up and running.

People lose jobs every day. It's part of the predictable, often tragic, ebb and flow of working life. These days, in fact, more companies are inclined to jettison workers first, and address other cost-cutting efforts later.

It's almost gospel for publicly traded companies to fire employees as a way to prove their "financial manhood" to Wall Street. Appearing to be serious about cutting costs and dumping workers—many of them, preferably—companies will try to send the message that they're not fooling around. There is no other way to explain the sudden jump in stock prices for companies that announce big layoffs. It's an ugly, time-proven strategy that's entirely too accepted among businesses.

Even privately held concerns often can think of no better short-term solution to a financial crunch than mass firings, just to get through.

But not so for small business owners Feuerstein, Cole, and the Avedesians; after the fires, which eliminated thousands of jobs, these owners, even though they didn't have the money to do it, made sure that all of their unemployed workers were paid and protected until the businesses had been rebuilt and the jobs re-established. One of the business owners protected his employees even when his company went into debt.

They did this while their ravaged businesses were generating no income and, in fact, required considerable expenditures to rebuild. When the businesses reopened, the employees all came back, after turning down job offers from other companies.

WHEN YOU CAN STAND THE HEAT . . .

It was December 1995, and Aaron Feuerstein had some tough decisions to make. His company, Malden Mills, was on life support after his key facility was destroyed by fire. One of New England's largest fleece-makers was on the verge of extinction.

They couldn't get their merchandise out, and it likely would be months, if not years, before they could accept product, manufacture it, and get it out again. In New England's intensely competitive textile world, Malden was the industry's dead-man-walking.

Advisors suggested that Feuerstein pack up, take his insurance check, and go home; it had been a good run, after all. But Feuerstein would hear none of it. The sixty-nine-year-old company founder had put too much time, effort, and money into Malden simply to walk away from his enterprise.

What's more, he couldn't betray his employees, who built the company with him. As he told reporters at the time, "What right do I have to destroy a major city just to get a few more dollars in the bank that I won't spend before I die? The money would only go to my children and spoil them."

To protect the nearly 3,000 workers at his Malden Mills factories in Lawrence and nearby Methuen, Massachusetts, Feuerstein did something unprecedented in those—or any—parts, and on a sweeping scale: Immediately after the fire, Feuerstein decided to continue paying each of his employees for the months it would take to rebuild the company and restart production.

Never mind that he was already getting pressure to move his mills to cheaper locales, especially overseas. One restructuring expert said that such a move could cut his labor costs in half, and maybe more.

In explaining his reluctance, though, he insisted again and again that the employees *are* Malden. Without them, "there is no Malden Mills."

He was able to put about half of them to work during the three months of reconstruction, but whether his employees were working full-time, part-time, or not at all, he paid and took care of every one of them.

That fierce loyalty to his troops instantly won him unintended fame. For example, Feuerstein was seated near then-first lady Hillary Rodham Clinton during Bill Clinton's 1996 State of the Union address. President Clinton used Feuerstein as a "symbol of hope" for sticking by his workers, rebuilding his mills, and paying their salaries while rebuilding his factory.

Regrettably, even after Malden Mills was operating at full capacity, Feuerstein still had plenty of problems. His customers had left him for other vendors. But even as the company's struggles increased, he continued to pay the people who had stuck with him and Malden Mills.

Finally, though, Malden's financial situation was so dire that he was forced to lay off 300 workers in 1998—something a publicly traded company would doubtlessly have done "years earlier."

The company fell into bankruptcy, but it's still working its way out, and unlike many in that position, it's doing so with intensely loyal workers, who are more than willing to make concessions to the man who under reduced circumstances had committed to each and every one of them, all those years ago.

Many MBAs will seize on Malden Mills's troubles as proof that being generous to workers when times are tough only makes things worse for the company, and its employees.

I studied Malden Mills's troubles quite closely and came to a very different conclusion. The problem wasn't corporate generosity, but bad timing. Slow sales of the company's well-known Polartec outdoor fleece and other soft fabrics were beyond any executive's control.

Rebuilding the mills and keeping the employees paid until they could work again gave Feuerstein peace of mind—the reassuring knowledge that the company had a workforce already in place and ready to go.

Had he not paid them during those months, they'd have gotten other jobs just to survive, and he'd have had to start a long period of hiring new employees, who'd need time to learn their jobs before Malden Mills could really be at full speed again.

Since the layoffs in 1998, there have been hopeful signs, and things are still hopeful today. "Made in America" has taken on a whole new meaning after September 11. And everything about Malden Mills is "made in America," an issue not lost on then Army General Tommy Franks, who ordered millions of dollars worth of the company's Polartec gear for the military. Thanks to that commitment, Malden has received $30 million in defense department contracts—and, according to Feuerstein, more are on the way.

It's too early to say, of course, whether multimillion dollar defense contracts alone will turn his business around, or whether there'll be a continued resurgence in demand for lightweight fleece in shirts, blankets, and military gear, as there appears to be now.

Malden Mills is also losing the fight against cheaper foreign competition. Feuerstein could have moved some of his mills overseas after the fire, reaping the benefits of much lower labor costs, but he refused to, preferring to pay more to keep his business in New England. Finally, the company is struggling in the generally tough economic environment for textiles that Feuerstein has no control over.

Whatever reorganization plans the now seventy-seven-year-old Feuerstein can persuade his creditors to adopt, they'll leave him with a reduced role in the company he built. But for his workers, having Feuerstein at Malden Mills in any capacity is motivating and inspiring.

They know that if the creditors decide on new management, a lot of jobs may be shifted overseas, but they also know that as long as their rugged, determined leader is part of the company, he'll fight as long as he able to stop any flow of jobs out of America.

For his part, Feuerstein will be the first to admit he made one mistake: He didn't file for a patent for some of his processes, and he accrued debt too quickly after the fire.

But he thinks better days are ahead for his company and his workers. Regardless of the future, Feuerstein always stood by them, when so many recommended that he simply walk away.

TALL TIMBER

Plenty of advisors told Milton Cole the same thing they told Aaron Feuerstein: Take the insurance money and run. Cole was in a similar situation; his self-built empire was also in smoldering ruins.

On Saturday, June 13, 1998, at about 3:00 P.M., Cole received a telephone call telling him that there had been a fire in one of Cole Hardwood's sheds.

"When I arrived at the lumber yard," he said at the time, "I felt the fire was under control as it was just one building. Somehow the fire got into the lumber shed west of the one that was burning, and within 30 minutes the fire was ablaze in the second lumber shed."

At that point, the fire could not be contained. Thirty-one fire departments were called out to deal with what some said at the time was the "hottest fire" in Indiana history.

"We lost eleven buildings and eight-and-a-half million board feet of inventory of hardwood," Cole recalled. Half of the company's lumber-handling equipment was gone as well. For Milton and his wife, Jean, the news couldn't be worse.

In 1986, they'd bought the sleepy, backwater lumber concern where Milton had worked for thirty years, and turned it into an international powerhouse, doing business in more than forty countries on every continent except Antarctica.

They had also branched out, adding another company, Indiana Dimension, Inc., specializing in cabinet and furniture component parts and moldings, as well as hardwood flooring. But everything fed off Cole Hardwood, and with that operation largely destroyed, Indiana Dimension would suffer too.

Milton Cole was well-insured, and after the fire, with more than half his business destroyed, the insurance company offered him nearly $14 million. That sum, and their considerable savings in the bank, would have allowed the then sixty-three-year-old Cole and his wife to live happily ever after.

But Cole wasn't thinking about his own comfort. Like Aaron Feuerstein's Malden Mills, Cole Hardwood represented more than Cole and his wife—it was the lifeblood of the community, and many people depended on its survival, especially the one hundred workers in Logansport, Indiana, who suddenly found themselves unemployed.

What amazes people to this day is why Cole moved so fast to re-build. Usually a decision of that sort takes time and, as Cole later admitted to National Public Radio, on the night of the fire he was leaning toward closing Cole Hardwood's doors.

"That evening if you would have asked me if I'd rebuild, I'd have probably said no," he told NPR. "But after I got a good night's rest, I got up Sunday morning, [and] I was re-energized, ready to go. And so, I knew I was going to rebuild."

In a revealing interview at the time with the Oklahoma City *Journal Record,* Cole said he owed it to the community to come back and make things right. "The community has just been so gracious to me," he said. "My employees, I just love them. They're just part of the family."

For Cole it was a practical decision as well as an emotional one. "We were running probably 70 percent efficient," he continued. "I just feel they made [the company], and I owed it to them. And we've done very well, and I'm just willing to share."

Cole told an Associated Press reporter later that his only true luxuries in life were a "couple of cans of Bud Light and a cigar" every Friday evening on his farm. As a result, he could afford to share with his workforce, and most importantly, he *wanted* to.

Those who knew Cole weren't surprised that he wouldn't take the cash and duck out. Partly, it was because the rough-and-tumble hardwood business was in his blood. He had grown up in Munford, Tennessee, where buzz saws were the rule, and sawdust was everywhere.

After Cole lost a couple of fingers and had one of his hands crushed, he went on to a lumber school in Memphis. The move proved prescient: It was there, in 1956, that he met John Schafer, the owner of a little hardwood operation in Logansport. Schafer offered Cole a job, and he took it.

The relationship proved fruitful. For the next thirty years, Cole learned the ropes from Schafer, every tiny detail and aspect of the wood business. He bought Schafer's small company outright in 1986, and things went brilliantly . . . until the fire.

Less than two days after the fire, Cole stood in front of his workers and said he would rebuild. But the topper for the crowd was his next promise: "No one would miss a paycheck. No one."

As Greg Baer, a lumber inspector with three kids, told the *Journal Record* at the time, "That really took the load off everybody. It would've been so easy for him to not go through all this again. But knowing him, it's no surprise."

As another employee said, "he's more concerned about his workers than he is for his business." Still another said of this ambitious, ebullient CEO: "He just put everyone in a good mood. The guy had to be feeling very anxious, very worried. But he was more concerned about us. He was putting it all on the line for us. We never forgot that."

As Cole told the *Journal Bulletin* about his employees, "They made the company. I didn't."

In the days that followed, Cole acted as chief company cheerleader, touring the grounds and greeting every worker, assuring them and on occasion, singing "Happy Birthday" to them.

I know quite a few chief executives who talk about how important the employees are to their companies, but I don't think there are too many who would sacrifice much, if at all, for them, whatever their "importance."

Cole's fierce loyalty was keenly rewarded as workers made sacrifices of their own for their boss in ways that were obvious, and in others that were not.

Today, this simple man has a thriving business. Cole Hardwood has emerged to become one of the nation's leading hardwood suppliers. Cole boasts about their accomplishments on the company web site, but it's the other things he brags about that really stand out. "I'm even prouder to say how we did it," he says. "We did it by serving our customers, large and small, meeting their ever-changing needs with constant solutions and innovations."

He goes on to say that Cole provides "The kind of quality that's only possible with commitment. From every department. From every person. Every day. Cole Hardwood, Inc., is a leader today and we'll be a leader tomorrow. That's a promise. A solid promise, of course."

Many executives make promises, but Cole *kept* his, with gutsy determination and a goal—to protect his workers and his company. He rallied around them and, today, they're still rallying around him.

Back in 1998, his company was on the brink of disaster; today it's an industry leader, because Cole had a good business model, and an even better personal one.

THE FOOD OF LIFE

I'm not one for shopping; I don't spend much time at the grocery store. I do like food, but the prospect of hunting it down in a store almost makes me want to consider a diet. Heaven forbid!

But I know that there are people, like my wife, Mary, who actually enjoy this experience. For them, grocery shopping has a special meaning. They notice the little things: not only the price of food, but its variety and quality as well. They remember how friendly or helpful the butcher is, the variety of vegetables, and the appeal of special store-made items. Mary will travel a long way to go to a store that provides just the right food and services, because in the end, she says, it's the little stuff that makes a big difference.

A store that caters to special needs gets a special response and solicits unshakeable loyalty from its customers. They adore their favorite grocery stores, and they go the extra mile to shop there.

Omni Foods has customers like that, who say there's no other store like them. For them, shopping at Omni Foods is darn near a religious experience.

In an era of supermarket chains and corporate mega-stores, Omni is a cozy oasis, where customer attention is paramount, and quality service is gospel. The management for the Meredith, New Hampshire-based mini-empire of three thriving grocery stores is a family affair. Actually, it's a father-and-son affair.

Jack Avedisian and his son Suren are a powerful combination, committed to great service, to the point of being maniacal about it. They live with the reality that people can shop for food at any number of stores these days. "It used to be the grocery store was the only place you could go," Suren told me. "Now there's Wal-Mart and [so] many others."

It's often said that large companies can beat little companies on the big stuff, but they have a tougher time competing on the special details, and that's where the Avedisians shine. For example, Jack and Suren always place organic or natural products alongside regular groceries. There are expanded sections of Hispanic, Greek, and Italian foods that cater to area neighborhoods. They carry the best beef, the best fish, the best chicken. Discerning customers know that Omni stores are a cut above, and the Avedisians make sure that they stay that way.

Credit Jack for getting the ball rolling: He started his supermarket career as a cashier at Star Market Company in 1950. Back then, there were only four stores in the Star chain. But the chain grew, and so did Jack's role in the company. From cashier, he moved through the ranks of store operations, merchandising, and advertising, until he eventually became an executive vice president. By the time he retired from Star Market in 1981, the company had more than sixty stores.

But while he was done with Star, Jack wasn't done with the grocery business. Upon his retirement, he purchased a Star Market location in Guilford, New Hampshire, and renamed it Jackson's Star.

Suren shared his father's zeal for the business. A graduate of Harvard Business School, he joined his father in 1989, after a fourteen-year career marketing packaged goods and software. That same year, they added another Boston-area location in the town of Weston.

A year later, they opened a third store, also called Jackson's Star, in Meredith, New Hampshire. And in 1993, they added a fourth, in Chestnut Hill, another Boston suburb.

By 1996, the Gilford store was closed, but the three that remained enjoyed almost cult-like appeal among their customers, who found the attention to detail and incredible selection second to none.

Friends say Suren's technological savvy helped the Avedisians monitor the details that Omni's customers value: "Providing quality perishables, great variety, and the best service in each store."

—————

Never mind that bigger, richer neighboring stores had scared smaller players away; Omni Foods enjoys wrestling with the big boys. In 1997, the Avedisians decided to open a 32,000-square-foot store right in the middle of "superstore alley," where giant Pathmarks and Stop-and-Shops dominated the scene.

"We realize that this is a very competitive area," Suren Avedisian told the *Boston Herald* at the time. "And yes, we are surrounded by superstores. But a lot of customers have told us that they like a store that's a little bit smaller and personal. They say it makes for a more pleasurable shopping experience."

Jack Avedisian was also quoted in the *Herald* article, saying, "We've ended up with everything the big guys have in a superstore, in a condensed version, and in a way that makes people more comfortable."

There, are of course, disadvantages for a small independent chain, and Suren doesn't dismiss the fact that bigger competitors have a certain price advantage. He told me, "Sure, we are aggressive on pricing and sales items. We compete with the Stop and Shop's every day of the week. I can't buy like they can, but we're still competitive. When a customer comes in and buys an all natural steak from us, it's going to cost them, but they keep coming back."

Suren explained the amazing customer loyalty and willingness to pay higher prices: "We try to cater to a more discerning population. We have a lot of natural meats and organic produce. Customers come to us looking for those alternatives. They know that when they come here to buy something, they are getting quality."

And for the Avedisians, good business is more than stocking the best food and offering the most helpful service. Maintaining exemplary, competitive grocery stores also meant taking care of their workers.

"We try and treat our people very well," Suren said. "We pay them accordingly. We get the store personnel involved in every detail of the business, and in every store remodel. We ask them, 'What are the items you want to carry. What don't you want to carry? What space can you live with? What can't you live with?"

Scheduling was flexible, and good behavior, especially helpful behavior, was rewarded. It's no surprise that turnover, a constant problem in the grocery industry, was much less of an issue at Omni Foods.

Kids who joined the staff stayed with Omni. Some who started in high school continued there while they went through college, not only for the benefits, but because of the support they got from their bosses.

Suren adds, "We try and treat people as we would like to be treated. We won't ask someone to do something that either we wouldn't do or haven't done ourselves."

The Avedisians constantly strive to make shopping and working at their stores a pleasurable experience. Omni doesn't just cater to its communities. Jack and Suren make each store's customers, employees, and communities the essential center of their entire operation. Those priorities were well-established by February 9, 2000.

On that date, everything changed. A massive fire in Chestnut Hill demolished a four-story building, and destroyed a neighboring hair salon, restaurant, eyeglass emporium, and dozens of small offices. Among the buildings hit was Omni's Chestnut Hill store.

"My father and I were standing outside watching the fire," Suren remembered. "We knew our store was okay, but the building next door was not." That four-story structure was in rubble.

Unfortunately, a wall joined the Omni store to the adjacent building ravaged by fire; the blaze had been so devastating, and the damage done to the wall the store shared with the ruined, broken building was so extensive, that the fire authorities were concerned that the wall wouldn't hold—knowing that if it collapsed it would bring down the Omni store. There were also worries about additional structural damage and the possibility that the building would have to be gutted.

With one building in ruins, and the Omni store held up on one side by a severely damaged wall that was basically unsupported, there was a vast amount of rebuilding to do and considerable concern about safety hazards.

After the fire, the authorities kept the Chestnut Hill store shut down, closed to customers and employees, as the city went about the planned rehabilitation of the building very carefully.

The owners hoped to reopen within a few weeks, but because the store shared the damaged wall with the gutted building, realistically, the reconstruction could take longer than everyone was hoping.

Jack and Suren were worried about how to proceed. They could replace their inventory, most of which was destroyed by fire hoses, to new products to sell when the store reopened. But that was a month away—at best.

More important, they didn't know what to do about their eighty-five employees at the Chestnut Hill store, twenty-five of whom worked full-time. Many had been there since the store first opened in 1993.

Suren recalled the company's early days for the *Boston Globe,* paying special attention to their appreciation of their employees: "We just didn't have anything concrete to tell them about when they could come back," he said. "A lot of people live paycheck to paycheck. We didn't want them to worry and we didn't want them to drift off."

Later he explained to me both his and his dad's thinking. "We knew they were nervous. Right then and there, that night, we told everyone, don't worry, your jobs are okay. It was a risk, no doubt about it. But we figured it would be three to five weeks before the store was back up and running, so why not?"

So Suren and Jack came up with a plan: They'd keep paying the eighty-five employees, and preserve their benefits. No matter how long it took, they would stick by them. They had been there for the Avedisians when they were building the company, and the father and son would stand by their employees as they rebuilt the store.

Tim Sarrasin, a supervisor at the Chestnut Hill store who began at Omni as a meat cutter, told the *Globe* that he wasn't surprised by his bosses' generosity. "I should be surprised, but I'm not. I knew myself, working for them for ten years, there would be nothing to worry about. I had to convince my wife, though."

Sarrasin and his coworkers could easily and quickly have found jobs elsewhere. The economy was strong at the time, and they would have been hired as soon as they made themselves available.

There is a certain cachet about being an Omni employee. Hiring any one of them in the grocery world is akin to nabbing a General Electric guy in the corporate world. Their reputation is that good, and their esteemed work ethic is well known.

A nearby Star Market, and at least two other area superstores were hiring, but Omni's workers weren't biting. "I couldn't find this job, with these people," anywhere else, Sarrasin said, so he stuck with Omni, along with virtually all his colleagues.

Almost immediately after the fire, they started pitching in wherever they could at other Omni stores, and even participated in the rebuilding process, helping out in any way they could.

Soon after the fire, there were so many of the Chestnut Hill workers helping out at the nearby Weston store that it seemed like Omni employees outnumbered the delighted customers, many of whom recognized the familiar faces.

Even the customers pitched in—if the Chestnut Hill facility couldn't serve them for the time being, they'd go to other Omni stores. They were that loyal, despite the inconvenience to many of them. But they were willing to make that longer drive to the two other stores, just to support the Avedisians.

"Our customers are very loyal," Suren told me. "They were calling the city. We had a trailer [at the sight of the fire] and a phone line in there. We were talking to customers all the time, talking about our reopening plans."

What the loyal and generous customers and workers didn't realize though, after the fire destroyed the Chestnut Hill store, was just how much the constant delays in reopening the store were costing the Avedisians.

"We kept pushing the demolition people to move faster," Suren explained. "From three weeks to get the company back in business, the schedule just kept getting pushed back." The fire apparently was so devastating, and the damage to the offending wall so difficult to fix, that city officials kept rescheduling the opening day. One month went by, then two, then three.

"I'll be honest," Suren told me. "We were getting worried." He knew that paying their people was the right and decent thing to do. But paying them indefinitely, in the face of constant delays and problems, was an entirely different matter.

"We did start talking about how much further we could go with this. At the beginning of the fourth month, when the rebuilding was getting significantly delayed, we kept asking ourselves, 'Can we go another month or two like this?' We would revisit that every two weeks."

But each week, they kept their promise. Although out of work, those employees weren't out of hope, and the Avedisians made sure, week after week, that their employees were provided for, and, more practically, that they wouldn't start pursuing the other jobs they could so easily get.

"Had this gone on for nine months, we might not have been able to do it," Suren explained. But in the meantime the family did not waver from their commitment. "There was no disagreement in the family," Suren said. "We all decided this was what had to be done."

So they continued paying their people, each week for nearly six months. That's how long it took to get the store back up and running.

By the time the store finally reopened on July 21, 2000, only five out of eighty-five employees had left for jobs at other companies. The rest had waited, worked at the other Omni stores, and helped as much as they could, wanting to come back to the store, and holding on as hard as the Avedisians had.

When the Chestnut Hill store was open again, and its workers could really get back to work, they were all truly grateful to return to their jobs. Suren and Jack were grateful as well—after all, loyalty is a two-way street. "If we had said to everyone, 'You're laid off,' we'd have had severe difficulty hiring these people back," Suren told me.

The employees weren't the only ones that were happy the company had stuck by them—the customers were thrilled as well. When the Chestnut Hill store reopened its doors that summer, it was as if those patient, loyal, devoted shoppers all raced to the store at the same time, in sheer joy.

Women kissed the store owners and clerks. Customers gathered in groups, talking in the aisles, catching up on all that had happened in the past six months, often pulling the employees into their conversations. Some of them were too busy enjoying the renovated Chestnut Hill store and each other to actually shop.

Suren Avedisian took it all in, happily. "This really isn't our store," he told the *Globe*. "It's theirs. It's their Omni Foods, their place to see many of their friends." The Avedisians found the reopening personally very rewarding.

For almost six months, customers had to go somewhere else, Suren recalled, and he remains extremely appreciative of those who came to help out, and who for those long months made even longer drives to shop at the other two Omni stores.

"I'm not going to say they all came back, but we kept plugging away at it, and a lot of them did come back."

The following January, the American Jewish Congress of the New England Region presented Jack and Suren Avedisian with a Special Recognition Award. The two were honored for their compassion toward their workers after the fire.

"The theme of the annual meeting was corporate responsibility," said Paul Dunphy, speaking for the American Jewish Congress. "The Avedisians exemplify that theme by moving quickly to allay concerns after the disastrous fire that occurred at their Newton store."

Today, Omni is among the most successful grocers in all of New England, thriving in a market of superstores and mega-complexes that were thought to be sure to bring about its demise.

When Suren looks back on the fire, he talks of the lessons learned from good deeds done. "Sure we kept pushing those demolition people to move fast," he remembers. "But I have no regrets about doing what we did. It was the right thing to do."

I asked whether he and his dad were ever tempted, even for a moment, to simply accept the fat insurance check. "Never," he answered. "There was no temptation at all to take the insurance money and run."

The family had too much time, effort, and money invested in the region. Sure, after the fire shut down one store, it still had two other thriving stores. But the Chestnut Hill store was special, and so were its customers, and, particularly, its employees. How could the family abandon any of them?

Unwavering loyalty, dedication, and commitment are simple credos, but they've held the family through its toughest times, and hold them together now. The Avedisians ignored financial advisors who warned them not to even think of paying workers when they're not working. Milton Cole ignored similar advice, as did Aaron Feuerstein, who at seventy-seven is still fighting to keep his company going.

They all risked huge financial losses. Feuerstein and his company actually went into bankruptcy, and then re-emerged because he wouldn't quit. But that they'd pay and support their unemployed workers for however long was necessary was never even in question. Their decisions were made in the heart, where notions about what's best for others register most clearly.

As owners of family businesses, with corporate and personal responsibilities integrated into their operations, they cared, of course, about their bottom lines, but when it really mattered, they cared more about the people who helped them achieve it. They showed them intense loyalty, and in return, were rewarded with the same.

Many of their employees have said that they would walk on hot coals for Milton Cole, Aaron Feuerstein, and Jack and Suren Avedisian. Doing a good deed can have that effect on people, and a positive response to misfortune can inspire and motivate a dispirited workforce.

Great men and women achieve most when success is most in doubt, when the odds are too daunting, and the obstacles seem insurmountable. It's by defeating their own fears that the victors go on to much greater triumphs.

Guided by good hearts, keen vision, and astute decisions, they build better companies by surviving the bad luck that eventually plagues every business, going on to accomplish much to enrich their employees, their customers, and their companies.

We can learn a lot from two grocers, a hardwood guy, and a textile mogul. Different industries, same theme: Give, even when it hurts.

You'll be surprised by the results.

CHAPTER 12

ON A WING
AND A PRAYER

Herb Kelleher is the third of the trio of great entrepreneurial visionaries whose remarkable life stories and careers I'm describing in this book.

I've always believed that heroes define history and are defined by their times. Kelleher is the earliest of these three entrepreneurs, launching his enterprise almost forty years ago, in the middle 1960s. That his new career and company would span five decades, and still be growing in the twenty-first century, is a tremendous testament to the power of his corporate vision, and his adaptability to a changing market.

Kelleher shares many of the splendid, entertaining, and triumphant qualities of Roger Ailes and Richard Branson. And just as they have their own unique characteristics, background, and range of achievement, so too does he. In fact, the story of Kelleher's company and career is colorful and outrageous enough to sound like a fictional saga, colored by the special glow of the wild American West. Kelleher, Branson, and Ailes powerfully demonstrate how great visionaries can have so much and so little in common. In contrast to Branson's international flare and marketing savvy, and Ailes's political sophistication, Kelleher is a figure right out of Texas folklore.

There are so many extraordinary stories about Herb Kelleher (about how he got his revolutionary concept for his company, and the crazy things he did in the years that followed), that they seem to be classic Texas tall tales—except that they're all true.

In 1966, Kelleher was practicing law in San Antonio, apparently happy to spend the rest of his life as an attorney. And then one of his clients, Rollin King, suggested to Kelleher an idea, reportedly dreamed up in a bar, for a new company that had nothing to do with running a law practice. Kelleher liked the business concept so much that he scribbled it down on a cocktail napkin.

That was the genesis of the company Kelleher would build, despite ferocious and protracted legal battles with potential competitors, which he would turn into one of the best-run businesses in the world, still beating its many opponents after all these years.

What makes his story even more remarkable is that thirty-three years after scribbling a note on a napkin, the widely loved CEO suffered and survived an experience more devastating than all the early court fights combined—and then went on to adopt a greater mission, which he faithfully executed, in his inimitable Texan way.

By the 1960s, the airline industry was well regulated and well protected, and the skies were ruled by the established behemoths, including United, American, Delta, Eastern, and Northwest, who protected their fiefdoms with medieval ruthlessness. In the conventional thinking of airline executives, there was neither room, nor time for any competing entity to enter the industry and become a threat.

As the market evolved over the decades, massive companies seemed to possess the only business model that worked—airlines were either colossal, or they didn't exist. Each of the major airlines had spent many years building and expanding their operations to grow to mammoth sizes. Any upstart airline would be too small to compete, and given the economies of scale, and the staggering costs involved, the expense alone would crush any small new airline. But what complacent CEOs and their executives didn't know in 1966 was that a San Antonio lawyer, energized by the intoxicated and intoxicating idea that his client Rollin King had given him, was developing his vision of an airline that could operate on a smaller scale, and effectively compete with the industry leaders.

Kelleher surveyed the industry's landscape and concluded that its prices were too high and its standards too low. The airlines were taking advantage of the American public, providing them with poor service, and themselves with fat profits.

His airline would reverse that equation—he'd provide great service at low prices. Kelleher decided to start a cut-rate airline flying to and from major cities in Texas, including Dallas, San Antonio, and Houston. And it would be cheap—*real* cheap; he asked for $20 to fly from Dallas to Houston, a fraction of what his rivals charged.

To maximize profit, he would keep costs very low, and turn the planes around quickly. The goal, inconceivable and simply ridiculous to airline executives, would be to get a plane in and out of the gate within twenty minutes. Even today, that's still close to impossible.

And Kelleher had precisely no experience in the airline industry.

But that was no deterrent. Kelleher had a vision, a true entrepreneurial spirit, and determination in spades. It appeared that he actually preferred to stare down huge obstacles, because the more challenges there were, the more fun he'd have.

A proud Texan and resident of the great American southwest, overlooked and dismissed by so many as being mostly a vast desert, Kelleher dubbed his new company Southwest Airlines. Rather than choosing a regal name like American or United, Kelleher intended to emphasize that his airline was deliberately—and advantageously—regional.

He was convinced that a regional carrier promising discount prices and friendly service could do very well in an area of the country where many fliers felt neglected and forgotten.

The difference at Southwest would be its attitude and its service. Southwest's passengers would get the benefit of an airline that reflected the personality and character of its energetic, passionate, fun-loving founder. He also planned to do more than democratize the air travel industry—he was going to turn it upside down, and have a blast doing it.

A consummate partier, Kelleher enjoyed his drink and his smokes. As he told one crowd: "Wild Turkey whiskey and Philip Morris cigarettes are essential to the maintenance of human life!" Kelleher, ever entertaining, also rode a Harley and did Elvis impersonations. To his mind, his exuberance made him even more qualified to be the first successful challenger to the airline industry in many years.

Later, when Southwest Airlines was off the ground and in the air, Kelleher had a meeting with Bob Crandall, CEO of American Airlines. When the meeting was over, Kelleher left Crandall's offices with Crandall's cigarette lighter in his pocket.

"He was quitting smoking, so I told him he didn't need them anymore."

Kelleher always knew how to endear himself to his competitors. When he was far enough along in his planning, preparation, and financing to begin operating Southwest, his giant rivals learned of his concept, and, up in arms, they took Kelleher to court to stop his new venture.

Despite their size and power, the idea of this little airline scared the industry's major players, because as crazy and unconventional as it sounded, they knew that it might work. And the huge airlines couldn't have a tiny airline, ferrying passengers around in Texas, sneaking away with their business. They understood that if Southwest caught on, they'd be under siege from armies of small, regional, low-fare airlines, each of them stealing pieces of their market share.

So the major airlines not only took Kelleher to court once, they sued him for more than *five years*. They had to, because Kelleher wouldn't quit—he'd spent his entire professional career as a practicing lawyer, and he felt comfortable in the courtroom. It's safe to say that the mere fact of the lawsuits encouraged him as well—why else would the airlines bother if they weren't anxious about the profitability of his idea?

He was willing to fight for Southwest's existence for the rest of his life, and was prepared to battle them for as long as necessary. That he would ultimately win was a certainty to him, and as a result he never considered giving in. As the assorted lawsuits dragged on, the airlines' legal expenses must have been considerable, but they knew that their businesses were imperiled if they didn't eventually win.

Finally, in 1971, a key court victory made it possible for Kelleher to get his upstart airline in the air. After six years of legal wrangling, his faith that America's system would eventually turn in his favor was justified, and he was able to savor his company's first flight.

Those years, however, had not been entirely wasted—they'd given him that much more time to thoroughly prepare for every aspect of the Southwest operation. And when the court at last allowed him to, Kelleher took the industry by storm.

He knew the executives at the major airlines were even more furious with him after he inaugurated his airline in earnest than they'd been in court, but he considered that an advantage as well. Their six years of worry and spite had exhausted them, and invigorated Kelleher, and his natural passion and energy were augmented by the time Southwest began booking passengers.

He'd always been optimistic and very confident about his airline business model, but he hadn't anticipated that people flying into, out of, and through Texas, would see the advantages of Southwest almost faster than he had.

Passengers jumped at the cheap fares and no-frills flights. The airline won a dedicated following of repeat fliers, and took on many passengers who'd never flown before.

As Southwest grew, led by a CEO whose antics added to his legend almost every day, its workforce expanded. The number of employees multiplied, and Southwest gained another huge advantage over its behemoth competitors: They built a team of the most highly motivated employees in the industry, then and now. They were clearly energized, and obviously enjoyed their jobs.

Kelleher, like Ailes at Fox News, knew how to build highly motivated teams that, while outmanned and outgunned in almost every conventional sense, had something special going for them—passion. It pervaded the Southwest workforce because of their CEO, who spewed passion like a volcano spewed lava.

Kelleher's style was infectious. Veteran employees kept each other relaxed and laughing, and new hires soon learned to do the same thing. He cheered his workforce on, telling them again and again that they weren't just doing a job, they were on a *mission*.

Kelleher told *Fortune* magazine in April 2000: "Our esprit de corps is the core of our success. That's most difficult for a competitor to imitate. They can buy all the physical things. The thing you can't buy is dedication, devotion, loyalty—feeling [that] you are participating in a cause or a crusade."

That's exactly what Kelleher was doing back in those early days, engaging and leading his workers against rigid and unyielding price ticketing structures that kept all but the savviest or richest passengers off planes altogether.

Inculcating the notion among employees that the company represents a cause instead of a profit margin is a common denominator among true entrepreneurial visionaries. It's also an important and fundamental difference between them and conventional CEOs, who get the results you'd expect from a conventional workforce.

These leaders instill in their workers a feeling that *anything* is possible, that old rules don't apply—that they make their own rules, the ones that best fit their enterprise.

And they make it clear that what's always important is a steady, productive, even catalytic flow of new ideas, and open discussion about their effectiveness and application.

In emphasizing to their workforce the value of imaginative, unconventional thinking, Ailes, Kelleher, and Branson are speaking from direct experience, as prophetic company founders and master builders.

They remind their employees that with the entire workforce contributing, their combined ideas will be valuable—for everyone. What's good for their company is good for them, too. And because their leadership shares with them, they know that they'll get to share in the rewards of a better business model, and a better business.

Kelleher didn't just tell his people that they were special, he said it publicly, and continues to more than thirty years later.

"Our primary customers are our employees," Kelleher told the Associated Press in 2002. "Your employees come first. If they're treated right, they treat the customers right and the customers come back for more. We want a company that's bound by love, where people smile because they want to, not because they have to."

As the *Houston Chronicle* reported in 1996, the message was unmistakable. "If you like the people of Southwest Airlines, you're going to likely fly it more often."

When a CEO considers his employees to be *his* most important customers, he's going to make certain that he gives and gets the best customer service possible, so that those buying tickets will keep coming back to fly with them again.

Kelleher, from the beginning, was very picky about the people he employed, and he's still astonishingly selective: Fewer than one in twenty applicants at Southwest are hired. As *Fortune* writer Katrina Brooker put it, "you've got better odds at Harvard."

Brooker summed up the Southwest hiring process, explaining that they're looking for people in Kelleher's mold. They want his cheerfulness and optimism, his sense of self-confidence and commitment, but most of all they want people who display his superhuman motivation.

Some of the employees already have similar qualities, while others learn them. *Every* employee benefits from having these qualities taught and reinforced, and so does Southwest and its passengers.

Few companies are so sweeping and intricate in their employee requirements. This goes for baggage handlers and mechanics to flight attendants and pilots. Everyone is rated by this personality test.

The lucky, elite few who are hired are sent to the "University of People," Southwest's training center in Dallas. There they cover everything from positive reinforcement to reading body language, which helps them deal with customers and fellow workers. It's Kelleher's vision, in classroom form.

At the University, and throughout their years of employment, workers continue to learn the value of working with each other in a constructive, positive manner. That seems obvious, but at too many companies, it's the obvious things that are lost, forgotten, or never taught. Southwest emphasizes civility and friendliness every day, as does its founder, no matter the circumstance.

As soon as a new employee starts at Southwest and actually *experiences* Kelleher, they immediately adore him. He makes each of his thousands of employees feel as though he knows them by name, and surprisingly often he justifies that perception—because he makes the effort to remember. It's an example one of those "little" things that are actually rather big to an employee, coming as it does, from the CEO himself.

No wonder they did something unusual themselves on Boss's Day in 1994, when the airline's 16,000 employees paid $60,000 to run a full-page "THANK YOU" ad in *USA Today*.

The ad said it all:

For remembering every one of our names.
For supporting the Ronald McDonald House.
For helping load baggage on Thanksgiving.
For giving everyone a kiss (and we mean everyone).
For listening.
For running the only profitable major airline.
For singing at our holiday party.
For singing only once a year.

For letting us wear shorts and sneakers to work.
For golfing at The LUV Classic with only one club.
For out-talking Sam Donaldson.
For riding your Harley Davidson into Southwest Headquarters.
For being a friend, not just a boss.

I can't imagine too many bosses being praised like that, and seeing those kind words splashed across an entire page of a major national daily newspaper. But such was their affection for Herb, and I have a feeling that given the chance, more than a few passengers would have chipped in some bucks for that ad.

What other airline, after all, pays as close attention to its customers? What other airline has mailed birthday cards to frequent fliers, or held in-flight contests for passengers with the largest hole in his or her sock, or challenged passengers to sing the company jingle on the plane's PA system?

For the employees, fun just came with the job, and the same was true for Kelleher, who took his CEO responsibilities seriously, but not gravely. He once remarked that executives who focused too much on the trappings of their office never get much beyond their office. His life is also more than his job. He's a great lover of history, and continues to be very well-read on the subject, sometimes applying his historical knowledge to his jokes.

Like Roger Ailes, Kelleher is blunt, but he's also very funny. I had the chance to cover some of his speeches, and they were never dull—and like Branson's, they were rarely scripted. Kelleher spoke from the gut, while his words resonated in the heart and worked through the funny bone. I always wondered what it must have been like for the company executive who had to share the dais with him, before or after Kelleher spoke.

Herb Kelleher doesn't fit the image of a chief executive, especially one presiding over an airline. He is boisterous and loud, and likes to rattle cages. In the clubby, often reserved world of airline executives, Kelleher wasn't just the bull in the china shop, he was an entire stampede, and his competitors just couldn't respond to some of his outlandish antics.

For example, he not only dressed up as Elvis, but once donned a leprechaun suit, and on another occasion came to a company function as Corporal Klinger, the cross-dressing oddball from *M*A*S*H*. He even went so far as to arm-wrestle another airline's CEO for the rights to a disputed advertising slogan.

Fortune describes how American Airlines CEO Bob Crandall took a potshot at Kelleher about a Southwest promotion featuring Sea World's Shamu the Killer Whale. Soon after, at a staff meeting no less, Crandall received a special delivery from Kelleher—a massive bowl of chocolate pudding meant to look like whale poop. The card read, "With love, from Shamu."

Even a prankster like Ailes couldn't match this level of shenanigans—discretion simply didn't permit it. After all, Ailes urged his own people to tone down his employees' jibes about departed anchor Paula Zahn, who had jumped to CNN, because they were getting too mean.

Something tells me Kelleher would have shown no such restraint.

⚏

Rival airlines noted Southwest's success, but most of them foolishly and self-destructively ignored it, blinded by conventional "wisdom." Executive thinking seemed to be that so many passengers flying at such ridiculously low fares was a phenomenon that was almost certainly unprofitable in the long run, and therefore came with a built-in termination date. All they had to do was to wait for Southwest to fail on its own.

As so often happens to conventional competitors watching or fighting an unconventional new company, by the time they realized that the founder's "crazy" vision was going to be enduringly successful, it was much too late for them to readjust and learn how to address the trend more effectively.

A few airlines did create their own versions of Kelleher's regional airline model, including USAirways' Metrojet, Delta Express,
and Continental Lite, but they discovered, to their financial detriment, that their prohibitively higher costs prevented them from out-
Southwesting Southwest.

But even if they could have competed financially, they lacked
two very important ingredients for success: Herb Kelleher's famous,
impassioned lunacy, and his spirited workforce, both of which Kelleher had predicted from the beginning they'd never be able to imitate.

He understood that he had ample business sense, but his magic
was his personality and commitment to people. Kelleher knew you
could have the best business plan in the world, but without eager
and willing workers to implement it, it's not much better than the
paper it's written on.

Like Ailes and Branson, Kelleher emphasized making his employees *want* to do the best job, rather than telling them to. No workplace is perfect, but it can be enjoyable, and that encourages the tens
of thousands of employees who work for the companies these men
founded, to do their best every day. This is the stuff of common
sense, not advanced Ivy League degrees, but none of the hundreds of
competitors who've challenged these CEOs and their companies over
the decades have been able or willing to mimic their success.

For some reason I don't get, it must be harder than it looks to be
what these three leaders are: Gutsy bosses who speak from their
heart as well as the mind, have a lot of fun as they direct their ventures, and show their loyalty. Kelleher was faithful to his troops, and
they gave the same to him in return. They gave when he didn't ask—
the full-page ad in *USA Today,* for example—just as when he did.

One year, he sent an urgent letter home to every worker, asking
them to help him think of and find ways to cut costs by some $55
million. Within days of receiving the letter, everyone from flight attendants to baggage handlers volunteered cost-saving suggestions,
including one group that decided to handle its own office cleaning.

The bottom line? Kelleher got most of that annual cost savings
realized in months. To this day, even with vast industry cutbacks

and no-frills service, Southwest's costs remain at least 20 percent below the industry average.

Bill Foote benefited from the same moving support at USG, and I've received the same, twice over, at PBS and Fox. I think I know how Kelleher must have felt as the cost-cutting suggestions kept pouring in from his employees.

His airline is a company consistently ranked tops in customer satisfaction, and a regular entrant on lists of the best places to work in America. What continues to make Southwest so outstanding year after year, decade after decade? For the employees, at least, it's not the money. Most earn up to a third less than their peers at United or American. But they do enjoy crucial benefits—company profit sharing and stock option programs—that allow them to narrow the pay gap significantly. Employees now own about 10 percent of the company's stock, and they continue to buy more.

The various profit-sharing programs augment their incomes, but the Southwest staff's diligence doesn't spring simply from their stake in the company. The fact is that they care deeply about their work; for example, it's not unusual to find pilots picking up wrappers or flight attendants helping the clean-up crews so that they can more quickly prepare the plane for boarding and get it up in the air.

Southwest's pilots clock nearly eighty hours a month, significantly more than the sixty-eight-hour industry average, and the airline's 7,400 flight attendants work even harder, notching 150 hours each month, nearly double the time their peers at other airlines put in.

The reason is simple: Southwest employees are motivated. They work hard, and don't complain.

For more than thirty years, Southwest has prospered while so many other low-cost carriers have failed. I'm sure an industry analyst could talk in more detail about the airline's low costs and quick turnaround times, and provide a more scientific analysis of the airline's successes. But for my money, the credit, or at least a good chunk of it, goes to the Southwest employees.

In *another* company that is 85 percent unionized, the relationship between labor and management would probably be strained at best and nearly warlike at worst. But at Southwest things are different—and better. The higher union membership gets, the more productive and harmonious employee-management relations are.

I think the reason is simple: Southwest workers don't see management as some amorphous being. They see one man—Herb Kelleher.

Like a folk hero, Kelleher probably seemed immortal to his employees. Somehow, they thought, he'd always be there for them, no matter how old he got.

But in August 1999, Kelleher revealed to the world that he had prostate cancer, the same form of cancer that killed my father. The same disease Joe Torre fought through.

At the same time he made the announcement, he sent a letter to all Southwest employees explaining the diagnosis and telling them that he expected a complete and full recovery. He further said that he'd decided to go public with the illness because it would have been impossible to keep secret.

Knowing the effect the news would have on his employees especially, Kelleher didn't make a big deal about his disease, calling it a "rather mundane, routine, and fairly insignificant case of prostate cancer." He even described the frightening diagnosis with classic Herb good humor. Noting his fondness for Wild Turkey whiskey and cigarettes, he said that prostate cancer was not the disease his doctors had thought he might get.

"I know that perhaps some members of the medical profession are going to be disappointed that it was prostate cancer," he told the *Dallas Morning News.* "But as far as I know, nobody has linked prostate cancer to smoking."

Because Kelleher's cancer was caught early, his prospects looked good. He has remained the picture of health, and maintained his sense of humor he's always had. He also maintained his hectic day-to-day schedule.

But clearly his employees were worried. Kelleher was more than the chief executive; he was the chief cheerleader. He was the guy who made them laugh hard, and work even harder.

Kelleher decided that he wasn't doing enough by just running the airline, and decided to launch a second campaign, building on his first one with Southwest, this time to help others who had the same disease, or are at risk of contracting it. He wanted to help as many people as possible to avoid his fate.

Within weeks of his diagnosis, he became a vocal advocate for regular prostate cancer screening, preaching the same message again and again: that prostate cancer is a largely curable disease, if caught early. But that's a *big* if. If a patient waits too long, the disease can spread and kill, usually within five years.

Meanwhile, the concern for Kelleher felt by every worker at Southwest was fervent and unceasing. They also had to learn to adjust to his growing absence as he slowly took himself out of daily operations. In March 2001, he resigned as chief executive and president at Southwest, but stayed on as chairman, as much to reassure his employees about his health and condition, as to have a say in the company's direction.

Into his positions stepped two well-seasoned, longtime associates—James Parker, vice president and general counsel, became chief executive and vice chairman of the board, and Executive Vice President Colleen Barrett became president and chief operating officer, becoming the first woman to hold such a title at a major airline.

The question going forward was whether a Southwest without Kelleher calling the shots would be the same Southwest. Analysts remain mixed in their projections. They know the airline is strong, and still commands the lowest costs in the industry, but there's no way to quantify the intangibles Kelleher brought to the job, or what the carrier will be like as it operates without its founder.

For Parker and Barrett, it's tough to follow a legend, as it was for Dana Mead. And for Southwest Airlines and its employees, it's tough to continue their great work after a legend has departed.

It's still too early to say, but I hope that we'll still see Southwest employees cracking jokes on planes and hiding in baggage bins as they used to. Without Herb setting the tone, that sort of behavior may now appear unruly, or even disruptive. Fortunately, though, Kelleher's good humor seems to have been inherited and perpetuated by the new management team, who were trained by the legend himself, just as Mead was trained by Michael Walsh.

It's too early to know how this new duo at Southwest will run the airline over the long term, but clearly, they've learned important lessons from Kelleher—that sometimes, it's okay to be disruptive, and it's okay to dress up in silly costumes, and it's okay to laugh, and joke, and kid, and send gag gifts to industry competitors, as long as you love what you're doing, and do it well.

An airline executive didn't come up with the leadership approach for an airline that evolved from a note on a cocktail napkin to a major industry competitor, and who continues to make his rivals look like relics that should have worked for the Wright brothers— when they were bicycle mechanics.

A San Antonio lawyer did.

United may have invited people to "fly the friendly skies," but Kelleher made that slogan his company' ethic. He made flight affordable and entertaining for millions of people, and by sharing his sense of humor, made it as much fun to work at the airline as it was to fly on it.

Even by the standards of the Southwest's folklore heroes, that's quite a legacy.

CHAPTER 13

MOUNTAINS TO CLIMB

The risks, ravages, and terrible tragedies that cancer causes have been one of the major themes of this book.

I have been moved to share the stories of cancer survivors, and those who've lost their lives or their loved ones to this horrible disease, because inspired by them all, many others, and my own experiences, I'm conducting my own passionate crusade to educate, foster understanding, and lend inspiration.

Even with all the advances that have been made in medicine and scientific research, cancer is still incurable if caught too late, and, of course, sometimes fatal as well.

However, as you know from the stories and actions of some of my heroes—Geraldine Ferraro, Evelyn Lauder, Joe Torre, Harry Pearce, Mel Stottlemyre, and Herb Kelleher—cancer can be successfully treated *if it is detected early on.*

To me, cancer best resembles a hydra: It takes many forms. In this small group of survivors, cancer attacked in *four* different forms: multiple myeloma, leukemia, prostate cancer, and breast cancer.

I was brought down for a while by advanced Hodgkin's disease, and the two survivors in the concluding stories I'm about to tell you were struck by *another* two forms of cancer: testicular semenoma and mouth cancer.

Cancer is dangerous and threatening. It can attack us from almost any direction, in almost any form. And depending on the timing, it can kill us, damage us, and cause great suffering. It forever changes our lives, and of all the people who are part of them.

That emphasizes the importance of awareness, knowledge, prevention, and early detection. While there's always the risk of recurrence, as happened with Ferraro, once cancer is in remission, patients stop being victims, and become *survivors* who can lead long and very productive lives, personally and professionally. Moreover, survivors can act *compassionately,* as they fight to stamp out the diseases that assaulted them.

I feel a tremendous need to help spread the word, and share the stories, information, and insights that can be gained from my years of confronting the illness. It's my hope and ambition that this sharing can potentially improve and perhaps even save some lives, and help maintain the quality of life for everyone who loves and cares about the people afflicted.

For these reasons, I'd like to tell you about two *multiple* survivors.

One of these people survived prostate and mouth cancer, after losing both of his parents to cancer, as I did. And the other overcame testicular semenoma three separate times. After the initial diagnosis, treatment, and remission, his form of cancer was so potent that it struck back twice more, until it was finally "defeated" with treatments that have kept the cancer in remission for an encouragingly long period.

Jon Huntsman and Patrick Byrne are similar in other ways as well. Fellow residents of Utah, each is an entrepreneur who built a smart, well-focused, very competitive, and profitable company. And both applied the same sheer grit and determination to launch their companies and keep them viable, despite tough competition. Huntsman started a chemical company that went on to become one of the largest privately held petrochemical concerns on the planet, while Byrne, a hardy and visionary Internet pioneer, rode the dot-com bubble like a surfer on a tidal wave. And then when the wave hit the shore, and the bubble popped, Byrne proved he could survive bumping along the bottom just as well as he could ride the crest. As thousands of other Internet businesses failed, Byrne hung on and rebuilt his business, leading it to new successes.

They may have displayed them in vastly different industries, but their fortitude, confidence in themselves and their companies, and refusal to quit are transcendental qualities that are valued in the business world, and every part of life.

It was the same courage and stamina that drove them to fight and defeat the bouts of cancer that came, recurred, and in Byrne's case, returned yet again.

Their compassion for the suffering of others inspired both of them, as it has all my heroes, to begin their own missions to help as many cancer victims and survivors as possible, hoping to save and improve their lives.

While they have much in common, they have their share of differences as well: Byrne's crusade was more focused on those who'd suffered the same form of cancer that he'd battled, while Huntsman's efforts were much broader and more ambitious, in that the war he waged was on behalf of increased treatment for and research of all forms of cancer.

Huntsman was born in poverty in Idaho; Byrne was an heir to great wealth, and had the advantage of a father and brother with relationships and contacts with some of the top business people in the world.

Huntsman built his own fortune; Byrne initially relied on his inherited and earned wealth, then went on to risk his own money on a business that ultimately would earn him a fortune all his own.

Huntsman is that true rarity: a born philanthropist, who from childhood to the present consistently devoted his life to assisting and supporting others through his efforts and his money. The nature of his philanthropy never changed—only the scope and level of his financial contributions. He shared his money when he had almost none, and he shared many millions more as he became a multibillionaire.

Byrne's philanthropic efforts began later, developing from his life experiences, but like Huntsman, once he began to use his money to support the causes he believed in, he never stopped.

In the end, what matters most is that they gave before they were savaged by cancer, and their characteristic, similar response, was to give even more, financially and emotionally, when they survived. They helped uncountable numbers of people in numerous and varied ways.

TALL TIMBER

Jon Huntsman is the man behind Huntsman Corporation, a vast petrochemical company that, according to *Forbes* magazine, has made him the forty-seventh richest man on the planet, worth more than $6 billion.

When the *Utah Deseret News* recently named him among the most influential people in the state, Huntsman was surprised. "I've never perceived myself as one who had great influence," he told the reporter.

A surprise to him or not, Huntsman's influence is real, and extends well beyond his business acumen.

Time magazine lists him as among the most generous philanthropists in the United States, and his greatest effort and most generous by far is the Huntsman Center Institute at the University of Utah Medical Center.

For him, the Center is the fulfillment of a lifelong dream to wipe out the disease that has burned through his family. Both of his parents died of cancer—his mother, in fact, died in his arms—and Huntsman himself has survived two bouts of the illness, prostate cancer and mouth cancer.

It's hard to quantify just how much money Huntsman has poured into the center. Conservative estimates now say that his contributions stand well north of $350 million, with millions more in pledges to come.

Huntsman has put his passion for finding a cure ahead of his passion for building a business, and he has used that business as the base for his numerous philanthropic efforts. Some say Huntsman built his massive petrochemical empire just to give money away, and he doesn't deny that.

He goes so far as to list charitable contributions in his company's mission statement, and his nearly 20,000 employees regularly rank among the most generous anywhere in donations to the United Way and other causes.

It matters little to him who gets the credit, just that the job gets done. Less than two years ago, his wife, Karen, and their nine children donated $350 million to various causes in Utah alone.

When talking with him, he rarely discusses himself. For example, he rarely, if ever, mentions the time that one of his children was kidnapped and the horrible ordeal when the FBI agent who was trying to save Huntsman's son was almost killed.

No, he focuses everything on his cancer center—building it, expanding it, nurturing it.

Friends say it is his all-consuming passion, even when it crosses political lines; critics say that he can have a sharp tongue but doesn't hold a grudge. Huntsman himself says, "I've tried to be very honest, open, and frank in any comments I've ever made."

A lifelong Republican, Huntsman says he has no problem crossing party lines to fight cancer. The one thing Huntsman wants is more federal matching grants for cancer research, and he'll support anyone, Republican or Democrat, who can deliver the funding. In fact, he's angered some in his own party by saying they're not doing enough in this area of policy, but Huntsman is more interested in his cause than partisanship.

That's why this former Nixon White House appointee is happy to work with any Democrat that comes along with a plan to help his cancer efforts. It's Huntsman's not-so-subtle way of pushing both parties to move immediately against what he calls the most lethal scourge in society.

Huntsman's work with any Republican or Democrat who actively supports his fight to help cancer victims is representative of the intense focus on helping others that's defined his entire life. He gave to causes even in his poverty-struck days growing up in rural Idaho. He used to pick potatoes to help his family make ends meet, and he mortgaged his house to buy his first chemical plant; but no matter how deeply in debt he was, he always was deeply committed to charity.

After receiving a scholarship to study at the University of Pennsylvania, he gave money to good causes from whatever odd jobs he was working to get through school.

After graduating from college, he joined the Navy, donating $50 of his $320-per-month salary to the poor.

Years later, in 1991—after losing both parents to cancer, and becoming a double cancer survivor himself—the ever-philanthropic, compassionate Huntsman decided to build a major medical center in Utah that would be devoted to ongoing, massive medical research of all types of cancer, including a hospital for treating cancer patients.

He wanted to make sure his friends and fellow residents of Utah had convenient access to the same outstanding care that's available to cancer patients in other parts of the country, especially the East and West coasts.

He immediately began soliciting likely prospects for funding, including drug companies and government agencies, to help make his dream a reality. Very few were interested in donating with a recession looming.

He also had to deal with many people's considerable doubts, as they wondered why patients would go to a cancer center in Utah when they could fly to any number of already well-known and well-established institutions in easily accessible major cities.

Huntsman found the logic faulty and risky. He knew that if he could assemble a high-tech, one-stop-shop for high-quality research and hospital care specific to cancer, he'd be pooling resources in a way never thought possible in that part of the country.

He didn't have support, belief, or funding, but he wasn't quitting that easily. As he went on to tell *People* magazine in December 2002, "I'll give what it takes, no matter what, to rid the world of this horrible disease." That meant taking out an eight-digit loan to keep his promise to fellow cancer sufferers that he wouldn't forget them and would build that center and hospital for them.

When he first began funneling money into the center's hospital section, Huntsman's goal, beyond the actual medical treatment, was simple: He hoped to provide a positive and relaxing environment for cancer sufferers, to help them clear their minds and make their battle a little easier. He emphasized comfortable interiors and large windows offering sweeping mountain vistas. Patients should feel at peace, he believed, and both the environment and the care providers themselves should provide that for them.

Once the center was built, it wasn't and isn't unusual to see Huntsman himself wandering the corridors checking in on patients, many of whom would not have been able to get the same quality of care on their own.

Also, because both of his bouts with cancer had caught him by surprise, Huntsman wanted the major research division of the center to keep pushing to develop new technologies that detect cancers much earlier, so that patients have a better fighting chance.

Rarely does he mention any of his own hardships with the disease, only that he wants to make sure others don't go through the same thing. To that end, Huntsman was able to use his influence and connections to secure a new weapon against cancer: a Positron Emission Tomography [PET] scanner.

Reports are that Huntsman, through his contacts at General Electric Medical Systems, heard about this relatively groundbreaking technology, which enabled doctors to find cancers months, and sometimes years, before they could using conventional methods. He got the president of General Electric on the phone, and a meeting soon followed, after which Huntsman and his research center and hospital moved up on the list for the portable scanner.

Because the PET scanner is on wheels, it can be easily transported, which is especially useful, because it can be brought to those who aren't healthy or strong enough to make a trip to the hospital or cancer center.

The *Daily Utah Chronicle* reported at the time about the case of lymphoma patient Michael Bulloch, a nineteen-year-old diagnosed with Hodgkin's disease—my form of cancer, but fortunately, it was less advanced when diagnosed in the young man. His doctors said that Bulloch required a PET scan to see if his chemotherapy was working to kill the large tumor in his lung.

The closest scanner was at the University of California at Los Angeles, and Bulloch's doctors weren't sure he could make the trip. But by then, Huntsman had gotten his own PET scanner and, as a result, Bulloch didn't have to risk a flight to LA. Huntsman had the scanner sent to Bulloch's hospital and got the satisfaction of knowing that his relentless pursuit of new technology had helped a young man to better fight his cancer.

Experts say it's hard to quantify how many lives the new scanner has already saved, but it's clearly helped people get the medical care that they require, and much sooner than would normally have been the case. And that's just from one high-tech machine that Huntsman got early on, because he had the power and connections.

The Huntsman Center Institute is distinguished by its highly admired cancer research division and hospital-care of patients. It's also known for the uniquely relaxing, positive, and spiritual environment that was so important to Huntsman, who felt strongly that cancer victims should feel at peace while being treated. Like Ailes, Kelleher, and Branson leading their impassioned workforces, Huntsman motivated and energized the doctors and other members of the hospital staff to concentrate on healing the cancer victims' minds and spirits as much as their bodies.

The PET scanner and everything else that Huntsman's Center offers has helped thousands of people fight cancer, saved lives, and prevented perhaps hundreds of unnecessary deaths. But what is immeasurable, and just as important, is how many people have had their hearts, minds, and emotions eased and healed because of a man who understood, to the core of his being, that cancer doesn't attack just a person's body; it goes to war against the entire being.

Today, Huntsman still actively pursues technologies and machines that might detect any and all cancers at their earliest stages, and treatments and therapies that can improve a victim's chances even more, aiding patients both physically and emotionally.

His goal is as it was more than a dozen years ago: keep building and expanding the center, its research and care, and transform Utah into a major cancer cure center in its own right, and give patients more choices beyond the respected and long-established big-city hospitals and institutes (with their big-city environment and attitude to match).

What Huntsman started, with his own money, and persisted with despite all the people who doubted his efforts was long thought impossible. But Huntsman's limitless generosity (and limitless bank account) said differently.

He doesn't think much of fellow billionaires who wait until they're dead to give their money away. There are too many people in desperate need of help now to justify hoarding vast piles of cash. It's selfish and even unintentionally cruel for billionaires to hang on to their money until death finally loosens their grip.

How many more lives could have been spared or saved if many more of the wealthy and not so wealthy, thought of their money as something to be used to help others today, and tomorrow, as soon as often as they can?

Huntsman hasn't lived his extraordinarily philanthropic life to make a point, but it's there. Anyone, at almost any income level, can give to others—and hopefully they will.

Wanting to give to the center and other good causes as many millions a year as he can, Huntsman still refuses to take public the very profitable company that generates the income he shares so generously. Additionally, over the past couple of years, the Huntsman Corporation has had numerous, very lucrative buyout offers, but Huntsman hasn't and won't accept them.

Shareholders can strongly affect what a CEO and a company do with "their" money. The CEO and the company he or she leads tend to think of revenue as theirs to make decisions about, but the shareholders are the real owners, and it's *they* who make the final decision. On his own, Huntsman has much more flexibility, and he has used every last inch of it.

BEYOND THE WEB

Patrick Byrne, Ph.D. was born in Utah, but in contrast to Jon Huntsman, who grew up in poverty and picked potatoes to help his family eat, Byrne, from the beginning, had all the advantages of a life of privilege.

His father is John Byrne, who has been head of GEICO Insurance and White Mountains Insurance Group; he has one brother in real estate, and another who's a hedge-fund manager.

As a teenager, Byrne, through his dad, developed a friendship with the world-famous investor Warren Buffett, whose almost unparalleled achievements have made his financial projections and comments as closely followed and eagerly accepted as the cryptic predictions of the Oracle of Delphi thousands of years ago.

Buffett is a man whose essential financial philosophy has always boiled down to enduring, steadfast patience. As a result, Buffett has sometimes watched the stock market and corporations for dozens of years before deciding that it's the right time to sell or buy stock in a particular company.

Another teenager might have simply bragged about and gloried in his friendship with the most legendary and successful investor in the world. But even at that age, Byrne was too mature and smart to lose the advantage of a unique education, even if all he learned was the more or less self-evident virtues of patience. Buffett applied it to investing. Byrne, then and now, makes it a defining element of his life—personal, academic, and professional.

While developing his patience, he also maximized the potential of his amazing intellectual gifts. He learned to speak Mandarin and at least four other languages, and, according to *Fortune* magazine, successfully translated Lao Tse's *Way of Virtue* during his senior year at Dartmouth.

He earned a doctorate in philosophy from Stanford and black belts in hapkido and tae kwon do. He went on to study moral philosophy at Cambridge as a Marshall fellow, and briefly took up boxing.

Byrne's bright future was upended, though, when, in his early twenties, he was diagnosed with testicular semenoma (the same cancer that Lance Armstrong fought before winning multiple Tour de France championships). Most frightening, Byrne's cancer had metastasized throughout his body.

His doctors told him that his chances of survival were less than one in five. Byrne, taking the long view, decided that those were acceptable odds, and he battled his way, steeled most likely by his double black belts and boxing experience, through a long series of treatments that finally pushed the cancer into remission.

His cancer, however, would not stay dormant for long, and the disease fought back, blasting his entire body. Byrne had to engage in a second battle more difficult, painful, and grueling than the first. And even if the recurrence wasn't as serious as his first bout with cancer, there was still the physical, mental, and emotional attrition that inevitably plagues even the toughest warriors when one battle follows another. But eventually he fought to another victory, and a second remission.

Throughout these years, Byrne concentrated on accumulating substantial and useful executive business experience, and accruing his own wealth. During his years as the CEO of High Plains, Byrne amassed a $100 million investment portfolio, and actively analyzed the market, looking for just the right entrepreneurial opportunity.

He had sterling academic credentials, superior intelligence, was fluent in five languages, had mastered two forms of hand-to-hand combat, and acquired the profound strength that comes from being a two-time cancer survivor. He had experience as a CEO, and considerable available funding. As he considered his options, Dr. Byrne was better prepared to create his own company than most.

He also had the unique advantage of having been taught about business by Buffett himself—as well as his own father, who had the depth of corporate experience that comes with being the CEO of two companies. Byrne learned, as well, from his brothers' experiences in their businesses.

Deciding what kind of company to start and in which industry, Byrne combined an entrepreneur's vision, a love of overcoming great challenges, and the intense competition inherent to investment banking.

Surveying the field, he determined that the Internet provided him the right opportunities and near-infinite room for innovation, new ideas, and fertile ground for a superb imagination fueled and guided by true intellectual brilliance. But as an Internet company founder and leader, Byrne is a different breed, drawn to the Internet not for the glitter of the moment, but the potential for the future, and greater opportunities to do business, and especially to help people.

It's a key distinction for Byrne, who puts great stock in being a cancer survivor, and feels that he has duties and responsibilities based on an appreciation of the importance of *people,* not profits.

Rival company leaders probably would have predicted, if asked, that with his distinguished credentials Byrne's new company would be one that operated at the highest technological, corporate, and scientific levels of Internet enterprises. They would have been wrong. Byrne was prepared to *invest* $20 million from his investment portfolio in his new company, and what he wanted was the best financial return on his investment, not corporate prestige and unimpressive profits. A high profit margin would enable him, like Jon Huntsman, to donate an enormous amount of money to his causes.

That Byrne would so scrutinize his prospective company's ability to turn a profit is another of those "little" things that seems so obvious, and but is so often overlooked or set aside. This was especially true during the Internet gold rush, when it seemed that everyone was dazzled by the brilliant *future*, and took for granted that profits, *big* profits, would come to every half-baked site on the Web. It took some time for investors to see returns on their Internet buys, but in the next few years the dot-com rocket carried them all higher and higher.

Byrne, though, didn't want the *possibility* of profits, especially in an industry that was so packed with startups and new competitors that fostered the feeling of being in the middle of a herd of cattle, with just about as much sense, and direction.

For Warren Buffett, and now for Byrne, patience was also a component of practicality. There were times when the best investment or business move was to take great risks, but the height of the Internet madness was not one of those times.

Byrne based his decisions about when to get into something, and when to get out, on experience, education, financial instinct, and attuned intuition. He made his decisions quietly, and always produced convincing financial and investment performances. Byrne was ready to sacrifice prestige for prudence and dependable profit.

The Internet company he created, Overstock.com, as its name indicates, focused on selling excess inventory of consumer items at deep discounts. He bought those overstocked products at equally deep discounts, from clueless Web-based businesses that didn't respect or appreciate Byrne's model.

The leaders of other Internet companies, often high-tech and state of the art, didn't *get* Byrne's back-to-basics model either. To them the fundamental, apparently elementary, nature of his business seemed more nineteenth century than twenty-first. It was practically prehistoric. Sometimes the CEOs and executives riding the Internet rocket pitied Byrne—he was *so* out of date.

Byrne didn't care at all about their opinions. By genetics, education, and experience, he had terrific business instincts, and they told him that the gold everyone sought was in his hills, and not theirs.

He based Overstock.com in Salt Lake City, in the state he'd grown up in and come back to, because it was a wonderful place to live and do business in. Because an Internet company is by definition global, the actual location of his offices was basically irrelevant (unlike that of his warehouse), and so he could well afford to base his company in Utah.

As he'd anticipated, Overstock.com grew, thrived, and took more and more market share, as other Internet companies with bad business models and big losses were constantly crashing and burning through their startup funding before they'd even come close to a single dollar in profit.

But as his business flourished, Byrne was again beset by testicular semenoma, which came roaring out of remission, and attacked his body for a *third* time. Like all cancer survivors, Byrne, from the time of his first diagnosis and successful treatment, had lived with the subdued but very real fear that his cancer could return at any time. When it did, his worst anxieties were confirmed, and a second series of treatments only elevated his worries. Two bouts with cancer meant that the odds were higher, emotionally if not medically, and that it could strike yet again.

Byrne may have felt as mistreated by life and fate as I did when I was diagnosed with MS seven years ago. My attitude has improved, as I've focused more on others and less on myself, but at some fundamental level, the sheer misery and pain of having both illnesses has never left me, and never will.

Byrne is probably a lot tougher than I am—my only black belts are in business news. Even so, I have to think that going through twenty-four to forty-eight months of treatment for a third time is horrendous by itself. Undergoing cancer treatment *and* simultaneously running a rapidly growing Internet business, for what turned out to be a long time, has to have been the worst kind of hell. After he finished the third round of treatment, he then "only" had to concentrate on his responsibilities as CEO, keeping the company moving in the right direction.

Having won three bouts with cancer, he must have known that his future might involve the strong possibility of additional attacks, and the disturbing knowledge that he could very well die in the event of another recurrence. That he was a three-time survivor was miraculous, and even with his remarkable physical stamina, there was only so much damage his body could sustain before breaking down completely.

Like Ferraro (who also fought a recurrence of cancer), Byrne faced the same physical limits when being treated with thalidomide; after a certain amount, the drug began to destroy, not heal, the body.

Byrne's three attacks and no less than twenty surgeries had already done major, cumulative damage, wiping eighty pounds off his hulking six-foot five-inch, 240-pound frame. Even if his cancer never came back, he had undergone serious physical strain. As he had each time before, when the treatments ended, he began a rigorous physical regimen to rebuild himself, to the degree that his body could sustain.

And he returned to his full-time duties at Overstock.com, with an even greater commitment and determination. It was his company, and however many years he had left, he and Overstock would make the most of them.

Byrne had also decided to make it his life's mission to transform the negatives of his multiple bouts with cancer into assets that would potentially enrich and enhance the lives of as many people as he could reach, and all the causes he'd become personally involved with and helped support financially.

As he wrote in a company press release in May 2000: "My own battle with cancer was one of the turning points of my life. I know I only survived because of the work of dedicated professionals and the commitment of scores of people who have participated in fundraising events."

By then, Overstock.com had lived through the demise of the dot-com bubble, and continued with more success than ever. To many, Byrne's company seemed like an endangered business species because of its rarity: It was an Internet survivor, the way its CEO was a three-time cancer survivor. That Byrne was able to keep himself and his company going through such difficult times, and have them both still standing, says volumes about his heart and spirit.

The Internet rocket soared, streaking through the business world exciting people to its possibilities, and crashed. There were few survivors, but Byrne was able to keep buying excess inventory from the companies that had failed, as well as those still in business, each selling for their own reasons. Byrne bought these companies' overstock during their entire ride, as they went up, floated on the bubble, and were pulled back down by financial gravity.

And because he always bought at such low prices, he could keep selling at low prices to consumers who came to his web site and company in ever-greater numbers.

Herb Kelleher would have respected Byrne's appreciation of the eternally vital importance of low costs and low prices, regardless of the industry's whims, and been amused by the fates of the other Internet companies who'd fared about as well as all the major airlines that had tried to copy his model.

Had they known or realized, the failed Internet companies would not have found it funny that they'd helped Byrne's company grow, prosper, and move steadily upward, even as they crashed to earth.

They probably wouldn't have understood either that it wasn't the Internet that had died and forced them to crash, but their bad business ideas, which wouldn't have survived at all during a business period governed by economic sanity.

Darwinism is part of business, regardless of the technology. And that's why Overstock.com has long-term prospects that are just as good as they were in the short term. Byrne created one of the fittest models for Internet business, and one most likely to adapt and prosper.

Another gift that Byrne enjoys, and is an important contributing factor to his success, is his photographic memory, for which he's famous. *Fortune* reports on a card trick he's mastered, where he studies a random deck, then recounts the cards, one-by-one, in either direction—remembering months later exactly the order they were in. That keen intellect helps explain Byrne's laser-like focus on financing cancer campaigns and awareness programs.

Whether or not he still tracks every penny of his financial worth, Patrick Byrne has a very good idea of his personal worth. He doesn't judge his life achievements by how much money he has, but by how much money and attention for cancer-awareness initiatives he has raised.

He stands in marked contrast to the Web's world of shallow goals, and even shallower promises. Byrne's values are major reasons for his personal strength and stamina, and Overstock's almost certain longevity.

Considering that he lost eighty pounds, his obsessive dedication to rebuilding his physical strength and endurance, specifically for the purpose of participating athletically in certain cancer-research fund-raising causes, including marathon bicycle riding, is truly heroic.

Byrne's long-distance bike tours may be a deliberate tribute to the inspirational Lance Armstrong, one of the greatest riders and racers in cycling's history. Only a year after being treated for the same form of cancer that's attacked Byrne, Armstrong came back to win the Tour de France, the greatest championship in cycling, twice more.

One of the cycling events that Byrne participates in is the Pan-Massachusetts Challenge, a cross-Massachusetts fund-raising ride that benefits the Jimmy Fund, which supports cancer research at Dana-Farber Cancer Institute in Boston. It's one of many bike tours and cancer awareness drives that Byrne has engaged in to increase the public's knowledge of and attention to the urgent need for significantly more funding for cancer research. In fact, he's already biked across the United States at least four times.

It's astonishing—the older Byrne gets, the more motivated and passionate he is, and the faster and harder he rides for his causes. He even puts his own money where his mouth is, challenging the Pan-Massachusetts Challenge to raise millions, and vowing to match a percentage of that with his own funds.

As a frequent guest on my show, Byrne remains an audience favorite. His enthusiasm for what he does comes through again and again. Who else but a three-time cancer survivor, his optimism buffered by beating back his illness, could talk so fervently about promising days for the Internet?

He follows the unwritten credo of many cancer survivors, including the heroes I've profiled, that they have an obligation to give others their time, money, and especially hope. What's special about Byrne is that he's committed to giving others all of those things— and more.

CHAPTER 14

STANDING TALL
WHILE SITTING DOWN

All Jim Langevin ever wanted to be, when he was growing up in Warwick, Rhode Island, was a cop, then maybe an FBI agent.

He was already a Boy Scout, when he participated in a special program that gave him a chance to work with the Warwick Police Department. He loved every minute of it. He'd ride along with them in their squad cars, taking in their conversations, their lingo, even their routines.

He was only eleven years old when he joined the program, but the more time he spent with the Warwick cops, the more he wanted to be just like them. He knew that some day he would be wearing their uniform. It was just a matter of time.

After four years in the program, Langevin was more determined than ever to realize his dream of a career in law enforcement. But then something happened—one of those random, inexplicable events life occasionally serves up for us.

While he was in the locker room of the Warwick PD, two members of the local SWAT team were examining a new gun not too far away from him.

The cops didn't know the gun was loaded. One of them pulled the trigger. The bullet, a .45-caliber automatic, ricocheted off a locker and pierced Langevin's neck.

He was instantly paralyzed. He would never walk again, and he'd lost almost all function from the neck down.

The bullet destroyed Langevin's dreams, and permanently changed his life—when he was only fifteen years old.

"Originally I was in and out of consciousness," he has told me about the ordeal. "I didn't realize the extent of the damage. I realized pretty early on I had been shot. It was several weeks later that I realized the extent of the damage."

At the time, Langevin was a student at Bishop Hendricken High School, in Warwick. He excelled academically and athletically, running in the cross-country team.

Learning that you're paralyzed—that the only physical activity you'll probably ever be capable of is moving your head, and *maybe* your arms, slightly—would be incredibly difficult for anyone. For a teenager, it was almost unbearable.

In some ways, the hardships he faced at such a young age are not unlike those who are diagnosed with devastating illnesses.

In other ways, Langevin's situation was worse, and far more complicated. Many life-threatening illnesses can be beaten, but Langevin's condition was permanent. Chemotherapy or radiation can't improve the life and body.

While advances have been made in spinal cord research, doctors are rarely able to reduce or eliminate paralysis, to regenerate nerves to enable paralyzed people to start moving and walking again.

And unlike the occasional pain, discomfort, and fatigue associated with most cancers and other major diseases, paralysis is very real, very constant, and very much in-your-face. The simplest tasks, from dressing and eating to picking something up, are impossible for the paralyzed person to do alone.

These constant inabilities, these everyday obstacles, are continuous reminders of your huge loss of function. And that you'll be enduring and suffering that loss the rest of your life.

Langevin remembers doing a lot of crying, wondering what would become of his life and dreams now that he was a quadriplegic.

I asked him if he was bitter or angry now, or if he had been after realizing the consequences of his injury.

"I don't ever recall being angry," he said. "Certainly a lot of sadness. I describe it in ways of going to a death. The life that I once knew I would never know again. Letting go was part of the grieving process, and that took time.

"Probably the hardest thing to deal with was giving up on the idea I was going to be a police officer," he said. "I had to come to terms with the fact that was no longer going to be possible."

I wondered if he was angry at the officers who had caused him so much pain—accidentally, of course—all those years ago in that locker room.

"No," he answered. "I've heard from them only time to time. I don't have any contact with them. But I'm not angry.

"Nobody wanted this to happen. It was a terrible accident and I know if any of us could have turned the clock back and had it not happen, we would have done it. But the reality was that was not possible. I have to deal with life not as I wish it to be, but as it is."

His tragic accident, the circumstances and his youth, generated a lot of local newspaper and television coverage, and a sympathetic, ongoing stream of support, concern, and heartfelt expressions of hope, even in the face of difficult reality.

It wasn't just the local residents who rallied to his cause, either. Langevin's condition moved folks all over Rhode Island, people who didn't even know him.

"My parents would read those cards and letters to me in the hospital," he said. "All this support touched me in a profound way."

But Langevin still had school to worry about. The shooting had happened in August, just before the start of his sophomore year.

For better than five months, he was in the Boston hospital. "My mom was insistent that I get tutored while I was in the hospital. She was determined and I was determined to graduate with my high school class."

But it wouldn't be easy. Langevin needed a lot of help, and he found more than a few teachers willing to offer it. Several volunteered to tutor him back up to speed. When he returned to school in February of the following year, he was taught by different tutors each day.

The months of tutoring helped Langevin continue his education, but he couldn't match the learning pace of his normal, fellow students who were going to class every day. "I was a year behind in my schoolwork," he remembered.

His mother appreciated the help her son was getting at school, but she made sure he did a lot of his own heavy lifting as well.

"The only way I could keep up and do my papers is I had to type them out," he told me. "And the only way I could type my papers was to weave a pen through my fingers and type out the words one letter at a time. I would beg my mother to do them for me, but she was a busy woman with a career of her own and three kids, and she wanted me to become an independent adult and she knew I would have to learn to do things my own way."

So he did. "I typed out every one of those papers myself," he recalled. "She taught me something."

Langevin appreciates what he learned from his mother, and the generosity that other people showed. "I just remember how my family was dealing with all this, and how several families in the area would come over with meals and baked goods for my family."

As the unusual outpouring of community and statewide support and compassion continued through the passing months, Langevin started to see the good in the bad.

He was surprised to learn that people throughout the town were holding fund-raisers for him. He peeked in on one of those events himself at the nearby Community College of Rhode Island.

What he saw there amazed him. Hundreds of people, most of whom he didn't know and didn't know him, gathered to help him and his family.

Whatever young Jim Langevin and his family needed, he would get.

It was more than the teachers volunteering to bring him up to speed after months of missed classes, not once charging his family for their efforts. Or others setting up education funds, or still others giving financial help for things like wheelchairs and support mechanisms. The people of Warwick, largely a working- and middle-class community, even pitched in money to help make the Langevins' house handicap-accessible. They raised most of the $30,000 needed to complete the project through volunteer campaigns, bake sales, car washes, you name it . . . anything any neighbor or friend, acquaintance, or even stranger could do to help out.

I'm not at all surprised that so many people—by the hundreds and thousands, eventually—wanted to help Jim Langevin. As someone who used to live in Rhode Island, I can attest to the big heart of our nation's smallest state. Rhode Islanders are a close-knit bunch. Jim was one of their own, a kid who got a bad break, and they were determined to help him get back. They couldn't make him walk again, but they could offer food, supplies, money, equipment, teaching, and maybe even hope again.

Although separated by ethnic backgrounds and money, Rhode Islanders share a camaraderie that transcends that of most other places where I've lived. The people who live here care for each other; quite literally, they look after each other.

Langevin agreed. "Rhode Island is a small, but neighborly, state."

And that neighborly feeling made a deep impression on him. It was behind his later decision to pursue public service. Jim Langevin realized early the tremendous good that could come from people banding together—people with their own problems, their own worries, and their own tribulations, who put all that aside to help a kid.

Little did that community know what it had unleashed.

Although Langevin was confined to a wheelchair, he planned to stand tall for all of them. He'd always been interested in government, so it seemed a natural progression from a career enforcing laws to one where he would be making laws.

But nothing came easy. As Langevin put it: "My parents may have given me this wheelchair, but I had to push it. The school gave me the books, but I had to study them."

Well, he did push, and he did study, and by May of that year Langevin was already mainstreaming at school, going to some regular classes. "In the end, I did graduate with my class."

He later went on to Rhode Island College; for a while he even continued to type his term papers—one letter at a time. "I finally wised up in college and paid someone a buck a page to do the typing for me," he laughs now.

His movement toward public service happened even faster than his education. In 1988, as a senior, he won election to the Rhode Island Legislature.

Soon he was commuting to Cambridge to earn a master's degree in public administration at Harvard's John F. Kennedy School of Government.

In 1994, he made his first run at statewide office, challenging a Republican incumbent for secretary of state. Langevin not only won, but at the age of thirty-three he suddenly found himself the country's youngest secretary of state.

With the power of his new position, and a passion to serve others inspired by the way they'd helped him, Langevin made the issue of government openness a personal crusade.

Voters loved him. Surprisingly, many of his colleagues didn't.

One of Langevin's earliest causes was encouraging public awareness of all state matters. Most General Assembly meetings and committee events, he discovered, were poorly publicized, if they were publicized at all. Committees were supposed to publicize meetings at least forty-eight hours in advance, specifying the time, place, and agenda for each gathering. But Langevin discovered that fewer than half of the meetings were publicly presented in that way.

How could people be part of the process, he wondered, if no one was letting them in on it?

Some of the assembly members tried to persuade him that Rhode Island's citizens were adequately served, that they had ample access to the machinery of making laws, Langevin discovered otherwise. In theory, citizens were free to address, and even testify to, any committee they so chose; in practice, however, it was quite another matter. The only place Rhode Islanders could go to learn about important state business, it turned out, was the State House library bulletin board. That's where committee meeting notices were usually posted—"if you were lucky," Langevin adds.

When he'd finished his investigations, Langevin prepared and released a report even more stinging than its title: "Access Denied: Chaos, Confusion and Closed Doors." It confirmed that the General Assembly was so sloppy in announcing its meetings that the public at large had no idea what was going on with the state's business.

The General Assembly leaders were furious with Langevin, even though he had decided to leave most names out of the report, highlighting the issue instead of any individual personalities who might have been pegged with blame.

Senator William Irons, a Democrat out of East Providence, considered Langevin a good friend, but he still criticized what he thought was the almost clandestine nature of this stinging audit-style report.

"It was done in the dark of night," he told the *Boston Globe* in April 2001. He argued that legislators hadn't been given a chance to respond to Langevin's report, before he released it.

Langevin's office had worked with a research team from Brown University in putting out the study, but even the new president of Brown got into the act, lambasting the title and tone of Langevin's report as inappropriate.

Langevin quietly rebutted all their criticisms.

What else would you call 52 percent of meetings not being adequately publicized but "Access Denied"? And isn't "Closed Doors" a fair description of some 236 bills—some on major issues, including the sale of private hospitals—that were acted on in committee without any advance announcement?

Langevin had alienated many of his colleagues; more important, he'd made his points to the public, and *for* the public. And as a result of his report the General Assembly changed its ways, taking much more care about publicizing meetings, and complying with all open meetings laws.

By making such information available by fax, and later on the Internet, Langevin had gone a long way in democratizing the lawmaking process.

He had also quickly transformed the function and role of the secretary of state into what he called the "people's partner in government." Langevin created the Office of Public Information, to make sure that all residents knew which committees were meeting and when. He provided comprehensive daily and weekly reports on all activities of the General Assembly.

The people of Rhode Island responded by easily electing Langevin to a second term as secretary of state.

While he was looking after the best interests of his state, Langevin was also thinking about the problems of disabled people. That made him pay particular attention to the design of the FDR Memorial that was being planned for Washington, D.C.

Langevin wasn't sure how many disabled Americans were involved in the monument to one of America's greatest presidents— a man who was himself disabled—but he wanted to be in on the design.

Langevin thought it was vital that those who were designing the memorial heard and understood the thinking and perspective of at least one representative of the millions of people with disabilities. So he contacted Senator Daniel Inouye, the cochairman of the FDR Memorial Commission, and lobbied hard to make the design portray FDR in his wheelchair. He argued that such a design would show the wartime president in a very human and heroic manner.

"It was important for me to see FDR portrayed as he was. He did have polio and he was paralyzed and he was in a wheelchair, and yet he served this country, as a great source of inspiration, and overcame great odds, and did it with great courage."

Many argued against depicting Roosevelt this way, but Langevin and those who agreed with his more human design carried the day.

Today, visiting the FDR Memorial is a stirring experience. Those who enter pass through panels of stone that ultimately reveal a wheelchair-bound president, who, though unable to lift himself with his own legs, was able to raise his nation's spirits and hopes when they needed it most.

That's the way Langevin wanted the world to see FDR. In a sense, that's the way he wants the world to see him as well.

When southern Rhode Island's Congressman Bob Wegand decided not to run for the U.S. Congress in 2000, friends urged Langevin to run for Wegand's old job.

The physical and political odds seemed daunting. A quadriplegic running for a seat in the U.S. House of Representatives? Would Rhode Islanders trust someone with such obvious disabilities to carry their political torch in the nation's capitol?

Langevin didn't have to wait long to find out. Nabbing a stunning 62 percent of the vote, he made history on the same day George W. Bush and Al Gore made history.

Major Tom Carmody, the Warwick police officer who had first told Langevin's parents about the shooting incident that had paralyzed their son, saw life coming full circle.

"The awful irony of this," Carmody told the *Boston Globe* in April 2001, "is that if the shooting hadn't happened, he would have been a police officer or an FBI agent. As much as it was a terrible thing, I think he's much more valuable to society where he is."

While the presidential contest would remain in doubt for more than a month, the shock waves from the country's smallest state were already being felt. Langevin would join Georgia Senator Max

Cleland, who lost both his legs and an arm in Vietnam as one of the capitol's two most prominent wheelchair-bound legislators.

Once the kid who was due something—*anything*—good, Langevin had become an American congressman, able now to concentrate on *doing* good for his country, just as he had for his state.

It had never been easy for him before, and working in Washington wasn't going to be any easier, possibly even harder. Among other things, the U.S. Capitol building is not handicap-friendly. The building seems to have miles of twisting halls, and dozens of impossible-to-navigate staircases. It's tough enough for any incoming freshman just to learn the political ropes. It's triply so for a guy in a wheelchair.

But Langevin had FDR as a constant inspiration, along with friendly colleagues who worked hard to make Langevin's job easier. They made the House chamber fully handicapped-accessible, even installing an accessible voting machine and podium. Langevin also had a broad-shouldered assistant to help clear a path for him when he needed to make House floor votes.

The simplest tasks are nearly Herculean for Langevin, but in Washington he accepted it all with good grace and good humor. He traveled in his battery-powered wheelchair, and used voice-recognition software to dictate letters and speeches, even legislation. An assistant at home helped him bathe and dress, and prepared his meals.

As a first-term congressman and the only disabled U.S. Representative, Langevin knew he was the focus of a great deal of attention, especially from the other 54 million Americans with disabilities. And a major portion of his crusading mission to improve the quality of life for all Americans, was getting involved in all disability-related issues.

It didn't matter that most Americans' disabilities are not nearly as serious as his. His cause was all-encompassing. He'd remember them, look out for them, and do all he could on their behalf.

Friends say that Jim Langevin is a living, breathing, and determined role model for the Americans with Disabilities Act. As
Langevin discovered, though, even that Act has left a great deal
undone.

According to a National Health Interview Survey, only 3 percent of Americans live in homes with any kind of accessibility fea-
tures. Most doorways are still too narrow, most shower stalls and
bathtubs still too insurmountable, most kitchen cabinets still too
high to reach, and most appliances still too difficult to maneuver.

And forget about elevators or stair-mounted lifts. Most houses
don't have them, and there's little evidence most major home-
builders will offer them.

But when he spoke to me, as he does so often with others,
Langevin quietly cites demographic shifts that might make builders
and planners change their thinking—for reasons of self-interest,
which sadly is still a stronger motivator than altruism.

The reason is no further than the mirror: We're getting older.
By 2030, the U.S. Census Bureau reports, one out of five Americans will be sixty-five or older.

That's why Langevin doesn't see the new improvements in the
House chamber's handicapped-accessibility as accommodations for
him alone. He's the first quadriplegic elected to Congress, but he's
certain he won't be the last, and he's determined to bring more disabled people into both houses of Congress.

As he fights his crusades and pursues his causes, Langevin does
so with passion, intensity, and good manners. Friends and colleagues
say that Langevin can be disarmingly charming, but a relentless force
when he's on a mission.

Rhode Islanders know from Langevin's years as their secretary
of state, and from his actions and decisions as a congressman, that
he is unwavering and passionate in his beliefs, even when they go
against the political grain, even within his own party. In this he reminds me of one of my other heroes who also served in Congress,

Geraldine Ferraro. His constituents know, as hers did, that even if his positions are controversial, they are heartfelt. They know that their congressman is there trying to do the right thing, against enormous personal and physical odds.

Some more conservative Rhode Island voters wince about being represented by a congressman who consistently receives top scores from the public interest group Common Cause. But Langevin considers those scores badges of honor.

And his decisions are made deeply personally, even when they might cost him politically. One good example is the furor over stem-cell research.

Langevin considered himself "pro-life," and many pro-life advocates saw him that way as well. Indeed, groups against abortion rights had donated more than $11,000 to his election campaign.

The anti-abortion groups and pro-life advocates were enraged by stem-cell research, because it involved the destruction of an embryo, which they saw as killing human life, almost murder.

But Langevin supported the research. And, while he admitted that this was "probably one of the most difficult decisions I ever had to make," he argued that his support was very consistent with his pro-life position.

He felt strongly that stem-cell research held the key to cures for scores of terrible diseases, from Parkinson's and Alzheimer's to diabetes and cancer. Even the possible repair and healing of spinal-cord injuries that kept people like him in a wheelchair could be aided by findings born of stem-cell research.

But that wasn't the only controversial, and deeply held, political position Jim Langevin held. Another was his strong support for gun control.

The accident that paralyzed him, of course, had happened because of the actions of two weapons experts on a police SWAT team, not because of criminals with guns. But Langevin knows that accidental shootings by armed policemen aren't really an urgent national issue.

The real issue is that there are too many unregistered guns on the streets, in the hands of otherwise law-abiding citizens—and especially in the possession of anyone who might use them for criminal purposes, or to commit acts of violence, including domestic violence.

That's why he pushes hard for greater precautions, including improved background checks and longer waiting periods.

He also wants more gun safety, even for guns that are legally owned and registered, because of the dangers of accidents or impulsive, violent behavior. For example, the requirement that every citizen who registers his gun ownership with the police must possess and show a trigger lock for every gun being registered, *at the time of registration.*

As he told National Public Radio: "I don't want to see what happened to me happen to a small child." He knows that even loving, gun-owning parents can be careless sometimes, leaving a gun or guns unintentionally loaded, or stored alongside the ammunition for the gun.

Langevin also prioritizes the bigger issue of dealing with terrorism—from how and when to engage the nation in counterterrorism, to anticipating risks, and preparing and taking pre-emptive precautions.

Soon after 9/11, this courageous first-term congressman and Rhode Island lawmaker became intensely involved in helping lead the congressional requests for an emergency backup plan. The goal was to make the necessary arrangements that would enable Congress to continue to function under any emergency circumstances.

After another terrorist attack, a national disaster, or any crisis or situation that currently could slow down or stop congressional operations completely—during a time of emergency when America would most need active, organized, functioning congressional leadership.

Langevin recommended a number of novel solutions, including running Congress via the Internet, exclusively or in combination with some form of wireless communications, that would make it possible for its members to communicate, coordinate, make decisions and take votes, even if they were isolated, physically, all over the country.

"I know that some members would not want to vote electronically or may not be familiar with the Internet," he told the Associated Press at the time. But despite that reluctance, Langevin knew that all of Congress had to face twenty-first century reality, negative and positive.

Terrorism and natural disasters could damage or destroy the Capitol building, depriving the body of a meeting place, and under such circumstances Congress might choose not to meet as a collective physical body of hundreds of members, who'd be an easy target for any follow-up attacks.

As Langevin suggested, the Internet, wireless computers, and cell phones, could be critical to ensuring that Congress could communicate and vote if its members were dispersed.

Langevin's congressional activism, crusades, results, and good fights (both won and lost), had the same effect on his constituents in 2002, when he ran for re-election: He was elected to a second term by a landslide.

That same year, Langevin's colleague, Senator Max Cleland, was defeated in his re-election campaign, leaving Langevin as the sole disabled person in Congress.

Later, he would talk to me about his close friend and mentor. "Having Max there was a great source of inspiration, and I do miss him.

"I remember when I came to Washington, I said, 'Max, you ramped up the Senate side of the Capitol, and I'm going to ramp up the House side of the Capitol.'

"I do hope that my election to Congress will empower others with disabilities to run for office as well. I may be the first quadriplegic in the House. But I won't be the last."

The courageous Langevin, who prized beliefs and values above political risks and gains, was among the minority in Congress who voted against authorizing the use of force against Saddam Hussein in Iraq in 2003, even though his Democratic Rhode Island colleague, Pat Kennedy, went the other way.

Langevin preferred a more measured, two-step approach that included armed action only if the United Nations Security Council approved it. Technically, he explained, *that* was the version that won in Congress. And technically, the president had succeeded in winning such a U.N. resolution, even though a second resolution, authorizing the coalition countries' eventual use of force, was never acted on.

"I apologize to no one for challenging the president to do this in the best way possible," he said.

"I would have liked to have seen a second resolution. I think this would have made the president's case stronger. But I still believe going through the United Nations was the best way to do it. We went the better way instead of the best way.

"I see it as my job to challenge the administration to do this in the best way possible. Use of force should always be a last resort."

Langevin isn't afraid to challenge the president of the United States. What matters much more to him are the folks who grant that power, to the president and to his constituents as their congressman.

He wants to give back to the people who gave so much to him—to the hundreds and thousands who gave money, equipment, schools lessons, and volunteered time to help a fifteen-year-old kid who suffered a horrible accident.

That incredible, generous, selfless support is what keeps him so politically involved. It's what keeps him a Democrat as well. "I grew up in a working class family and it makes me committed to such families and wanting to give people a hand up."

There is a sense of urgency that drives Langevin, an impatience with the established, often protracted give-and-take of politics. There are too many important things to be done, and never enough time to do them. Time should never be wasted. And in his opinion, it too often is, especially by politicians.

Langevin was driven to get things *done* when he was in the Rhode Island General Assembly, and he's even more driven during his service in the U.S. Congress.

He doesn't care if he steps on toes, or rattles colleagues of both parties. He doesn't do these things deliberately, but if fellow Congressmen and others are in his way when he's trying to get political action—if they don't work with him or move aside fast enough.

He'll do whatever it takes to help *his* people, *his* constituents, the very people other legislators back home were neglecting when they refused to publicize General Assembly committee meetings. The same people who had a dickens of a time figuring out complicated voting machines, until *he* changed the machines for them, making voting as easy a physical process as it should be, and giving a lot more people a reason to vote—without having to struggle with such undemocratic machines.

He has never forgotten those people: He is driven by his care for them, and so he marches on. And he marches under *many* banners: In Congress, as a board member for the Rhode Island American Red Cross, the Warwick Shelter, the Rhode Island March of Dimes, the Knights of Columbus, the Lions Club, and Save the Bay.

I asked him about his state colleague in the House, Patrick Kennedy. What kind of relationship do they have?

"I'm happy for Patrick that he has done so well for himself. We get along great and we're very good friends. There's no internal competition. My first and foremost priority is to serve the people of the second congressional district. Of course, I look out for the entire state. Patrick and I look out for Rhode Island."

As part of that trust—looking out for the smallest state with the biggest heart—Langevin keeps a schedule that would run ragged the healthiest of men. How a guy almost completely paralyzed does and continues doing as much as Langevin does, amazes and inspires his colleagues and his constituents.

Part of Langevin's "secret" is that he's extremely committed to maintaining optimal physical conditioning so he can have the strength and stamina to do all the work he does.

Despite his huge congressional workload—and because of it—he never misses a single physical therapy session. He keeps his muscles toned, so that his body can sustain and energize his sharp mind.

As Jim Langevin pushes forward with his demanding work-out—one that always pushes the body limits of what a quadriplegic can do—he thinks about the paralysis he's lived with for more than two decades, and his enduring hope for medical advances.

His intense workouts are evidence that he's not simply waiting for those potential advances to arrive someday. He's advancing himself as much as he can. Even sustaining his amazing stamina and conditioning is a feat in itself; few healthy people with full use of their bodies have the heart and determination to exercise as hard as he does, and continue that intensity of exercise for year after year after year.

And over the past twenty years, he *has* extended his body's lim-its. When he was first paralyzed, the doctors told him he'd almost certainly be a true quadriplegic, able only to move his head.

But his mother's typing lessons pushed him onward, and proved something to him. They were tedious, arduous, painful—but productive.

As he realized then, and told me later, he'd learned for himself the lessons his mother had intended him to learn, without telling him what they were, or even that she had greater ambitions for him than she was revealing.

Since then he'd learned to use a computer; by the time we had our interview, he was able to feed himself.

No, he's not waiting for the scientists and doctors. He's going to keep moving on, while they do whatever they're doing, just as he does in Congress, as his colleagues waste time in what seem like cir-cular, endless debates that never result in decision.

There's still the hope that one day, maybe soon, maybe much later in his life, there'll come a time when his paralysis can be treated the way diseases are now—that his range of movement could be in-creased, his pain diminished.

Jim Langevin's hope, like his exercise regimen, never ends.

Colleagues say he carries a mustard seed in his pocket—a gift from a close friend. In the Bible, the mustard seed is the symbol of possibilities, the potential for greater things. For Langevin, it's a constant reminder, a metaphor for his life of great triumphs realized through great adversity.

"Challenges shouldn't derail you," he told me. "They should empower you. For me, that's meant a new way to fight the bad guys." From the policeman he wanted to be, protecting the law, to the congressman he is now, making the law. "We all get knocked off our paths, but we all have the power to get right back up."

Langevin's been back up for many years now, and with his popularity, longevity, experience, commitment, and endurance, his future holds plenty of possibilities. His name is raised frequently as a potential governor or senator. He remains extremely popular in a state known for looking fondly at mavericks.

Rhode Island's Republican Senator Lincoln Chafee, for example, votes more often with his Democratic colleagues, and on issues from tax cuts to spending cuts, remains a thorn in the administration's side. Rhode Islanders like their politicians that way. Another advantage for Langevin.

For his part, he says he's happy where he is.

"I've learned never to look beyond tomorrow. You never know what life is going to bring. I don't know what the future holds. I don't pay attention to all that talk. I just enjoy my job serving in the United States Congress."

For now, that's his only focus: the people of Rhode Island. He looks after them. They revere him.

A practicing Catholic, he talks a great deal about faith. "You have to have faith and believe in yourself. I have a deep faith in God and that everything will work out."

He summed it up this way: "You have to think bigger and imagine new horizons." Borrowing a line from Ernest Hemingway, he observed that the world breaks everyone, and many become stronger in the broken places.

Jim Langevin may have more broken places than most, but they are just physical breaks. Mentally and emotionally, he is incredibly sharp and enormously agile. His friends know it. His political opponents know it.

Jim Langevin may yet walk again. But for his hopeful and concerned friends and constituents, it doesn't really matter.

In their eyes, he's standing pretty tall as it is.

FINAL REFLECTIONS

I remember asking my oncologist, after I first discovered I had cancer, why I had to suffer. "It's easy," he answered. "Because everyone does."

He was right then. He is right now.

But it took me a while to understand the deeper meaning of what he'd said. Yes, we all suffer—but we don't have to suffer alone, or get so focused on our own pain that we don't think about the pain that everyone else is going through.

What I finally came to realize is that life is better, and can become good again, in ways large and small, if we stop thinking only of ourselves. If we become more sensitive to what's happening in the lives of the people around us—family, fellow workers, friends, even people we don't know personally, but know about, individually, or as part of a group, organization, or other companies.

And as we come to know who is suffering and why, we can think about how we might be able to help *them* deal with life's inevitable and too numerous hardships.

I know that pain is selfish. When we feel it intensely, we're almost forced to think about ourselves, and often only about ourselves.

Emotional suffering and physical pain can monopolize our awareness, dominate our lives, and distance us from other people.

But we don't have to let our hardships control and isolate us. We can take back that control, endure our pain, set it aside, and look around, be more aware of the big world that we've forgotten about or ignored for a while.

Yes, I learned—but only after having lost sight of my place in the world because my cancer and treatments kept getting my attention. In time, even this big-ego news anchor became humble enough to see how much he really was only a bit player on a very big stage.

I'm glad I learned that. I'm also glad I learned there is a lot of good in sharing with each other what we're experiencing as a result of our difficulties, and doing what we can to help.

No one likes getting sick. Or losing loved ones. Or getting hurt. Or fired. Or seeing businesses destroyed. Or dreams dashed. No one *chooses* any of these things. But we have to deal with them when they happen, as they always do, in every life. Tragic events are part of the essential, unchanging unpredictability of life. "Everybody suffers."

I know we'd love to be able to change the basic nature of life, to turn back the clock. To return to when we were well or our relatives were alive, or go back to the cozy innocence of childhood, before the very real and haunting hardships of adulthood began.

But life doesn't work that way, no matter how much we wish it did. Life gives and it takes. It takes and it gives.

During my past sixteen years of cancer remission, and seven years of MS, I have thought more about others, helped, and tried to help, and always wanted to do more.

In writing this book, I've thought a lot about the lives and life-changing events of the particular people I've profiled, and wondered about how different their lives would have been if I could have done what's impossible to do:

- If I could bring back Duffy's son. If I could warn him on that sunny Tuesday September morning, not to go to work.
- If I could have helped Milton Cole prevent that fire.
- Or told Evelyn Lauder sooner about that cancer festering in her.

- Or Geraldine Ferraro about that very different cancer bubbling in her.
- Or let Rhode Island Congressman Jim Langevin know that the gun was loaded, so he could leave the Warwick police locker room before the bullet was fired.

Ironically, though, as you know from Langevin's story, by almost any measure his old Warwick friends and Rhode Islanders are much better off because he *didn't* leave—despite the fact that Langevin himself is physically so much worse off. They now enjoy a state government that's more open, and have a hell of a fighting congressman, more determined than ever to make sure their voices and opinions are heard and their interests looked after.

More to the point, though, they all have higher-quality lives because of the actions he took, and the decisions he made, *after* he was paralyzed.

Everyone suffers. But that doesn't mean we can't change our lives and the consequences of what happens to us. All of us can find the right ways to make life at least a little better, for others and ourselves, Sometimes much better, as Langevin did.

None of the heroes we've visited in this book deserved what happened. They were victims of circumstance, but they didn't remain victims.

They took control of their lives and made the most out of what had happened—not for themselves, but for other people. Through their compassion and selflessness, they made their suffering a transforming, new beginning of their lives.

Their pain and suffering made them think more about other people, and what others were experiencing and enduring. They made decisions and took actions, and did what they could do to ease the suffering and pain of others.

They also tried to help people improve their lives, and give them more reason for hoping and living.

My heroes are survivors, and they're ambitious. They want to help a lot of people, as many as possible for as long as possible.

They started and dedicated their lives to missions, crusades, and causes, and they contributed to all the good work that other people were already doing.

As I wrote in the opening pages, I truly think we are defined in life not by how we handle all that goes well, but how we deal with all that does not. It is one thing to assume you have conquered the world, and quite another to appreciate that the world hasn't conquered you.

I see over and over again that when bad things happen to good people, they somehow carry on, instead of being victimized and immobilized.

Years ago, my life seemed hard. Life's unfair, I used to say. But I learned that others were suffering more, sometimes much more. I also learned that most of these people were fighting the good fight, clinging to the slimmest of hopes with the biggest of hearts.

Since then, I've changed my attitude and what I say. Instead of feeling self-pity when life makes some part of my life crash, I say *That's okay,* and start thinking about what I can *do.*

The power of hope, compassion, and inspirational actions and lives is amazing—and life-changing.

Harry Pearce overcame the sure death sentence of leukemia, and went on a personal—and company-supported—mission to assist leukemia patients and save lives on an unprecedented scale.

Gerry Ferraro came out of retirement, after a long and distinguished political career, to make a big political difference once again, this time with her education crusade about her form of blood cancer.

When he's not running his congressional colleagues ragged with his passionate political causes, Jim Langevin, quadriplegic and wheelchair-bound, works out, and thinks about a day when he may walk again.

He doesn't care what people say about the medical odds for spinal-cord injuries. He's been fighting against even bigger odds for more than two decades now, and winning.

In the end, the best lesson I learned from all of my heroes is that a life of *doing* good is more important than having a lot of fine things.

Stocks are nice, but taking stock of what has real value is far more rewarding. Fancy homes are beautiful, but solid emotional foundations are more beautiful. Running a company is a worthy professional pursuit, but keeping good company is a worthier lifetime goal.

Good family. Good friends. Good works. These are part of a life that's truly good.

The goal for our journey through life, then, for however long we're here, is to make living worthwhile, meaningful, and more enjoyable for all of us.

Rich and poor. Powerful and not so powerful. We all come into this world, and we all leave it. It's what we do in between that defines and motivates us, and influences the lives of the people whose lives intersect our own.

A good attitude doesn't make illness disappear, but it does make the disease more bearable.

A chuckle doesn't make you live longer, but you have more fun while you're living.

And a smile can't bring a burned factory back, but it can make you think about rebuilding.

Hardships, suffering, and pain can ravage your life, and dangerous diseases can damage your body. But none of them can hurt or destroy your heart if you keep it repaired, pumping, and loving.

The beauty and value of a life dedicated to doing good is inestimable, and the beneficial influence on the lives of others immeasurable.

More than possessions, conquests, or triumphs in the boardroom, good lives can be as simple as just decency in every room.

In the end, a life of doing good is about more than money. Much more.

ACKNOWLEDGMENTS

Setting out to write a book is one thing; continuing your job and your private life while you're at it, well, that's quite another. I've been very lucky on both fronts to be surrounded by people who weren't only supportive, but helpful. They trudged on doing their thing, so I could take my stab at this literary thing.

First and foremost, thanks to my wife Mary, who put up with this long process just as she has with so many of my physical travails. And thanks to my daughter Tara, who put up with her mother putting up!

And to Pat and Kay Cavuto, who taught their son the value of meaning over money and being good over just doing good. They're gone now, but not one day goes by that I don't appreciate all the valuable things they taught me, including the very lessons learned in this book.

It's amazing through all this that I was still able to put out a daily and weekend show. But then again, I wasn't doing all the heavy lifting. Far from it. My thanks to Gresham Striegel for keeping *Your World* on top each day, and Gary Schreier for doing the same each weekend with a bloc of powerful shows. They're fantastic guys who know how to rally the reporting troops.

And what troops! Talk about your on-air all stars, from David Asman and Brenda Buttner to Terry Keenan, Dagen McDowell, and Stuart Varney. There's a reason we've got the most watched business show. And they're it.

Thanks as well to my colleagues Jennifer Altheide, Merideth Beasley, Holly Cerelli, Amanda Gershkowitz, William Gregson, John Huber, Susannah Jabbour, Hilda LaPolla, Alison Moore, Cheryl Moritz, Cynthia Newdel, Michele Nunes, Pam Ritter, Jason Rosenberg, Sam Sayegh, Tia Tiryaki, Rafael Uribe, and Andrew White.

Of course, it's one thing to have great people plugging along every day. It's really nice having someone there to get the big picture right. My thanks to Roger Ailes, the captain of the Fox News ship, for always standing by us, even when we weren't getting any numbers. And to Rupert Murdoch for making all this possible, long before anyone had any numbers! And to my friend Beth Ailes, who's always been in my corner through thick and thin!

I know very well that I couldn't be writing about people surviving hardships if I didn't have some damn good doctors who helped me survive a few of my own. So to Drs. James Salwitz, Richard Nissenblatt, and especially now, Saud Sadiq, for always being there and always offering hope, my deepest thanks and gratitude.

Books are funny things, of course. You can come up with an idea, but it takes a pretty shrewd visionary to get the big picture right. Judith Regan, my publisher, is that and so much more. Thanks for giving me the focus I needed to write, and the inspiration I needed to continue writing. Who better to help her along in that process than one of the best editors I've ever encountered in the business, the always calm and calming Calvert Morgan. And thanks especially to another incredible editor and visionary, Paul McCarthy, who helped string some of my crazy ideas into yes, crazy, but thanks to him reasonably coherent copy. But a good book doctor does more than that, and Paul did. He as much saw my mission as he did my manuscript, melding the two, uniting the two, and lifting the two. The end result is as much a reflection of me the person, as of me the TV anchor. Paul saw that and delivered on that, even during those early drafts, when my copy was far from that. Then there's my erstwhile assistant Anita Garay, who kept me focused on what I had to do at work, and what I had to do here. And to my lawyer and friend Bob Barnett, who steered me through this process as he has my career, many thanks.

And to my sister Arlene Krauter and my brother Ron Cavuto, thanks for always caring in my darkest days. May this book give hope to those, like you, who believed, even when I did not.

INDEX